Veg-Feasting

in the Pacific Northwest

*A complete guide for vegetarians
and the curious*

Vegetarians of Washington

Book Publishing Company
Summertown, Tennessee

Editors:	Amanda Strombom
	Stewart Rose
Managing Editor:	Griggs Irving
Cover and Interior Design:	Edwina Cusolito
Map Design:	Timothy J. Fargo
	Anne I. Johnson
Cover Photos:	C.B. Bell, III
	Seattle skyline and snowy mountain

Book Publishing Company
P.O. Box 99
Summertown, TN 38483
1-888-260-8458
www.bookpubco.com

Printed on recycled paper in Canada.
All rights reserved.

ISBN 1-57067-160-5

09 08 07 06 05 <u>04</u>   6 5 4 3 2 <u>1</u>

The material in this book is not a substitute for professional medical care. Please consult your physician before making any changes to you diet, lifestyle or medications.

The Book Publishing Co. is committed to preserving ancient forests and natural resources. We have elected to print this title on New Leaf Ecobook 100, which is 100% postconsumer recycled and processed chlorine free. As a result of our paper choice, we have saved the following natural resources:

48 trees (40 feet tall)
14,000 gallons of water
8200 kw hours of electricity
120 pounds of air pollution

We are a member of Green Press Initiative. For more information about Green Press Initiative visit www.greenpressinitiative.org.

Library of Congress Cataloging-in-Publication Data

Veg-Feasting in the Pacific Northwest: a complete guide for vegetarians and the curious /
    by Vegetarians of Washington.

        p. cm.
    ISBN 1-57067-160-5
    1. Vegetarian restaurants—Pacific, Northwest—Guidebooks.
    2. Farmers' market—Pacific, Northwest—Guidebooks.   3. Vegetarianism.
    I. Vegetarians of Washington.
TX907.3.P323V44 2004
647.95795—dc22
            2003027057

Contents

Acknowledgements

We would like to thank the farmers and manufacturers, the distributors, the brokers, the retailers and restaurateurs who form the vital links in our food chain.

The Vegetarians of Washington would also like to acknowledge our reviewers who visited the many restaurants and natural markets featured in this book including: Holly Anderson, Sid Anderson, Kathy Barry, Jessica Dadds, Michelle Daugherty, Erica du Bois, Lana Fletcher, Gary Einhorn, Shaeleen Gilson, Griggs Irving, Lainey Kahlstrom, Randy Kimbler, Luna Marcus, Casey McDonald, Bud & Trish Nicola, Kati Peters, Joanna Pirie, Ken Pirie, Janice Renck, Susan Rose, Rich Schmoeller, Beth Ullman and Liz Ward, with apologies to anyone we may have overlooked.

We thank all our article authors for their time and commitment, our associate editors Mary Ann Hagan, Jonathan Laden and Alice Smith, and also Christa Goddard, Priya Niralay, Brett Wallick and others whose generous efforts helped create this book.

Special thanks to the Vegetarian Resource Group and the Provender Alliance for their support and encouragement.

Our ultimate thanks is to all the volunteers and members of Vegetarians of Washington for their support of the organization and its mission.

Introduction

Food is there to be enjoyed! There's no doubt about it.

However, many people feel that they're caught in a bind. They want to enjoy delicious food, but at the same time they worry that the food they most enjoy is the least healthy for them. Many people also feel that the idea of consuming animals for food weighs heavily on their minds, but resign themselves to eating meat, thinking that it's us or them. When people discover how environmentally unsound animal agriculture is, they often say "But I have to eat to live!"

In light of all this, Vegetarians of Washington would like to offer you this deal. You can enjoy the most delicious food you can imagine, and at the same time greatly improve your health, while easing your conscience about the animals and the environment. Sound good? We think so too, so we wrote this book to enable more people to get in on a good deal.

Let's talk about enjoying our food first. We admit it, we love great tasting food and we'll accept nothing less. The fact is that vegetarian food has come in to its own as the most desirable of cuisines, attracting the world's most noted chefs and cookbook authors. The food and restaurant industry has caught on and we'll guide you to the region's best restaurants and grocery stores. We'll help you learn the secret of delicious food and how to get started with a kitchen make over. We'll grab you by the taste buds and we won't let go!

The land, the air and the water are so much a part of our lives. There's a good feeling that comes from helping to sustain the environment. While some people think of helping the environment by recycling, we think of enjoying a veggieburger! The satisfaction of eating in a way that protects the environment makes the food taste even better.

Today's factory raised animals have a much rougher time than they used to. The animals are our friends, so let's give Elsie the Cow a well deserved vacation. While good old Elsie is enjoying her vacation, we can also enjoy ours in excellent health. It's another win-win situation.

Trying new foods and learning as you go will give you a chance to be creative. The secrets of success on your journey are to be willing to experiment with new foods, to be willing to learn, to proceed at your own pace and to just do the best you can. We take the optimistic approach. However far you come on your journey makes you that much further ahead.

Just who are those vegetarians anyway? The big news is that vegetarians are everywhere these days and, in fact, they have always been an important part of our society. They have made contributions in all walks of life throughout history. Examples include Albert Einstein in science, Thomas Edison in industry, baseball and football stars in sports such as Hank Aaron the homerun king and Desmond Howard, the Superbowl MVP, Paul McCartney of the Beatles, and founding fathers such as Benjamin Franklin. But most vegetarians are not famous. They're the people who live next door, the lady who sits next to you at work or the guy standing behind you in line at the movies. They're everyday people.

Vegetarians of Washington was founded by everyday folk. We welcome everyone whether you're a vegetarian, a beginner or just curious. We're having a good time discovering new and tasty foods, and we invite you to join in the adventure and the fun.

"Many is the time that the chef has come out to relate his delight at having the opportunity to be creative and prepare a vegetarian meal. The result can be a dish that is truly inspired."

PART ONE

Dining Out

Dining out is one of life's true pleasures. There are so many good restaurants to choose from, each specializing in a different cuisine and atmosphere. As more people discover the many benefits of a vegetarian diet, there has been a steady increase in the number of vegetarian restaurants throughout the Pacific Northwest. There is also a growing trend for general restaurants to offer more vegetarian options.

Dining at a totally vegetarian restaurant is easy since you have a wide selection to choose from. You will often find that most items on the menu can also be made without dairy or eggs if requested. Most of the vegetarian restaurants are used to receiving special requests and many include dairy and egg alternatives on the menu.

Most Indian, Thai, Chinese and Vietnamese restaurants have many tasty vegetarian options to choose from. However, other cuisines should not be overlooked. Often Ethiopian and Middle Eastern restaurants have good vegetarian choices on their menu. Bean burritos and enchilladas are a good choice at Mexican restaurants, although they do tend to include a lot of cheese. Tip: ask for whole beans to avoid those cooked in lard.

Vegetarian food is also showing up in some surprising places. Many steak and seafood houses are now offering some rather tasty dishes to attract the vegetarian customer. At the very least, you can get a veggie burger in many American and fast food restaurants these days and even a veggie dog at many baseball stadiums.

Using this guide to local restaurants, we hope you will always have plenty of delicious choices available. But on occasion, you will need to eat at a restaurant with few, if any, vegetarian options. If there is nothing you feel comfortable ordering on the menu, we recommend that you ask if a special meal could be prepared, and specify what you would like, choosing ingredients that you see are available from the menu. Chefs are often happy to receive such special requests. Many is the time that the chef has come out to relate his delight at having the opportunity to be creative and prepare a vegetarian meal. The result can be a dish that is truly inspired.

There have never been so many dining options for vegetarians to choose from. We encourage you to enjoy the adventure of finding tasty vegetarian options when dining out!

"In choosing a vegetarian diet as part of our strategy for healthy living, we can be confident that the scientific evidence gives credence to our efforts" — see page 123.

Restaurants in Washington

BAINBRIDGE ISLAND

Sawatdy Thai Cuisine

8770 Fletcher Bay Road • Bainbridge Island • (206) 780-2429

VegFriendly • Thai • Lunch Tue-Fri • Dinner Tue-Sun • Closed Mon • Full service, take-out • Entrées $5-10

This elegant Thai restaurant is rated as one of the best restaurants on Bainbridge Island, and is listed in several Best Places guides. It serves a wide variety of Thai and South East Asian dishes, with many vegetarian options. You can also request any meat based dish be served with tofu replacing the meat. Special sunken table for large parties at the end of the room. Make reservations.

BELLEVUE

Acapulco Fresh

1360 156th St NE • Bellevue • (425) 747-1054

VeryVegFriendly • Mexican • Daily lunch & dinner • Take out & counter ordering services

Using fresh ingredients daily and no lard, MSG or can openers, makes this Mexican fast food restaurant a favorite for the health-conscious. The Baja Combo, vegetarian upon request, is a combination of grilled veggies, fajita style, with choice of corn or flour tortillas. With the rice, beans, sour cream, guacamole and chips on the side, a filling meal can be had for a very reasonable price. All you can eat salsa bar. Whimsical southwest décor.

California Pizza Kitchen

595 106th Ave NE • Bellevue • (425) 454-2545

VegFriendly • Pizza & pasta • Daily lunch & dinner • Entrées around $10

This popular family-friendly pizza restaurant chain has a long list of pizza choices, with over a third being vegetarian. Choices include Vegetarian with Japanese Eggplant, Wild Mushroom or Southwestern Black Bean (Tostada) pizzas. There are also several pasta and focaccia sandwich options. If you're vegan, ask them to hold the cheese. Service is quick and efficient.

Chantanee

150 105th Ave NE • Bellevue • (425) 455-3226 • www.chantanee.com

VeryVegFriendly • Thai • Daily lunch & dinner • Daily • Full service & take out Entrées $5-10

Because the owner is a vegetarian, that menu alone lists 40 items and the portions are very generous. It is reported that the spring rolls are wonderful and there are 12 on the plate. Coconut soup is superb and chock full of tofu and veggies. Phad Mee tofu is perfectly spiced and a hit. Best of all, the service is unbelievable. Fresh orchids on every table and a huge bouquet of them in the spotless (women's) restroom.

Chutneys

938 110th Ave NE • Bellevue • (425) 467-0867 • www.chutneys.com

VeryVegFriendly • Indian cuisine • Lunch (with buffet), dinner • Entrées $10-20

A large portion of the menu is vegetarian. The vegetable Pakoras are just perfect and their fire roasted Eggplant Bharta has a wonderful smoky taste. Every dish sampled is delicious. The elegant décor is very tasteful and the convenient location a bonus. The Chutneys restaurants in Seattle have a similar reputation, although they are now separately owned.

India Gate

3080 148th Ave SE (Eastgate) • Bellevue • (425) 747-1075

Very VegFriendly • Indian • Daily lunch & dinner • Sun dinner only • Entrées $5-10

Bellevue has so many wonderful Indian restaurants and this one does not disappoint. Dishes are perfectly executed and the portions are substantial. The Saag Paneer is creamy and is perfectly spiced. The Eggplant Bhartha is smoky with a hint of tomato. The Vegetable Samosas are the best around, especially with the coriander mint chutney on top. Don't forget the rich and dreamy rice pudding.

King and I Thai Cuisine

10509 Main St • Bellevue • (425) 462-9337 • www.howspicy.com/kingandi

VeryVegFriendly • Thai • Open daily • Entrées $5-10

From the extensive vegetarian menu Tom Ka Gai stands out (coconut broth with tofu and mushrooms) but the Phad See Ew is SUPERB! Its wide rice noodles and broccoli are perfectly spiced in a flavorful sauce. Both brown and white rice are offered. The décor is noticeably artistic.

Mayuri Indian Cuisine

15400 NE 20th St • Bellevue • (425) 641-4442 • www.mayuriseattle.com

VegFriendly • North & South Indian • Lunch & dinner • Full service or take out Entrées $5-10

A beautiful, friendly family restaurant where vegetarian, vegan and non-veg can be happy. Dinners are well-sized, and the Thali dinners are enormous. The staff is warm and willing to help make changes and suggestions for vegan diners. There is often live entertainment, noted on their website. The restaurant is associated with Mayuri Grocery in Redmond. The owner is a devoted vegetarian. A local favorite.

Mediterranean Kitchen

103 NE Bellevue Way • Bellevue • (425) 462-9422

VegFriendly • Middle Eastern • Daily lunch & dinner • Full service, take out and catering • Entrées $10-20

People stand outside shivering in the winter to be able to enjoy this restaurant which has seven vegetarian main dishes and virtually all vegetarian appetizers. Portions are gargantuan and service is attentive and friendly. The enormous Meze platter over-flows with 6 delicious appetizers which could make a filling dinner for three hungry adults. Baskets of pita bread keep coming and the various soups are always vegetar-ian and hearty with loads of flavor. The homemade Baklava is delicate and light.

Moghul Palace

10303 NE 10th St • Bellevue • (425) 451-1909

VegFriendly • Indian• Luncheon buffet Mon-Sat • Dinner daily • Entrées $5-10

This restaurant offers a selection of vegetarian entrées that are made with organic spices and can be ordered as mild, medium, hot or extra hot. A variety of breads are cooked in a charcoal clay oven.

Natures Pantry Juice Bar

10200 NE 10th St • Bellevue • (425) 454-0170
15600 NE 8th St (Crossroads) • Bellevue • (425) 957-0090

VegFriendly • Juice, Salads & Deli • Open Daily all day • Entrées less than $5

For a quick healthy meal, you can't beat Natures Pantry Juice Bar. There is a large selection of fresh organic juices and smoothies, where you can add special ingredi-ents such as spirulina or wheat germ. Choose from salads, wraps, noodle dishes and sandwiches for a light lunch or quick evening meal. Seating is mostly at the bar.

Pho An Nam

2255 140th Ave NE • Bellevue • (425) 644-4065

VeryVegFriendly • Thai & Vietnamese • Mon-Fri lunch & dinner • Sat dinner only Closed Sun • Entrées $5-10 • Full service & take out.

This tasteful and serene jewel-box restaurant has 12 wonderful vegan/vegetarian dishes to choose from. There is an organic vegetable menu and tofu may be substi-tuted for the meat in any dish. Try favorites like Phad Thai vegetables, Thai noodles with vegetables, bean sprouts, ground peanuts, turnip and scallions, Tom Yum Tofu Soup with lemon grass, thai spices and tangy lime. Portions are well-sized; service is friendly. Customize your level of spiciness.

Taco Del Mar

677 120th Ave SE • Bellevue • (425) 646-9041
14808 NE 24th St • Bellevue • (425) 644-5055
See review - Seattle

Thai Chef
1645 140th Ave NE • Bellevue • (425) 562-7955

VegFriendly • Thai • Daily lunch & dinner • Entrées $5-10

The entrées are sure to please both vegetarian and non-vegetarian fans of Thai food. Great appetizers. Family friendly.

The Thai Kitchen
14116 NE 20th St • Bellevue • (425) 641-9166

VeryVegFriendly • Thai • Daily lunch & dinner • Full service & take out
Entrées $5-10

The vegetarian menu has soup, appetizers and a few select entrées. The meals are served as spicy as you want and are flavorful. Friendly courteous staff provides fast service.

Udupi Palace
15600 NE 8th St • Bellevue • (425) 649-0355

Vegetarian • Indian • Daily lunch & dinner • Full service • Entrées $5-10

Nestled between a doll store and a bakery at one end of Crossroads Mall, Udupi Palace is a truly authentic Indian vegetarian experience. With clean simple décor, and all Indian dishes, such as Cashew Pongal and Masala Dosa, this restaurant is especially popular with the local Indian population.

Zen Yai Noodle House
15400 NE 20th St • Bellevue • (425) 378-1100

VegFriendly • Thai • Daily lunch & dinner • Full service or take-out • Entrée $5-10

Dining in this tranquil and upscale décor, you'll find many items on the menu available in vegetarian and vegan options. Favorites are several soup selections, the Vietnamese Hand Rolls and Eggplant with Basil. Several soup selections are vegetarian.

World Wrapps
228 Bellevue Square Mall • Bellevue • (425) 635-0103 • www.worldwrapps.com

VegFriendly • International Fast Food • Lunch & dinner around $5 • Special menu for kids.

World Wrapps is a gift to vegetarians! It's incredibly flavorful, vegetarian fast food that's healthy too. There are five vegetarian sandwich wraps available - Bombay Curry Veggie, Tofu Mushroom Teriyaki, Bean & Cheese, Baja Veggie and Portabello Mushroom and Goat Cheese. Vegans, the cheese can be left out of most of the dishes. The smoothies are rich and fruity, with ingredients like blackberries and mangos. It's fast food, but tastes like it isn't.

Zoopa

Bellevue Square Mall • Bellevue • (425) 453-7887 • www.zoopa.com

VeryVegFriendly • American Buffet • Eat in or take-out • Special kids menu & high chairs

Fresh and healthy food in a convenient all you care to eat buffet format. Most items are vegetarian and there are many vegan items available. Many items such as prepared salads, dressings and soups are labeled vegetarian, low fat or fat free. Vegans may want to check out the web site for specific information on soups and bakery ingredients. The website also offers special features, nutritional information, discounts, catering menus and offers. The dining rooms are large and cheery with servers to help clear dishes making this an excellent choice for informal parties and large family gatherings.

BELLINGHAM

Casa Que Pasa

1415 Railroad Ave • Bellingham • (360) 738-TACO

VeryVegFriendly • Mexican • Daily 11am-midnight • Entrées $5

Known for being inexpensive with huge proportions. Vegetarian dishes are clearly classified. Specialty burritos weigh in at one pound for under $5. About half the burritos on the menu are vegetarian, with some vegan options. Relaxed atmosphere full of music and color with a friendly and accommodating staff.

D'Anna's Deli Café & Catering Co

1307 11th St • Bellingham • (360) 752-3390

VeryVegFriendly • Traditional Italian home cooking • Daily breakfast & lunch
Most entrées below $5

This quaint, two-story café is very accommodating to both vegetarians and vegans alike. Sandwiches can be prepared on homemade vegan focaccia bread. There is a wide variety of mostly vegan, all vegetarian soups. The deli is equipped with an espresso bar and also offers an assortment of bottled beverages and wines. The owners, a vegetarian couple, offer a welcoming atmosphere that is inviting to everyone.

The Lemon Grass Restaurant

111 N Samish Way • Bellingham • (360) 676-4102
www.lemongrassbellingham.com

VeryVegFriendly • Thai • Mon-Fri lunch, daily dinner • Full service & take out
Entrées $5-10

Alleged to be the best Thai food in town! The warm, exotic, inviting atmosphere is not to be missed. Excellent vegetarian and vegan choices on the menu, all including salad. Necessary accommodations will be made for vegan/vegetarian requests as the staff is familiar with these diets. There is usually no more than a 20-30 minute wait on weekends, and it is well worth it. Parking is free, which is rare for many restaurants in Bellingham. High chairs for kids.

The Old Town Café

316 West Holly St • Bellingham • (360) 671-4431

VeryVegFriendly • Breakfast & lunch daily • Full service • Entrées $5-10

The Old Town Café has a traditional and cozy atmosphere. With a menu almost entirely made up of vegetarian meals, there are also some excellent vegan options. They serve an assortment of juices, espresso drinks, omelets, salads and sandwiches made up of natural, local and organic products. Delicious pastries made on site. Avoid the hustle and bustle of everyday life and step into the slow-paced, relaxed environment of the Old Town Café.

Supon's Thai Cuisine

1213 Dupont St • Bellingham • (360) 734-6838

VeryVegFriendly • Thai • Daily lunch & dinner • Full service • Entrées $5-10

Located on the outskirts of Bellingham, Supon's Thai Cuisine is a casual restaurant with great service. Though the sauces aren't usually made vegetarian, they will be happy to remake the order. This is especially helpful if ordering Phad Thai or other common dishes with previously made sauces. The spring rolls are vegan and excellent. Good assortment of bottled juices and other drinks. High chairs for kids.

Swan Café (Community Food Co-op)

1220 N Forest • Bellingham • (360) 734-8158 • www.communityfoodcoop.com

VeryVegFriendly • Eclectic deli • Items under $5

Located inside the Community Food Co-op, the Swan Café offers items from tofu cutlets and tempeh salads, to vegan desserts such as fudge, cake and other pastries. All items are clearly and accurately labeled if vegan or vegetarian. The espresso bar carries both soy and rice milk, and offers a variety of delicious smoothies that can be made vegan. Casual atmosphere and friendly service. Non-members charged 6.5% on all items, but if you're a member of another co-op in Washington, this should be honored.

Taco Del Mar

122 East Magnolia St • Bellingham • (360) 734-0313
4277 Meridian St • Bellingham • (360) 255-2254
See review - Seattle

BOTHELL

Pen Thai Restaurant

10107 Main St • Bothell • (425) 398-7300 • www.penthai.com

VegFriendly • Lunch & dinner • Closed Sun

Like its sister restaurant, Chantanee in Bellevue, the vegetarian menu alone lists 40 items and the portions are very generous. It is reported that the spring rolls are wonderful and there are 12 on the plate. Coconut soup is superb and chock full of tofu and veggies. Phad Mee tofu is perfectly spiced and a hit. Best of all, the service is unbelievable.

Taco del Mar

22833 Bothell-Everett Hwy • Bothell • (425) 481-0737
See review - Seattle

BREMERTON

Taco Del Mar

7058 State Hwy 303 NE • Bremerton • (360) 307-8226
See review - Seattle

BURIEN

Schuller's Bakery

15217A 21st Ave SW • Burien • (206) 244-0737

Vegetarian • Café • Lunch Tues-Fri • Dinner Friday night • Saturday breakfast only
Closed Sun, Mon

The area's most delicious, creative and diverse bakery, Schuller's Bakery is a vegetarian's dream come true, particularly for those who love incredible fresh baked goods and organic foods. Special favorites are the lasagne, foccacia sandwiches, stromboli and quiche. Another excellent choice is the soup of the day or a selection of the specialty pasta salads. Some favorite treats are the cinnamon rolls, chocolate chip cookies and a chocolate cream pie that is unbelievable. Schuller's also offers some groceries including organic produce, coffee, croutons and locally made specialty items. Enjoy the comfortable, relaxed atmosphere. It's well decorated and features local art.

Taco Del Mar

116 SW 148th St • Burien • (206) 243-4675
See review - Seattle

CENTRALIA

Berry Fields
201 S Pearl • Centralia • (360) 736-1183

VegFriendly • American • Breakfast & lunch • Full service & take out
Entrées $5-10

Black bean veggie burgers. Ask for meatless stir-fry. They bake and sell their own oat bread. Friendly efficient service.

GG's
2501 Haviland St • Centralia • (360) 736-7242

VeryVegFriendly • Mediterranean • Breakfast & lunch • Closed Sun • Full service, take out & delivery • Entrées $5-10

Unusual soups, sandwiches, salads and entrées - wholesome and delicious. Proprietors are vegan so they are adaptable to your preferences. Casual, quality atmosphere.

Panda Inn
806 Harrison Ave • Centralia • (360) 807-2088

VegFriendly • Chinese • Daily lunch & dinner • Entrées $5-10

Vegetarian dishes in each category of Chinese food. Will substitute tofu for meat in many dishes. Large pleasant room with many tables.

CHEHALIS

Aldente
545 N Market Blvd • Chehalis • (360) 740-8000

VegFriendly • Italian • Tue-Sat lunch & dinner • Closed Sun & Mon
Entrées around $10

Rich and wonderful food. All the pasta dishes on the menu are vegetarian and they are very willing to accommodate vegans. Friendly, helpful and efficient service.

Market Street Bakery & Café
492 N Market • Chehalis • (360) 748-0875

VegFriendly • Eclectic • Snacks & lunch • Daily 8:30am-5pm • Full service & take out • Entrées under $5

The wonderful breads freshly baked are their highlight. All soups except clam chowder are veggie.

Plaza Jalisco
1340 NW Maryland • Chehalis • (360) 748-4298

VegFriendly • Mexican • Daily lunch & dinner • Full service & take out
Entrées $5-10

Small and crowded but food is so delicious that many local people go there. Waiters are efficient and friendly. Most speak English. They have recently added a veggie selection to the menu, including vegetarian enchiladas, burritos and fajitas. Painted multicolored outside and inside.

COLLEGE PLACE

His Garden & Bakery
28 SE 12th • College Place • (509) 525-1040

Vegetarian • Deli • Mon-Thurs 7:30am-7pm, Fri & Sun breakfast & lunch, closed Sat

An excellent vegetarian deli where about half the choices are vegan. Soups, sandwiches, vegan cheese, 'Haystacks', burritos. Eat there or take home. The bakery makes lots of whole grain breads from fresh ground flour.

Walla Walla College Cafeteria
32 SE Ash • College Place • (509) 527-2732

Vegetarian • Cafeteria • Daily when class is in session • Limited hours in summer

Vegan eats are also available in this youthful setting where all the food is meat-free, including the make-your-own Mexican meal table. Soups, salads and pastas of course.

COVINGTON

Taco Del Mar
27116 168th Ave SE • Covington • (253) 630-4393
See review - Seattle

ELLENSBURG

Valley Café
105 W 3rd • Ellensburg • (509) 925-3050

VegFriendly • Eclectic • Lunch & dinner daily • Entrées $5-10

You can eat well at this 1938 classic Art Deco bistro. Seven out of twelve entrées are cheese and butter rich vegetarian meals. A majority of the tasty appetizers and large salads are fully vegetarian.

EVERETT

The Sisters

2804 Grand Ave • Everett • (425) 252-0480

VegFriendly • American • Mon-Fri breakfast & lunch • Closed Sat & Sun

This cozy family-owned and operated restaurant has walls covered with local artists' work. They offer buttermilk hotcakes, soups, salads, their own nut burger, hummus and pita bread. Many menu items can be veggie upon request. Friendly, comfortable, informal setting.

Taco Del Mar

1723 Hewitt Ave • Everett • (425) 303-0300
See review - Seattle

FEDERAL WAY

Marlene's Market & Deli

31839 Gateway Center Blvd S • Federal Way • (253) 839-0933
See review - Tacoma

Taco Del Mar

2020 S 320th • Federal Way • (253) 839-9113
See review - Seattle

FORKS

Plaza Jalisco

90 Forks Ave • Forks • (360) 374-3108
See review - Chehalis

GIG HARBOR

Taco Del Mar

5500 Olympic Dr • Gig Harbor • (253) 857-7807
See review - Seattle

ISSAQUAH

Acapulco Fresh

1480 NW Gilman Blvd • Issaquah• (425) 313-1542
See review - Bellevue

Bamiyan

317 NW Gilman Blvd • Issaquah • (425) 391-8081

VeryVegFriendly • Afghani cuisine • Daily lunch & dinner • Entrées $10-20

There is a separate vegetarian menu with six entrées. Very unique and tasty food. The Ashak dumplings, filled with scallions, cilantro, parsley and chives, are delightfully hot and spicy. The Badenjan Borani, fresh eggplant sautéed, baked and topped with tomato sauce, is delicious! Vegans: it's OK to bring your own soy yogurt for a topping as yogurt is used as a sauce extensively, but can easily be left off upon request.

Noodle Boat

700 NW Gilman Blvd • Issaquah • (425) 391-8096

VeryVegFriendly • Thai • Mon-Fri lunch • Daily dinner • Full service or take-out Entrées $5-10

A delightful little restaurant located near the major shopping area on Gilman Blvd. Their food is delicious and light. In addition to their vegetarian menu, the staff is very helpful and receptive to creating vegan options. Outdoor seating is available during warmer weather.

Taco Del Mar

730 NW Gilman Blvd • Issaquah • (425) 837-3755
See review - Seattle

KELSO

Plaza Jalisco

400 West Main • Kelso • (360) 425-7476
See review - Chehalis

KENMORE

Acapulco Fresh

6016 NE Bothell Way • Kenmore • (425) 482-0334
See review - Bellevue

Bastyr University Cafeteria

14500 Juanita Drive NE • Kenmore • (425) 823-1300 • www.bastyr.edu

Vegetarian • Cafeteria • Breakfast, lunch & dinner • Closed school holidays Entrées reasonable

Off the main path and in a university setting, anyone is welcome here for the all vegetarian, frequently vegan cafeteria food. There is always a fresh salad bar, soup and homemade baked breads and deserts. All this in the setting which has been the "heart of natural medicine for 25 years." Be sure to take a walk through their medicinal herb and vegetable gardens.

KENNEWICK

Toeshi Teriyaki & Korean
7935 W Granville Blvd • Kennewick • (509) 734-9339

VegFriendly • Korean • Lunch & dinner • Closed Sunday • Entrées $5-10

This is a family owned and operated restaurant that is very authentic and they happily accommodate vegetarians and vegans. Most items are prepared from scratch. Their kim chee and sautéed tofu is reported to be the best in the Tri-cities. Vegetable Fried Rice is a local favorite. Clean, relaxed and family friendly.

KENT

Circo Circo
23223 Pacific Highway S • Kent • (206) 878-4424

VegFriendly • Mexican • Daily lunch & dinner • Full service

The vegetarian co-owner ensures that you will find a vast selection of truly lard-free, simple and tasty vegetarian food. If you are vegan, ask them to hold the cheese. The vegetable fajitas are a great choice for vegans - hot, sizzling. The portions are huge and the décor down-home café. Very family friendly.

Paulos
23810 104th Ave SE • Kent • (253) 850-2233

VegFriendly • Italian • Closed Sun • Lunch $5-10 • Dinner $10-20

Italian food on the lighter side with a large number of vegetarian choices for the ovolacto vegetarian. Any pasta dish can be made meatless upon request. A vegan soup is sometimes offered. The antipasto plate or salad, minus the meat and cheese, is a particularly good choice. Ask your server for help in accommodating your diet choices.

Spiro's Greek Island
2215 1st Ave S • Kent • (253) 854-1030

VegFriendly • Greek • Lunch $5-10 • Dinner $10-20 • Closed Sun

The vegetarian choices are limited, but the food is good; the atmosphere is warm and friendly. Try the Falafel Platter which can be extra-spicy. Baba Gannouj, (smoked eggplant spread) and hummus (fava bean spread) are always good choices. The pita bread is homemade, fresh and hot out of the oven. For vegans, hold the feta cheese which is sprinkled on almost everything. Weekend nights there are colorful belly dancers, entertaining a packed house. Very child friendly.

Taco Del Mar
25616 102nd Place SE • Kent • (253) 852-5210
21110 84th Ave S • Kent • (253) 395-1070
See review - Seattle

Wild Wheat Bakery
202 First Ave S • Kent • (253) 856-8919

VegFriendly • American • Daily breakfast & lunch • Entrées $5-10

Wild Wheat has a few good vegetarian options, but what options they are! Delicate and smokey acorn squash pasta is a celebration of unexpected flavors. Ask them to hold the cheese and it's vegan. There's also a vegan Italian roasted vegetable grinder (sandwich). Yum! Sunday brunch is always a treat with great traditional breakfast fare. Every kind of baked dessert you can think of, freshly made by the pastry chef every morning. Mile-high chocolate mousse, strawberry tarts, decedent three-chocolate cakes... the list goes on.

KIRKLAND

Café Happy
102 Kirkland Ave • Kirkland • (425) 822-9696

Vegetarian • Taiwanese-style Chinese • Daily 9am-9pm • Dine in or take out
Entrées under $6 • Cash only

A small family-owned restaurant near the Kirkland waterfront. Excellent choice for vegetarian and vegan food, including vegetarian breakfasts and vegan lunches and dinners. Dishes are made fresh and light, with over 40 menu items to choose from. Descriptive pictures help the menu. They also serve dairy ice cream and have fresh-made juices.

Circo Circo
12709 NE 124th St • Kirkland • (425) 821-9405
See review - Kent

Meze
935 6th St S • Kirkland • (425) 828-3923

VeryVegFriendly • Middle Eastern • Breakfast, lunch & dinner • Closed Sun
Full service, take out and catering • Entrées $5-10

Virtually all the appetizers and many of the main dishes are vegetarian. One major favorite is panini with hummus, roasted eggplant, roasted red pepper, grilled onion, feta and parsley. People rave about the falafel. Fresh squeezed orange juice and lemonade and of course baklava in three flavors! Owner/chef Abraham loves to chat with customers.

Shamiana
10724 NE 68th St • Kirkland • (425) 827-4902
See review - Seattle

Taco Del Mar
104 Central • Kirkland • (425) 828-3002
12551 116th Ave NE • Kirkland • (425) 820-5763
See review - Seattle

The Thai Kitchen
11701 124th Ave NE • Kirkland • (425) 820-5630

VeryVegFriendly • Thai • Daily lunch & dinner • Full service & take out
Entrées $5-10

The vegetarian menu has soup, appetizers and a few select entrées. The meals are served as spicy as you want and are flavorful. Friendly courteous staff provides fast service.

Thumra Thai Restaurant
12549 116th Ave NE (Totem Lake W) • Kirkland • (425) 821-0577

VegFriendly • Thai • Mon-Fri lunch & dinner • Sat dinner only • Closed Sun
Full service & take out • Entrées $5-10

This small unassuming Thai restaurant just west of the Totem Lake exit off I-405 has no separate vegetarian menu. However, there is a highlighted area at the bottom of the menu stating that most dishes can be made using tofu or vegetables. The Tum Yum Soup was "yum in the tum" and had a spicy lemon grass base with tofu and mushrooms. Pud See Ewe, wide rice noodles with fried tofu and broccoli in a wonderful sauce, is a winner. The Pud Thai (Thailand's signature dish) was also done to perfection. High chairs for kids.

World Wrapps
124 Lake Street S • Kirkland • (425) 827-9727 • www.worldwrapps.com
See review - Bellevue

LACEY

Emperor's Palace
7321 Martin Way SE • Lacey • (360) 923-2323
See review - Olympia

Taco Del Mar
730 Sleater-Kinney Rd SE • Lacey • (360) 491-9564
See review - Seattle

LYNDEN

Taco Del Mar
8195 Guide Meridian • Lynden • (360) 354-5737
See review - Seattle

LYNNWOOD

Mediterranean Kitchen
3333 184th St SW • Lynnwood • (425) 774-6595
See review - Bellevue

Taco Del Mar
1291 205th N • Lynnwood • (206) 533-8226
4201 196th St SW • Lynnwood • (425) 673-4607
See review - Seattle

Taster's Wok
15128 Highway 99 • Lynnwood • (425) 787-6789

VeryVegFriendly • Chinese • Daily lunch & dinner • Full service & take out
Entrées $5-10

The separate vegetarian menu features a selection of dishes that use vegetable product "fake" meats, including "chicken," "pork," and "salmon," as well as a wide selection of tofu dishes. Although the fake meat product contains egg whites, Taster's Wok is very accommodating to vegans and will substitute tofu in those particular dishes. It has a nice comfortable atmosphere and very friendly servers. It's a favorite for PAWS staff.

MILL CREEK

Taco Del Mar
1402 164th St SW • Mill Creek • (425) 743-5668
See review - Seattle

MONROE

Taco Del Mar
19656 State Route 2 • Monroe • (360) 794-6560
See review - Seattle

MORTON

Plaza Jalisco
200 Westlake Ave • Morton • (360) 496-6660
See review - Chehalis

MOUNT VERNON

The Deli Next Door
202 S 1st St • Mt Vernon • (360) 336-3886

VeryVegFriendly • Deli • Daily 8am-9pm

Not really next door, but actually in the Skagit Valley Co-op, one of the friendliest, all product natural food stores in this agricultural area. In addition to the expected soups and salads and lots of vegetarian sandwiches, The Deli has specials like Veggie Samosas and Falafal Nuggets. Take your eats upstairs to the mezzanine and relax watching the activities in the store floor below.

MUKILTEO

La Cascada Acapulco
801 2nd St • Mukilteo • (425) 348-9569

VegFriendly • Mexican • Daily lunch & dinner • Entrées $5-10

The beautiful hand painted scenes of Mexico surround you inside La Cascada. The service is fantastic, and a basket of chips and homemade salsa is on your table almost as soon as you sit down. There are many vegetarian options—vegan if you ask that they hold the cheese. This is one of the few Mexican restaurants around that doesn't use lard in their food. Black Bean Enchiladas are delicately spiced, with a red hot sauce on top. If you ask them, they'll even make vegan fajitas, and they are sizzling hot and fun to eat. At the end of the meal, they bring a complimentary deep-fried tortilla chip sprinkled with cinnamon sugar, topped with raspberry jam and a dollop of whipped cream. An amazingly rich treat! If you're a vegan, ask them in advance to hold the whipped cream.

NAHCOTTA

Moby Dick Hotel & Oyster Farm
Sandridge Rd south of Bay Ave • Nahcotta • (360) 665-4543
www.mobydickhotel.com

VegFriendly • Mediterranean • Dinner Thurs - Mon • Entrées $11-21

If you stay at this charming 8 room B&B hotel you will be treated to delectable breakfasts featuring fruit and homemade breads. Open to the public for dinner, every meal has vegetarian selections such as Lasagna with Asparagus, Wild Mushrooms and Garlic Sauce, Yellow Split Pea Soup with Cumin and Lemon. Menus change twice a month to take advantage of seasonal availability of vegetables and fruits supporting organic farming and sustainable agricultural practices.

NAPAVINE

Plaza Jalisco
120 Birch St SW • Napavine • (360) 262-0243
See review - Chehalis

OLGA (ORCAS ISLAND)

Doe Bay Café
Point Lawrence Rd • Olga (Orcas Island) • (360) 376-2219

Vegetarian • Natural • Seasonal three meals • Closed in winter • Phone ahead

This remote mossy old cabin resort has a setting to die for and a laid-back restaurant overlooking the bay and adjacent dell. Meals are delicious and inventive. Eat between the daily guided kayak trips or big hot tub, sauna or massage.

OLYMPIA

The Lemon Grass Restaurant
212 4th Ave • Olympia • (360) 705-1832

VegFriendly • Chinese & Vietnamese • Daily lunch & dinner • Full service
Entrées $5-10

Beautiful, flavorful food, fresh, hot and perfectly spiced. Innovative ingredients make the food fun and interesting, like the Purple Passion, made with Asian eggplant, jicama, green beans, tofu, basil and a yellow bean and garlic sauce. The vegetarian items do not contain fish sauce like most Thai restaurants, so rest easy. Go with a friend and split one of the many exotic choices such as Lemon Grass Garden, Ginger Vegetables, Swimming Angel or Jungle Prince.

Emperor's Palace
400 Cooper Point Rd SW • Olympia • (360) 754-2188

VeryVegFriendly • Chinese • Daily lunch & dinner • Entrées $5-10

Vegetarian food delivered! A separate vegetarian menu of about 30 items offers tasty traditional Chinese fare like hot and spicy Ma Po's Tofu with diced tofu stir-fried with peppers, onions and tomatoes in a rich spicy brown sauce. The hot and sour soup is a treat, and vegan. The Broccoli and Mushroom With Ginger Sauce has just the right amount of zip. The Cashew Vegetables are extremely rich and flavorful, swimming in cashews and sauce. Emperor's Palace is a great excuse to put your feet up at home, and call your meal in.

Le Voyeur
404 East 4th Ave • Olympia • (360) 943-5710

Vegetarian • Eclectic • Daily lunch & dinner • Full service • Entrées $5-10

Get ready for the best vegetarian home cookin' within a 100 mile radius! Try an open faced tofu sandwich with mushroom gravy, the Sloppy Hippie with tempeh and grilled onions, chicken fried tofu with home fries, or another of the many vegan choices. Their salad dressings and gravies are masterpieces. The décor is funky and extremely casual. For entertainment, wear your Birkenstocks, hang out with the 20-somethings, watch the cooks (the kitchen is almost part of the dining room), drink your water out of Ball canning jars, and go to the little lounge in back and listen to local bands. Extensive, reasonably priced wine list.

Olympia Food Co-op
3111 Pacific Ave SE • Olympia • (360) 956-3870
921 N Rogers • Olympia • (360) 754-7666

VegFriendly • Deli • Open Mon-Sat 11am-8pm • Closed Sun

This co-op features a grab and go deli, with six different menu rotations with several vegetarian and vegan options, including Cilantro Pesto Pasta, Smoked Tofu Sandwich, Curried Tempeh and Nori Rolls. Organic foods are used whenever possible.

Saigon Rendezvous

117 West 5th Ave • Olympia • (360) 352-1989

VeryVegFriendly • Chinese & Vietnamese • Daily lunch & dinner • Full service
Entrées $5-10

A huge vegan menu with over 75 choices makes this vegetarian heaven. Soy based "meat" imitations are a specialty here, with items like "Prawns" with Lemon Grass, BBQ "Pork," and Kung Pao "Chicken." Tofu is also plentiful. Try the Tofu with Peapods - the colors are beautiful and the flavors great. The large appetizer platter is amazing, with five types of hors d'oeuvres, served at the table with a flaming mini-caldron to cook the skewers of Teriyaki "Beef." With great food, lots of choices, and friendly service, it's a real find.

Santosh

116 4th Ave W • Olympia • (360) 943-3442

VegFriendly • Indian • Daily lunch buffet and dinner • Entrées $5-15

Specializing in northern Indian cuisine, this classic Indian restaurant serves up plenty of vegetarian choices.

PORT ANGELES

Café Garden

1506 E 1st St • Port Angeles • (360) 457-4611

VegFriendly • American • Daily breakfast, lunch & dinner • 6:30am-8:30pm

Start the day with pancakes or veggie omelets and scrambles, creative salads, pasta and stir-fries offered for other meals.

Thai Peppers Restaurant

222 N Lincoln St • Port Angeles • (360) 452-4995

VegFriendly • Thai • Daily lunch & dinner • Full service & take out

One block from the Victoria ferry, the friendly staff will guide you through the 20-plus vegetarian items such as tofu curries and stir-fried veggies, all with those enticing Thai flavors.

PORT TOWNSEND

Khu Larb Thai

225 Adams St • Port Townsend • (360) 385-5023

VeryVegFriendly • Thai • Daily lunch & dinner • Full service & take out
Entrées $5-10

Everything that a Thai restaurant should be, pleasing vegetarians, vegans and meat and fish eaters at the same table. There is a vegetarian entrée for every letter of the alphabet. The signature spices are used in generous, well balanced amounts.

Vegetarian Tom Kha soup is as hearty as it is tasty, with lots of vegetables and tofu, a meal in itself. Classic Phud Thai without egg stands as a vegan treat. Curries are all delicious and the Spicy Eggplant is not to be missed. Lovely, thoughtful ambiance, unobtrusively good service and live jazz vibraphone on the weekends.

The Food Co-op Kitchen & Juice Bar
414 Kearney • Port Townsend • (360) 385-2883

VegFriendly • Deli & juice bar • Daily breakfast & lunch • Entrées $5-10

If you really want to "go native" this is the most vegetarian and vegan friendly place in town and organic is standard here. It is where local artists, construction crews, earth mothers, wooden boat sailors and massage therapists all meet to eat. There are choices here for meat eaters too, but the emphasis is veggie, and there are several excellent vegan live food selections. The 'live' palak paneer is expensive but quite nice as is the raw food pizza. Or have a delicious and generously custom made sandwich. There is a small area for sit down snacking inside the store. The juice bar is great, and there's not a tourist in sight.

Fountain Café
920 Washington St • Port Townsend • (360) 385-1364

Veg Friendly • Northwest eclectic • Daily breakfast, lunch & dinner
Entrées $10-20

This cozy, casually elegant little place is well worth visiting one block off the beaten tourist path. The vegetarian biscuits and gravy are the best you are likely to find anywhere; large homemade biscuits served with a generous amount of fennel and wild mushroom gravy. For a fine lunch or dinner try a black bean burger or portabello mushroom burger. The seafood crepes are excellent ordered with no seafood but extra mushrooms and spinach. You really can't go wrong here, though it is a much easier place to be vegetarian than vegan. Excellent wine list and service is always good.

The Land Fall
412 Waterfront St • Port Townsend • (360) 385-5814

VegFriendly • Eclectic • Daily breakfast & lunch • Full service or take out
Entrées $5-10

Peculiar architecture, funky atmosphere and great location overlooking the Point Hudson Yacht Harbor make it a favorite of locals and boaters for casual dining. It serves delicious confetti cole slaw and has backyard picnic tables for warmer days. There is a special vegetarian penalty. If you don't want to eat hamburger for lunch, expect to pay $1.50 extra for a veggie burger! The veggie quesadillas are the best vegetarian item on the menu.

Lehanis Deli & Coffee House
221 Taylor St • Port Townsend • (360) 385-3961

VeryVegFriendly • Deli & coffee house • Daily breakfast & lunch • Cafeteria or take out • Entrées $5-10

A very pleasant little coffee house which is both vegetarian and vegan friendly where you can get a delicious organic soy milk latte and some really nice soups, treats and snacks in both vegan and vegetarian choices mostly from local organic produce. Vegan chocoholics can indulge here. Some evenings there is live acoustic music or poetry reading.

Otters Crossing Café
130 Hudson St • Port Townsend • (360) 379-0592

Veg Friendly • Creative family style • Breakfast & lunch • Closed Mon-Tue Full service or take out • Entrées $5-10

On the far point, across the yacht harbor from town, in one of the historical old white Point Hudson buildings with a fine view of the small harbor (yes, otters do live under them and raid the boats of incautious yachtsmen). At this charming, out of the way place, you can get a vegan breakfast of oatmeal with soymilk, and there are plenty of veggie choices. Classic Port Townsend nautical ambience with an ever changing water view and breakfast all day.

The Salal Café
634 Waterfront St • Port Townsend • (360) 385-6532

VegFriendly • Northwest eclectic • Daily breakfast & lunch • Full service & take out • Entrées $5-10

A long standing commitment to vegetarian dining, overall it's a fine place to eat with good service and a pleasant sunny atmosphere in an old building right on the main tourist drag.

Sweet Laurette & Cyndee's Café & Patisserie
1029 Lawrence St • Port Townsend • (360) 385-4886

VegFriendly • Bakery & Northwest eclectic • Daily breakfast & lunch, Sun brunch, closed Tues • Full service or take out • Entrées $5-10

The food is creative and trendy. For lunch, have a delicious grilled vegetable Panini, the vegatini sandwich, the vegan delight, or a large salad served with a choice of several soups, at least one of which is vegan. Any meal with meat will be served without for $1 off. They have excellent expresso, served almost too beautifully to drink, and great chai as well. French toast fans may just find Sweet Laurette's Stuffed French Toast to be the best.

POULSBO

Vege Restaurant
18713 State Hwy 305 NE • Poulsbo • (360) 697-2538

Vegetarian • Vietnamese • Open Mon-Sat lunch & dinner, closed Sun
Entrées $5-10

A favorite on the peninsula, this restaurant offers authentic Oriental vegan fare. Owned by devoted vegans, they have translated their values into one great tasting dish after the other. Large and varied menu. Try any of the faux meat dishes for a real treat. Conveniently located, easy parking.

PUYALLUP

Bangkok Thai Restaurant
520 39th Ave SW • Puyallup • (253) 445-8040

VeryVegFriendly • Thai • Daily lunch & dinner • Full service & take out

Family owned and staffed, you'll get the feeling that you're an honored guest in their home when you have a delicious vegetarian lunch or dinner. There is a section of the menu that is specifically vegetarian and any dish on the menu can be prepared for you with tofu substituting for other ingredients. Special requests are honored for vegan diners as the staff is sensitive to nutrition, religious or philosophical requirements. The portions are generous and served family style.

Taco Del Mar
3827 1/2 S Meridian Ave • Puyallup • (253) 841-7658
10929 Canyon Rd • Puyallup • (253) 537-1335
See review - Seattle

REDMOND

Acapulco Fresh
16330 Cleveland St • Redmond • (425) 883-3510
See review - Bellevue

Haveli
16564 Cleveland St • Redmond • (425) 883-4443

VeryVegFriendly • Indian • Daily lunch (buffet) & dinner • Full service & take-out
Entrées $5-10

There are 21 vegetarian entrées on the menu plus many breads, some soups and numerous appetizers that are meatless. Try the Saag Paneer and Eggplant Bhartha, both perfectly spiced, with fluffy basmati rice. The onion Kulcha (onion stuffed nan) was flavorful and filling. Have some chai tea for a perfect end to a comforting meal.

Taco Del Mar
8074 160th Ave NE • Redmond • (425) 883-8822
See review - Seattle

RENTON

Pabla Indian Cuisine
364 Renton Center Way SW • Renton • (425) 228-4625

Vegetarian & Kosher • East Indian • Daily lunch (buffet) & dinner • Full service
Entrées $5-10

One of the few vegetarian, kosher restaurants in the Seattle area. The cuisine is from
the Punjab region of India and is deliciously, richly spiced. It's located in a little
strip mall in Renton, and has typical strip mall décor. But don't let that fool you.
The food is great, and their lunch buffet is one of the best around. It usually has
two or three vegan entrées, with many more lacto-vegetarian items. The Thali Dinners offer a sampling of eight or so dishes, and are a great alternative for those who
like variety.

RICHLAND

Aioli's Restaurant & Wine Bar
94 Lee Blvd • Richland • (509) 942-1914

VegFriendly • Mediterranean tapas • Lunch & dinner • Entrées $5-10

Many dishes on the menu are vegetarian and the very friendly staff is willing to
adjust other dishes to your vegetarian or vegan needs. Excellent wine selections. For
much of the year there is outside seating overlooking the Columbia River.

Taco Del Mar
1308 Lee Blvd • Richland • (509) 943-7500
See review - Seattle

SEATAC

Bai Tong
15859 Pacific Highway S • Seatac • (206) 431-0893

VeryVegFriendly • Thai • Daily lunch • Dinner only Sat-Sun • Entrées $5-10

Bai Tong is a northwest legend. It was originally opened to exclusively feed the crew
from Thai Airways, with chefs brought in especially from Bangkok. For the last
10 years or so, it's been open to the rest of us, too. The food is fantastic, and very
authentic. It is extremely vegetarian-friendly, with no fish sauce hidden in any menu
item. There is a separate vegetarian menu but your choices are unlimited because
almost any item on the menu can be made with tofu instead of meat. This place is a
must-visit!

Agua Verde Paddle Club & Café

1303 NE Boat St • Seattle • (206) 545-8570 • www.aguaverde.com

VeryVegFriendly • Mexican • Lunch & dinner • Full service & take out
Entrées $5-10

The choices for vegetarians are abundant, with no lard or other hidden animal ingredients. The Empanadas de Flor de Calabaza (squash blossoms, zucchini, epazote (an herb) and Oaxacan cheese) is a favorite. So is the De Hongo (portabello mushrooms, tomatoes and onions sautéed with guajillo chiles, cotija cheese). The yam open faced tacos are wonderful. Be sure to order some of their side dishes, like Pineapple Jicama Salsa or Corn & Cactus Salad. Delicious! A very inexpensive place for the entire family. Reservations recommended.

Araya's Vegetarian Place

4732 University Way NE • Seattle • (206) 524-4332

Vegan • Thai • Daily lunch & dinner • Full service, take out & buffet
Entrées $5-10

You know the fresh rolls stuffed with cool tender spinach and sweet peanut dipping sauce will be perfect. On cool winter days, the mushroom or hot and sour soup will be amazing. After all that, will you have room for an entrée? Warm and cozy with friendly servers and funky decorative hangings.

Bahn Thai Restaurant

409 Roy St • Seattle • (206) 283-0444

VegFriendly • Thai • Lunch Mon-Fri • Dinner daily

Long a favorite part of Seattle's authentic Thai restaurant scene, Bahn Thai offers an extensive list of vegetarian and vegan entrées.

Bamboo Garden

364 Roy Street • Seattle • (206) 282-6616 • www.bamboogarden.net

Vegan & Kosher • Chinese • Daily lunch & dinner • Full service & take out
Entrées $5-10

When asked, "So what do vegans eat?", bring them here. They will be deliciously overwhelmed with over 100 menu items, all vegan and all kosher. There are creative and traditional Chinese sauces, crisp veggies, thick doughy noodles, and faux meats that are so real you will keep checking the menu just to be sure. Soft chatter and quick moving servers let you know that you are in a popular place without feeling crowded.

Café Flora

2901 East Madison • Seattle • (206) 325-9100

Vegetarian • Gourmet • Lunch & dinner • Closed Mon • Entrées $10-20

Although all of Café Flora's menu is completely vegetarian, many non-vegetarians are repeat customers coming to enjoy more fine gourmet dinners. The dishes are prepared using seasonal vegetables and although the menu changes regularly, there are always standard options such as the French dip sandwich and the curry (veg) burger. The presentation of dishes is outstanding and very colorful. The interior is decorated with vibrant colors, new artists' work is displayed throughout, and the interior atrium with seating around a fountain creates a very pleasant atmosphere. Popular Sunday brunch.

Café Long

12517 Lake City Way NE • Seattle • (206) 362-6259

VegFriendly • Asian • Lunch & dinner • Closed Sun • Entrées $5-10

Authentic oriental foods with a wide choice in vegetarian dishes. Salads, faux meats such as chicken and ham, tofu and 27 vegetarian dishes give a wide choice to vegetarian customers. It is small and cozy.

California Pizza Kitchen

401 NE Northgate Way • Seattle • (206) 367-4445
See review - Bellevue

The Canal Pan Asia Grill and Bar

235 Broadway Ave E • Seattle • (206) 328-0515

VegFriendly • Lunch & dinner • Entrées $5-10

The Canal offers vegetarian entrées with nutritious vegetables and tofu based dishes. Seating is spacious and the staff is gracious. Most of the dishes can be customized as vegetarian on request.

Carmelita

7314 Greenwood Ave N • Seattle • (206) 706-7703

Vegetarian • Eclectic • Dinner only • Closed Mon • Full service • Entrées $10-20

Gourmet vegetarian cuisine at this popular Phinney Ridge bistro with vegan alternatives for every course. Excellent service and great selection of food. Desserts served in generous portions, enough to share.

Chutneys

1815 N 45th St • (Wallingford) • Seattle • (206) 634 1000
605 15th Ave E • (Capitol Hill) • Seattle • (206) 726 1000
519 1st Ave N • (Queen Anne) • Seattle • (206) 284 6799
See review - Bellevue

Cyber Dog

909 Pike St • Seattle • (206) 405-3647

Vegetarian • Hot dogs • Daily, 9am-midnight • Full service & take out
Entrées $5-10

Giving a new reputation to the hot dog, these are all vegetarian, mostly vegan, totally crazy and absolutely yummy. Start the day with a Breakfast Dog (served all day) like the Banana Dog, or the Bratwurst (ovo-vegetarian), topped with breakfast-type things like vegetarian bacon or hollandaise sauce. There are also pastries and gourmet coffees. Later try the Laika Dog, with Russian Eggplant Caviar. Or the DoggiLama with masala and Cumber Yogurt Sauce. The Lamour, a "Lovely French Dog" is smothered in fondu and vegetables. And it's all wrapped up in an art-filled internet café. Fantastic!

Elysian Brewing Company

1221 E Pike St • Seattle • (206) 860-1920

VegFriendly • PubGrub • Daily lunch & dinner • Entrées $5-10

A great choice for a vegetarian or vegan in the mood for a microbrew experience. About a third of the menu is made of great vegetarian, mostly vegan choices, with usually a vegan soup of the day. Sandwiches feature field roast, a lentil based meat substitute in a variety of tangy sauces and there are old favorites like rice and beans, veggie burgers and pasta. The Elysian also brews many varieties of its own draft beers (vegan!) Try the beer sampler tray or non-alcoholic Elysian root beer and ginger beer.

The Globe Café & Bakery

1531 14th Ave • Seattle • (206) 324-8815

Vegan • Coffeehouse • Breakfast, lunch & dinner • Closed Mon • Entrées $5-10

In the Capital Hill area offering inexpensive vegan meals in a small informal dining room. The daily menu is written on a chalkboard by the front counter and customers have to get their own silverware and water. Portions are quite generous and the food is hearty and delicious. Be sure to try the vegan desserts.

Good Morning Healing Earth.

901 NE 55th St • Seattle • (206) 523-8025

Vegan • Home cooking • Late breakfast, lunch & dinner • Closed Mon
Entrées $5-10

Tucked away in a brightly painted "U District" house with an extremely bohemian atmosphere offering a menu that is entirely vegan. The daily feature is soup, salad, rice and bread (plain or topped with crushed garlic) or you can choose from one of their many sandwich/salad/homefries combo or a pasta and veggie dish. The biscuits with mushroom gravy are a meal in itself. Comfort food at its best.

Gravity Bar

415 Broadway • Seattle • (206) 325-7186

VeryVegFriendly • Eclectic • Daily late breakfast, lunch & dinner • Full service
Most $5-10

Avant garde healthy food with fun décor, like the Flintstones and Jetsons collided, really more of a bar with stools. The food is wholesome and fantastically delicious with lots of vegan choices. A favorite is the RV1 with the Works (brown rice, steamed veggies, grilled tofu and your choice of sauces like Lemon Tahini or Peanut Sauce). The Bathing Rama is great with fresh steamed spinach and perfectly spiced peanut sauce. Their Tempeh Burger is a better alternative. Fruit juices made fresh while you watch. The Wheat Grass grows in flats and is so fresh, it doesn't have time to even know it's been mowed and squeezed into your glass.

The Green Cat Café

1514 E Olive Way • Seattle • (206) 726-8756 • www.greencatcafe.com

Vegetarian • Daily breakfast and lunch • Full service

At Capitol Hill's friendliest vegetarian café you can start the morning with tamale pie or tofu scramble. For lunch, the Buddah Bowl offers you brown rice topped with grilled vegetables and covered in lemon tahini sauce. Inventive sandwiches and salads. All washed down with Ginger Blast or Wonder Juice.

Hillside Quickie's Shop

4106 Brooklyn Ave • Seattle • (206) 632-3037

Vegan-organic • Sandwich shop • Mon-Sat lunch & dinner

Intentionally low key but notably high profile sandwiches made from home-made seitan, tempeh or tofu. Raves for their Crazy Jamaican Burger which is grilled plantain, onions and tofu. Famous is their Macaroni & Yease, and the seitan 'steak', mashed potatoes and vegan gravy. A brunch suggested is the polenta and vegan French toast. The foods created and offered by this African American family go on. See the Tacoma listing for Quickie Too.

Himalayan Sherpa Restaurant

4214 University Way NE • Seattle • (206) 633-2100

VegFriendly • Nepal/Tibet/Indian • Mon-Sat lunch buffet & dinner • Closed Sun
Entrées $5-10

Great vegetarian choices, particularly on Tues and Fri lunchtimes. Vegans may want to ask about dairy free dishes. Dall Bhaat Tarkary and Bhendi (Ocra/Ladies Fingers) Masala are tasty choices. Try some Chang, authentic Tibetan beer. Chants and tranquil Himalayan music fill the air, while authentic wall hangings and paintings of majestic mountains with sun drenched stupas surround you with the sights and sounds of Tibet, Nepal and Northern India.

Kabul Afghan Cuisine

2301 N 45th • Seattle • (206) 545-9000

VeryVegFriendly • Afghani • Daily, dinner only

Five time winner at "Bite of Seattle." A unique culinary experience bringing a subtle blend of spices, home recipes and photography to transport you to the Afghan city of Kabul. Try the Bolani Turnovers with herbs, potatoes and tomato sauce; Shornakhod: chickpeas and kidney beans in a lemon-vinegar dressing; Qorma-I Tarkari: cauliflower, carrots and potato with dill, turmeric and cumin; Bodenjan Borani: eggplant with tomato sauce and mint. The mango sorbet dessert is specially made for Kabul. Wine available. Live sitar music some nights.

Kitaro Japanese Cuisine

1624 N 45th St • Seattle • (206) 547-7998

VeryVegFriendly • Japanese • Daily lunch and dinner (lunch only on Wed) Entrées $7-13

Vegetarian sushi is the specialty of this wonderful Japanese restaurant, with about 20 different vegetarian choices such as burdock root or tofu with garlic and avocado. Every dish on the extensive menu can be made vegetarian by substituting tofu for meat where necessary. There are also noodle soups, stir fry noodles and many vegetarian rice dishes such as the vegetables and tofu teriyaki, all available with brown rice if you prefer.

Kwanjai Thai

469 N 36th St • Seattle • (206) 632-3656

VeryVegFriendly • Thai • Daily lunch & dinner • Full service & take-out Entrées $5-10

The restaurant, run by a Thai family, is situated inside a tiny house where the atmosphere is bursting with energy, yet it is very cozy as all the tables are placed close together. The food comes quickly, and most entrées can be prepared vegetarian by omitting the fish sauce and asking for tofu instead of meat. A favorite dish is the eggplant with tofu.

Lucky Palate

307 W McGraw St • Seattle • (206) 352-2583 • www.luckypalate.com

Vegetarian & Vegan • Eclectic • Home delivery, take out & storefront meals

A popular home delivery service of delicious gourmet vegetarian or vegan meals on a weekly basis. Choose from two to six meals per week with or without dessert, or order a la carte. The owner/chef is author of *The Accidental Vegan* cookbook. The storefront is open off and on for grab-and-go meals and a selection of homemade groceries.

Mediterranean Kitchen

366 Roy St • Seattle • (206) 285 6713
See review - Bellevue

10 Mercer

10 Mercer St • Seattle • (206) 691-3723

VegFriendly • Continental/American • Daily lunch & dinner • Entrées $10-20

10 Mercer is a hot spot with fabulous food and an even better wine list. Every night there are at least two vegetarian entrées, like Wild Mushroom Risotto (for lacto-vegs) or Ratatouille (for vegans if you request they hold the parmesan). The chef stands in front of the stove for 20 minutes and stirs creamy rich risotto laced with Chanterelle mushrooms, just for you. The Spinach Cannelloni is surprising, with the earthy taste of Shitake mushrooms and spinach, with a minced black olive garnish. Seasonal ingredients like grilled pears, pumpkin seeds and other earthly delights dance in your mouth and on your salad plate. All of their salads can be made vegan.

Mighty-O Donuts

2110 N 55th St • Seattle • (206) 547-0335 • www.mighty-o.com

Vegan • Donut & coffee shop • Breakfast thru lunch • Sit in or take out

These are big, rich cake donuts, so moist, dense and delicious that you will be reminded why you drink coffee in the first place. A friendly neighborhood coffee house, with some sandwiches and juices, newspaper strewn tables, comfy chairs, couches, soothing folk music and excellent espresso. Try the chocolate coconut. Unbelievable!

Phoenecia at Alki

2716 Alki Ave SW • Seattle • (206) 935-6550

VegFriendly • Mediterranean • Dinner only • Closed Mon • Full service
Entrées $10-20

On Alki beach in West Seattle, offering several options for vegetarians, such as salads, pizza and pasta dishes. Instead of relying strictly on the menu, let Phoenicia's owner, Chef Hussein Khazaal, select a dish for you which can be a vegetable curry entrée as a very flavorful and satisfying vegan meal.

Quazis Indian Curry House

473 N 36th St • Seattle • (206) 632-3575

VegFriendly • Indian • Daily lunch & dinner • Full service & take out
Entrées $5-10

This restaurant serves a superb Eggplant Bharta (request without cream if vegan). Their Vegetable Pakoras are vegan as is the Spinach Naan and Aloo Paratha, very welcome since in most restaurants Naan bread is not vegan. Opened in 2002, the atmosphere is quiet. Seats are surrounded by vases on the wall with fabric undulating above and across the walls.

Rose Club Café

3601 S McClellan St • Seattle • 206 725 3654 • www.theroseclub.net

VeryVegFriendly • Café • Daily breakfast, lunch and dinner, except Sun dinner
Full service & take out • Entrées $10-20

Across from the park in the beautiful Mount Baker neighborhood, this small independent restaurant serves up a delicious seasonal menu using organic ingredients wherever possible. Come in for breakfast and try the tofu scramble. Enjoy fresh made soups and sandwiches for lunch, or select from a range of delicious entrées such as mushroom tacos, ravioli or pizza for dinner.

Rovers

2808 E Madison St • Seattle • (206) 325-7442 • www.rovers-seattle.com

Vegfriendly • Dinner only • Closed Sun-Mon • 5-course set menu • Full service
Must reserve

High-end, exclusive restaurant offers one 8-course and two 5-course set menus, one of which is always vegetarian. The menus change slightly every day, and with 24 hours notice, they can provide a vegan menu. Set back behind the storefronts on the west side of Madison Street, you will feel like you have walked into a private house as you enter the several small cozy rooms of the dining area, with traditional elegant décor. While the portions are small, each course is exquisitely presented and very flavorful. By the time you've enjoyed all five dishes, plus a dessert plate and tea or coffee, you will feel comfortably satisfied and delightfully indulged.

Shamiana

2255 NE 65th St • Seattle • (206) 524-3664

VegFriendly • Indian cuisine • Daily lunch & dinner • Entrées $10-20

With festive décor and family friendly smiles, Shamiana offers good service, delicious appetizers and moderate portions for all. The vegetarian menu is small but offers very tasty food with vegan options that include vegetable curry, eggplant dishes and more.

Silence Heart Nest

5247 University Way NE • Seattle • (206) 524-4008

Vegetarian • Indian plus • Lunch & dinner • Closed Wed • Full service
Entrées $5-10

Though the Indian curries and chutneys are truly delightful, people come from far and near for the spectacular "Neat Loaf," mashed potatoes and gravy. Waitresses wear traditional Indian attire and Indian music plays in the background. You will be charmed by the menu and the relaxing Sri Chinmoy art on orange and blue walls. Vegans will find several selections to their liking in this small but pleasant location.

Sound View Café
1501 Pike Pl • #501 • Seattle • (206) 623-5700

VegFriendly • Cafeteria • Daily 8am-5pm

Located downstairs in the Pike Place Market, this health-minded restaurant has an unusual variety of vegetarian specialties. Enjoy watching the ferries in Puget Sound while sitting on a stool by the window, enjoying great food!

Sunlight Café
6403 Roosevelt Way NE • Seattle • (206) 522-9060

Vegetarian • Ethnic eclectic • Daily breakfast, lunch & dinner • Full service
Entrées $5-10

One of the first vegetarian restaurants in Seattle and still a relaxed setting with tasty selections. A good casual meeting place and excellent value.

Super Bowl Noodle House
814 NE 65th St • Seattle • (206) 526-1570

VeryVegFriendly • Thai • Daily lunch & dinner • Entrées $5 - 10

A tiny gem, a bit north of UW serves huge portions of Phad Thai, always wonderful and less sweet than most Thai restaurants. It's hard not to always re-order the Vegetarian M-80 – a huge bowl of spicy soup noodles (choice of egg, thin or thick rice noodles) full of tofu plus many veggies. Fresh or fried, the spring rolls are amazing and the service is the best! It's a family affair and spotlessly clean.

Taco Del Mar
1033 65th NE • Seattle • (206) 729-0670 • www.tacodelmar.com
12311 Lake City Way NE • Seattle • (206) 363-9151
3526 Fremont Pl N • Seattle • (206) 545-8001
1815 N 45th St • Seattle • (206) 545-3720
8004 Greenwood Ave N • Seattle • (206) 706-4063
6101 15th Ave NW • Seattle • (206) 297-4446
725 Pike St • Seattle • (206) 628-8982
1165 Harrison St • Seattle • (206) 624-2114
1520 Broadway • Seattle • (206) 328-4868
107 1st Ave • Seattle • (206) 467-5940
2136 1st Ave • Seattle • (206) 448-8877
823 Third Ave • Seattle • (206) 467-4878
2932 4th Ave S • Seattle • (206) 521-8887
2401 Utah Ave S • Seattle • (206) 343-0552
4740 42nd Ave SW • Seattle • (206) 938-1413

VeryVegFriendly • Lunch & dinner • Entrées under $5.

Vegan fast food? Yes, it's true! Try Taco Del Mar for a colorful, fun restaurant known for fresh and quality ingredients as well as a healthy fast food alternative. There are many vegetarian options and a vegan burrito right on the menu. Don't forget to try the smoothies and the chips and salsa, they are excellent. The friendly staff will quickly prepare your food right in front of you. Perfect for kids.

Tawon Thai

3410 Fremont Ave • (206) 633-4545 • Seattle • www.tawonthai.com

VeryVegFriendly • Thai • Daily lunch & dinner

Their new vegetarian menu offers a surprising number of appetizers, soups and entrées made without eggs or fish sauce. For a wonderful Thai feast try the savory Pad Woon Sen, stir fried bean thread noodles with pineapple, celery, green onion, nappa cabbage, bell peppers and tofu, or the Pad Kee Mou, stir fried wide noodles with broccoli, tomatoes, basil and chili sauce. There are great desserts to choose from such as sweet black sticky rice in coconut milk, coconut, mango ice cream, and the tasty pairing of white rice and mango.

Teapot Vegetarian House

125 15th Ave E • Seattle • (206) 325-1010

Vegan & Kosher • Asian • Daily lunch & dinner • Full service & take-out
Entrées $5-10

Many of the Teapot menu items feature mock meat dishes. Start a meal with their spring rolls or the mushroom and lettuce appetizer. The very popular rose drummettes are served with a table brightening sweet and sour sauce. There are a variety of Asian favorites, like Yaki Udon, Szechuan "Beef" and an array of soy based stir fries. The "Rama Garden" of fresh veggies are steamed to crisp perfection and served with a tofu and peanut sauce. The thick "House Noodles" with the heaping pile of vegetables is a local favorite. Count on a healthy, hearty meal at a moderate price. The ambience is very comfortable. A softly glowing neon outline of a teapot covers the ceiling, lending a quirky air to the large dining room. Live music is featured on Saturday nights.

Thai on Alki

1325 Harbor Ave SW • Seattle • (206) 938-2992

VeryVegFriendly • Thai • Daily lunch & dinner • Full service • Entrées $5-10

Enjoying a beautiful view across the bay especially at night of the downtown Seattle skyline, you will find many vegetarian appetizers and entrées. On request they will make eggless vegan dishes. The service is prompt and prices are reasonable.

Thai Kitchen

2220 Queen Anne Ave • Seattle • (206) 285-8424

VeryVegFriendly • Thai • Daily lunch & dinner • Full service & take out
Entrées $5-10

A very pleasant ambience in the living room of an old house with lots of outdoor seating as well. The Thai spices are subtle but pleasant. Pud Thai and Yellow Curry are excellent. There are about 35 vegetarian choices and the service is fine and prompt.

Vegete

131 15th Ave E • Seattle • (206) 325-1733 • www.vegeterestaurant.com

Vegetarian • Deli-cafeteria • Daily 10am-8pm • Eat there or take-out
Entrées $5-10

Established in 2002, this vegetarian deli is a delightful addition to the many veg-friendly restaurants and cafés in the Pacific Northwest. The sandwiches are out of this world, especially the BLT ("bacon," lettuce and tomato). The deli serves traditionally non-veg items (using meat analog products), creating comfort food like French dip sandwiches. Items can be made vegan, too. The savories are very good with lots of vegan options. Incredible bakery.

World Wrapps

528 Queen Ann Ave N • Seattle • (206) 286-9727 • www.worldwrapps.com
1109 Madison St • Seattle • (206) 467-9744
7900 E Greenlake Drive • Seattle • (206) 524-9727
2750 NE University Village • Seattle • (206) 522-7873
222 Yale Ave N • Seattle • (206) 233-0222
601 Union St • Seattle • (206) 628-9601
400 Pine St • Seattle • (206) 628-6868
701 5th Ave-Columbia Tower • Seattle • (206) 340-0810
See review - Bellevue

Zao Noodle Bar

2590 University Village • Seattle • (206) 539-8278 • www.zao.com

VeryVegFriendly • Asian noodle bar • Daily lunch & dinner • $5-10

"Health & Wisdom in a Bowl" portends the complex balanced flavors in their noodle bowls but start off with a vegan appetizer like Crispy Tofu Fries with three sauces or Roasted Wasabi Peas. Entrées have innovative ingredients like soy-lime dressing. The Monk's Vegetarian Delight or the Vietnamese Rice Noodles with Five Vegetables are recommended. Portions are huge and the food is "scrumptious."

Zoopa

Northgate Mall • Seattle • (206) 440-8135 • www.zoopa.com
See review - Bellevue

SEQUIM

Khu Larb Thai

120 W Bell • Sequim • (360) 681-8550
See review - Port Townsend

SILVERDALE

Taco Del Mar

2244 NW Bucklin Hill Rd • Silverdale • (360) 307-8226
See review - Seattle

SPOKANE

China Best

226 W Riverside Ave • Spokane • (509) 455-9042

VegFriendly • Chinese • Daily • Full service & take out

Over 20 vegetarian menu items, with some vegan options. Try the Buddha's Delight, a mélange of vegetables, water chestnuts and mushrooms in a soft sauce, or have their fried eggplant or sautéed string beans, done with very little spice but a sweet-and-sour sauce. Every dish is freshly prepared to order and there are vegan options.

Mizuna

214 N Howard St • Spokane • (509) 747-2004

VeryVegFriendly • Eclectic • Lunch Mon-Fri, dinner Tues-Sat • Closed Sun
Full service

Next to old brick walls, with candles on the table, you can enjoy items like butternut pecan canalone or Indian tandor curry tofu. There is a selection of organic wines.

Niko's

725 W Riverside Ave • Spokane • (509) 624-7444

VegFriendly • Greek/Middle East • Daily lunch & dinner 11am-10pm • Full service

There is a very large selection of vegetarian items such as spanakopita and their mushroom and tofu entrée.

Peking Palace

11110 E Sprague Ave • Spokane • (509) 924-3933 • www.pekingpalacespk.com

VegFriendly • Chinese • Daily lunch & dinner • Entrées $5-10

Chinese without MSG. All the traditional dishes available with vegetables, such as Vegetable Chow Mein, Lo Mein, Chop Suey or Fried Rice, and some special vegetable and tofu dishes. Tofu can be substituted for meat in any dish.

TACOMA

East & West Café

5319 Tacoma Mall Blvd • Tacoma • (253) 475-7755

VegFriendly • PanAsian • Lunch & dinner • Full service & take out • Entrées $9-12

An elegant restaurant that prides itself on its fresh local produce, high standards with no MSG and healthy flavorful cooking. Mostly Thai and Vietnamese cuisine along with a few Indian, Korean, Malaysian and Indonesian dishes are offered with a variety of vegetarian dishes like curries, soups and salads. NonVeg dishes can be customized as completely vegetarian or vegan. Customers are encouraged to order dishes they prefer and not on the menu.

Marlene's Market & Deli

2951 S 38th St • Tacoma • (253) 472-4080 • www.marlenesmarket-deli.com

VegFriendly • Natural foods • Open daily • Take out

A welcome in-store deli/restaurant which, in addition to soups and salads, offers tasty plates of pasta and sandwiches such as their vegan Field Roast or Avocado Delight or vegan bologna! There is a pleasant table area for a relaxed before or after shopping meal.

May's Vietnamese Restaurant

2514 N Proctor • Tacoma • (253) 756-5092

VegFriendly • Nouvelle Vietnamese • Lunch & dinner • Closed Sun
Entrées $5-10

May's was rated 3 stars in the *Tacoma News Tribune's* "Top Ten Restaurants of 1999." May specializes in Vietnamese "Nouvelle Cuisine" influenced by Chinese, Thai and French cooking resulting in dishes that are light, full of flavor and low in fat. May's offers a good variety of vegetarian dishes. Only vegetable oils are used to prepare the entrées. No starch or MSG used here.

Quickie Too

1324 Martin Luther King Ave S • Tacoma • (253) 572-4549

Vegan-organic • Sandwich shop • Mon, Wed, Fri, Sun 11am-8pm

Intentionally low key but notably high profile sandwiches made from home-made seitan, tempeh or tofu. Raves for their Crazy Jamaican Burger which is grilled plantain, onions and tofu. Famous is their Macaroni & Yease, and the seitan 'steak', mashed potatoes and vegan gravy. A brunch suggested is the polenta and vegan French toast. The foods created and offered by this African American family go on. See the Seattle listing for the Hillside Quickie.

Taco Del Mar

4009 Tacoma Mall Blvd • Tacoma • (253) 472-6256
1908 Pacific Ave • Tacoma • (253) 572-8393
5738 N. 26th St • Tacoma • (253) 761-7425
2700 Bridgeport Way W • Tacoma • (253) 566-0555
See review - Seattle

Wendy's Vietnamese Restaurant

430 East 25th St • Tacoma • (253) 572-4678

VegFriendly • Vietnamese • Daily lunch & dinner • Entrées $5-10

In the food court of Freight House Square. Same great taste but a smaller version of the full restaurant, Wendy's II.

Wendy's II Vietnamese Restaurant

5015 Tacoma Mall Blvd • Tacoma • (253) 471-0228

VegFriendly • Vietnamese • Daily lunch & dinner • Entrées $5-10

A great choice for vegetarian and vegan cuisine in Tacoma. Winner of several awards, including 3 stars, *Tacoma News Tribune* winner of the 1994 Golden Fork Award. The food is tasty as well as healthy with no MSG used. Try the Tofu Salad Roll, the Sai Dai Tofu or the Black Bean Tofu with Vegetables.

Zoopa

1901 South 72nd St • Tacoma • (253) 472-0900 • www.zoopa.com
See review - Bellevue

TUKWILA

Taco Del Mar

17410 Southcenter Pkwy • Tukwila • (206) 575-8587
See review - Seattle

Zoopa

Strander Blvd at Southcenter Plaza • Tukwila • (206) 575-0500 • www.zoopa.com
See review - Bellevue

TUMWATER

Plaza Jalisco

5212 Capital Blvd • Tumwater • (360) 709-0287
See review - Chehali

Taco Del Mar

555 Trosper Rd SW • Tumwater • (360) 753-6100
See review - Seattle

VASHON ISLAND

Homegrown Café

17614 Vashon Hwy • Vashon Island • (206) 463-6302

VegFriendly • Café • Daily breakfast, lunch & dinner 7am-9pm

Natural home-style cooking with a flair. Many vegetarian and vegan choices like Mediterranean Pasta with Artichokes or Brown Rice and Lentil Curry. The home-made Boogle Burger is highly recommended as is the Tofu Scramble.

WENATCHEE

Taco Del Mar

142 Easy St • Wenatchee • (509) 665-9500
See review - Seattle

WOODINVILLE

Taco Del Mar
13780 NE 175th Ave NE • Woodinville • (425) 398-8183
See review - Seattle

YAKIMA

El Porton
420 S 48th Ave • Yakima • (509) 965-5422

VeryVegFriendly • Mexican Family • Daily lunch & dinner

"Healthier Dishes" are showcased as a separate, totally vegetarian part of the extensive menu. Try Fajita Vegetarian, a huge sizzling pan with a bright variety of eight roasted vegetables with rice and beans and choice of corn or flour tortillas; it's vegan if you ask for no cheese and sour cream. The mystery spiced Cheese and Spinach Enchilada is excellent, as is the Chile Relleno, a rich mild poblano wrapped in the right balance of inner and outer flavors. Vegan Margarita!

ZILLAH

El Porton
905 Vintage Valley Pkwy • Zillah • (509) 829-9100
See review - Yakima

"Fish carry their share of fat and cholesterol and they also have a knack for bioconcentrating toxic chemicals in their muscles."

"Vegetarians have just 1-2% of the national average of levels of certain pesticides and industrial chemicals [in their bodies.]"
– see page 159

Restaurants in Oregon

ASHLAND

Ashland Food Co-op

237 N 1st St • Ashland • (541) 482-2237 • www.ashlandfood.coop

VeryVegFriendly • Deli • Open daily during normal store hours

If you're hungry, 3 blocks from Ashland's main drag is the Ashland Food Co-op full-service deli, bakery and juice bar. Indoor and outdoor seating provides the perfect place for breakfast, lunch or dinner. There are vegan, vegetarian and omnivore selections. Also features many wheat and/or dairy-free products.

Pilaf Restaurant

10 Calle Guanajuato • Ashland • (541) 488-7898 • www.globalpantry.com/pilaf

Vegetarian • Mediterranean • Lunch & dinner • Full service or take out
Entrees $5-10

Innovative as well as traditional dishes, drawn from the cuisines of the Mediterranean, Middle East and India using local organic and international ingredients. Pita sandwiches, panini, pitzahs, salads, Sicilian fries, mezze sampler plates, pasta dishes, as well as daily specials complemented by microbrews, wine, world famous "illy caffe" espresso, Global Pantry Chai and Mediterranean Cooler. Colorful, elevator accessible dining room faces famous Lithia Park.

ASTORIA

The Columbia Café

1114 Marine Dr • Astoria • (503) 325-2233

VeryVegFriendly • Natural foods • Full service • Breakfast & lunch daily, dinner Wed-Sat

This small bohemian restaurant is vegetarian apart from the few fish entrees offered for dinner. There are plenty of delicious meals to choose from including rice, vegetable and tofu dishes, bean burritos, homemade pasta, and other international options. Salsas are made from all types of fruits and vegetables. Delicious crepes with a variety of fillings, vegan chilli and French onion soup are their specialties.

BEAVERTON

India Direct

16205 NW Bethany Ct • Beaverton • (503) 690-0499 • www.shopindiadirect.com

Vegetarian • Indian • Lunch and dinner • Full service & take out • Entrees $5-10
Closed Mon

India Direct is an Indian grocery store with a small café in the back. The menu is limited, but 100% vegetarian. The food is incredibly good, but a little spicy. India

Direct caters to the Indian community so the food is authentic. Seating is at the counters, in a bar stool style. The café seats only about 10 people. If you have to wait, you can do some grocery shopping in the store where you can find every kind of spice imaginable.

Swagat Indian Cuisine

4325 SW 109th Ave • Beaverton • (503) 626-3000 • www.indogram.com/swagat/

VegFriendly • Indian • Daily lunch (buffet) & dinner • Full service & take out
Entrees $5-10

The full range of traditional north and south Indian dishes are offered at this traditional Indian restaurant, but their specialties are from Madras and southeast India. The classic lentil flour dosas are crepe style pancakes, over a foot wide, which are stuffed with a vegetable curry. The all-you-can-eat buffet is a great choice for lunch.

Taco Del Mar

11729 SW Beaverton-Hillsdale Hwy • Beaverton • (503) 646-5898
www.tacodelmar.com

VeryVegFriendly • Lunch & dinner • Entrees under $5

Vegan fast food? Yes, it's true! Try Taco Del Mar for a colorful, fun restaurant known for fresh and quality ingredients as well as healthy fast food alternatives. There are many vegetarian options and a vegan burrito right on the menu. Don't forget to try the smoothies and the chips and salsa, they are excellent. The friendly staff will quickly prepare your food right in front of you. Perfect for kids.

Thai Orchid Restaurant

18070 NW Evergreen Pkwy • Beaverton • (503) 439-6683
16165 SW Regatta Ln • Beaverton • (503) 617-4602
www.thaiorchid.citysearch.com

VegFriendly • Thai • Daily lunch & dinner • Full service • Entrees $5-10

Traditional Thai food that is fresh, flavorful and healthy with no msg or hydrogenated oil added. Choose from more than 40 vegetarian options including choices such as Pad Nam Prik Phao (with chili jam, eggplants, bell peppers, onions and sweet basil leaves), Gaeng Pa Nang (with Pa Nang curry, green beans and kaffir leaves) and the traditional Pad Thai. Level of spiciness can be prepared to your liking.

CORVALLIS _____

China Delight

325 NW 2nd St • Corvallis • (541) 753-3753

VegFriendly • Chinese • Open daily for lunch and dinner • Full service & take out
Entrees $5-10

Healthy, delicious vegetarian entrees including their famously addictive sesame tempeh. The service and atmosphere is friendly, and almost all of their dishes have a vegetarian option. Meal choices go beyond your typical to such as vegetarian "pork chop," tofu with rosemary, and Da Vinci tofu.

Feast Alternative (in First Alternative Co-op)

1007 SE 3rd St • Corvallis • (541) 753-3115 • www.firstalt.coop

VegFriendly • Deli • Daily 9am-9pm

This co-op makes delicious dishes for their deli. All ingredients are organic and local whenever possible. Easy meals such as torte verde and caramelized onion lasagna, salad bar, fresh made-to-order sandwiches, hot pizza and soups. Fresh vegan and vegetarian bakery items daily. In and outdoor seating available. Full details of ingredients are helpful.

Intaba's Kitchen

1115 SE 3rd • Corvallis • (541) 754-6958

VeryVegFriendly • International • Lunch & dinner • Closed Mon • Full service & take out • Entrees $5-10

A special blend of organic world cuisines, their almost exclusively vegetarian/vegan menu offers a unique variety of delectable entrees including BBQ tempeh kabobs, tofu stroganoff, seitan stew and stuffed portabello mushrooms. For lunch, treat yourself to one of the wood fired lunch wraps such as the basil almond pesto, cashew hummus or roasted shiitake mushroom. Their wood fired pizza cooked in a beautiful earthen oven can be made to order with an appetizing selection of vegetables and even tempeh chorizo or "To-Feta."

Nearly Normal's

109 NW 15th St • Corvallis • (541) 753-0791

Vegetarian • International • Mon-Sat, all three meals • Closed Sun • Full service & take out • Entrees $5-10

Affectionately called "Gonzo Cuisine," from vegan breakfast burritos to gonzo pad thai or "tempehchangas" to BBQ tempeh burgers, there is not a customary plate on the menu. The organic soups, salads and daily specials are each their own exceptional, unique meal. This funky yet classy restaurant supports a thoughtfulness in preparation and presentation of food, where original vegetarian recipes are invented behind the counter, born from "creative chaos."

Taco Del Mar

1915 NW 9th St • Corvallis • (541) 738-0540 • www.tacodelmar.com
See review - Beaverton

Café Yumm!

296 E 5th Ave • Eugene • (541) 484-7302
130 Oakway Center • Eugene • (541) 225-0121
1801 Williamette St • Eugene • (541) 431-0204 • www.cafeyumm.com

Vegetarian • American/International • Daily for three meals • Full service &
take out • Entrees $5-10

Based around their signature sauces, they have developed a distinctive style of
healthy, sustainable vegetarian meals. Rice and beans have never been prepared in
so many delicious ways on a single menu. You can choose between the likes of a
Yumm! wrap with tofu, or a Chilian zucchini corn stew and rice dish. Great care
is given to the quality of the recipes and ingredients which highlight sustainable,
organic and truly Yummy! meals. Soups, salads and finger foods are also offered,
as well as their sauces and marinades.

Cosmic Pizza

199 W 8th • Eugene • (541) 338-9333
1432 Willamette Ave • Eugene • (541) 338-9337

VeryVegFriendly • Pizza • Open daily • Take out or order in with free delivery in an
electric vehicle

A pleasant organic pizzeria with a heart. Create your pizza with vegetarian Canadian
bacon or pepperoni or just go for a choice of organic vegetable toppings and add
cheezy tofu topping. This all goes on a gluten free crust made from potato and rice
flour. Owner Joel encourages folks to bring a board game and stay for the evening.
Locals will order Genesis Juice, Rusty's Handbuilt Cookies, and vegan cheesezecake.

Holy Cow Café

1222 E 13th Ave at U of O Student Union • Eugene • (541) 346-2562
www.holycowcafe.com

Vegetarian • Café • Phone for hours • Closed Sat-Sun

Organic vegetarian gourmet food at affordable prices. Ethnic comfort food from
around the world, plus an organic salad bar and grab-and-go selections, fair trade
teas, homemade soups and breads. Family owned to provide right livelihood by
offering healthy international comestibles low on the food chain. Great taste. Lively
ambience in a college setting.

Keystone Café

395 West 5th Ave • Eugene • (541) 342-2075

Vegetarian • American/International • Daily for breakfast & lunch • Full service
Entrees $5-10

This popular hangout boasts a uniquely Eugene décor and menu centered around
an impressive array of vegetarian breakfast items which are served all day. Keystone

also offers a creatively thought out selection of vegan dishes. Reasonable prices and well-prepared organic meals are a few reasons why Keystone is repeatedly voted one of Eugene's favorite vegetarian restaurants. Try the vegan French toast or the vegan power breakfast to find out why everyone loves this neighborhood mainstay.

The LocoMotive
291 E 5th St • Eugene • (541) 465-4754 • www.thelocomotive.com

Vegetarian • Dinner only • Wed - Sat at 5pm • Reservations recommended
Entrees $12-15

Voted Best Vegetarian Restaurant in Eugene (*Eugene Weekly* poll). Fine dining for the vegetarian gourmet. A lovely setting with delicious food, using organic ingredients whenever possible. Owners Lee and Eitan have lived around the world and the food reflects a wide variety of cuisines. The menu changes weekly, with half the choices being vegan.

Lotus Garden
810 Charnelton Ave • Eugene • (541) 344-1928

Vegan • Chinese • Lunch & dinner • Closed Tues & Sun

Founded by a Taoist practitioner serving a variety of delicious, high protein, faux meat dishes as well as a great many vegetable dishes. The most popular are reported to be Hunan veggie beef, spring rolls, pot stickers, wonton soup, mushu "pork" and the veggie shrimp dishes.

Morning Glory Bakery & Café & Out of the Fog Coffeehouse
450 Willamette St • Eugene • (541) 687-0709

Vegetarian • Café & Coffeehouse • Daily for breakfast & lunch

A happy combination where the socially and earth conscious gather to share thoughts on important issues, have a vegetarian breakfast or lunch (vegan on request) and sip socially responsible organic shade-grown Café Mom coffee. The eclectic menu features delicious tofu scramble with soysage, Tofu Luna sandwich, Triple Lucky Noodle dish, homemade flatbread and vegan baked goods and much more.

New Day Bakery & Café
345 Van Buren Ave • Eugene • (541) 345-1695

VegFriendly • Bakery & Café • Daily for three meals • Full service & take out
Entrees $5-10

This little bakery in the heart of Eugene's cultural hub serves a wide variety of cheap meals. From tofu scrambles and veggie fajitas to tempeh sandwiches and vegetarian tamales, New Day Bakery serves more than just excellent bakery items. Fast, friendly counter service, generous veggie options and an eclectic atmosphere make this café a great choice for any meal.

New Odyssey Juice & Java

1004 Willamette St • Eugene • (541) 484-7411

Vegetarian • Open Mon-Sat for three meals, lunch only on Sundays, some evenings for special events • Entrees all under $5

An energetic center for fresh squeezed organic raw juices and smoothies and/or organic free-trade, shade grown Café Mom coffee. Enjoy daily meal specials. Most food can be prepared vegan. Their soy sirloin has converted many. One of the biggest sellers is the BLT made with hickory smoked tofu. Many Mexican style options, also quiches, lasagnes and mock shepherd's pies. They enthusiastically support Performance Art, in particular electronic computer music, much of which is created and performed with laptops on premises.

Planet Goloka

679 Lincoln St • Eugene • (541) 465-4555

Vegetarian • Café • Dinner Mon-Thurs, lunch & dinner Fri; Sat brunch only

Experience a little bit of Hindu culture: sip fresh squeezed juice, herbal enzyme elixirs, or kava juice while watching culture films from India. All organic vegan dishes (with cheese options). Daily specials include stir fry, quiche and lentil dal. Try the coconut kava waffles topped with blueberries and coconut tofu crème. Handmade tapestries add to the relaxing ambiance.

Sam Bond's Garage

407 Blair • Eugene • (541) 431-6603

Vegetarian • Pub grub • Daily 4pm-late

Eat, drink, breathe and dance. Pizza by the slice, appetizers, soups, salads, along with great micro-brews, juice and soft drinks. Kids welcome till 8:30pm. Entertainment nightly.

Sundance Salad Bar & Hot Buffet *(in Sundance Natural Foods)*

748 E 24th at Hilyard • Eugene • (541) 343-9142

Vegetarian • Breakfast, lunch & dinner • Open daily

A traditional natural food store that also offers a self service salad bar and hot buffet with many imaginative vegan and vegetarian hot dishes. Reported to be the "best deli for a vegan meal anywhere around." There are vegan offerings daily and vegetarian pizzas. Restaurant quality food at deli prices.

Sweet Life Patisserie
755 Monroe St • Eugene • (541) 683-5676

Vegan • Patisserie • Open daily

A beautiful dessert café known and loved by vegans especially for the vegan "cheeze" cake and vegan chocolate cake. Products are gluten and margarine free and made from scratch with organically grown ingredients where possible. The place to go for thoughtful wedding and birthday cakes.

Taco Del Mar
3510 W 11th Ave • Eugene • (541) 344-4067 • www.tacodelmar.com
See review - Beaverton

Taste of India
2495 Hilyard St • Eugene • (541) 485-9560

VegFriendly • Indian • Daily lunch & dinner • Full service and buffet • Entrees $5-10

Authentic with so many vegetarian and vegan options. Servers are willing to modify most dishes. Pleasant ambiance and delectable food.

Toby's Tofu Palace
At the Eugene Saturday Market and area street & country fairs and music festivals. No phone, just be there.

This is a booth which has reappeared at Saturday Market for decades because folks have always flocked there for its unusually appealing foods such as the Tofu Tia, an especially scrumptious taco with tofu, sprouts and a secret red sauce which can be expanded to the Tia Special which the addition of avocado, onions and vegan sour cream. One unique product is Toby's Tofu Paté which makes a fabulous eggless egg salad sandwich. Finish off with a blueberry tofu "cheesecake" washed down with the Palace Cooler. As for the specific address, just follow the crowds. It wouldn't be Saturday Market without Toby's.

GOLD BEACH _____

Savory Natural Food Café
29441 Ellensburg Ave • Gold Beach • (541) 247-0297

VeryVegFriendly • Café • Closed Sundays

Very special homemade vegetarian soups, mostly organic sandwiches, salads and smoothies for indoor seating or take out. Hummus, cranberry chutney, pesto and such are deli items. Muffins baked daily. Home of the "Complete Meal Cookie."

GRESHAM

Taco Del Mar
2469 SE Burnside Rd • Gresham • (503) 674-9867 • www.tacodelmar.com
See review - Beaverton

Thai Orchid Restaurant
120 N Main Ave • Gresham • (503) 491-0737 • www.thaiorchid.citysearch.com
See review - Beaverton

HILLSBORO

Thai Orchid Restaurant
4550 NE Cornell Rd • Hillsboro • (503) 681-2611 • www.thaiorchid.citysearch.com
See review - Beaverton

HOOD RIVER

China Gorge Restaurant
2680 Old Columbia River Dr • Hood River • (541) 386-5331
www.chinagorge.com

VegFriendly • Szechwan & Hunan • Lunch & dinner • Closed Mon

Enthusiastically, "Oh yes, we have lots of vegetarian foods. We serve tempeh, our eggrolls are vegetarian, lots of vegetarian Chow Meins and many other things like Crispy Eggplant." Locals love it. Just east of downtown, across the Hood River with a view of the Columbia River. Vegan options.

Mother's Market Place
106 Highway 35 • Hood River • (541) 387 2202

Vegan • Home cooking • Tiny counter & take out • Closed Fri at 3pm & all day Sat

Inside this small vegan store is a great place to pick up quick, hot, freshly prepared and self-serve vegan eats like fresh steamed tomales, creamy (nut cream) asparagus soup, or vegan pizza. Sandwiches in the summer. There is a fresh juice bar and you could eat at the tiny counter which overlooks the Columbia River.

Sixth St Bistro and Loft
509 Cascade • Hood River • (541) 386-5737

VegFriendly • Northwest eclectic • Daily lunch & dinner • Entrees $10-20

Menu varies with the season. Some vegetarian choices always available and they are all extraordinary, like the local wild mushrooms from the nearby forests. Classic meat-based dishes can be made with tofu. Many appetizers are actually vegan. You can "veg out" with their artichoke dip, rustic bread and the huge and succulent seasonal greens salad. The menu celebrates the foragers, farmers and orchards who supply them (all organic). Cozy restaurant under, happy bistro above with vegan microbrews!

Taco Del Mar
112 Oak St • Hood River • (541) 308-0033 • www.tacodelmar.com
See review - Beaverton

McMINNVILLE

Wild Wood Café
319 N Baker St • McMinnville • (503) 435-1454

VegFriendly • Café • Breakfast & lunch • Closed Tues • Full service

Family-owned restaurant specializing in breakfast. Try the wildwood toast with granola, a potato plate, or an omelet with avocado, olives, salsa and cheddar cheese. A wide range of veggie burgers, veggie melts and salads are available for lunch. They make their own breads, granola, soups and salsa.

NEWPORT

Oceana Natural Foods Cooperative
159 SE 2nd St • Newport • (541) 265-3893 • www.oceanafoods.org

VeryVegFriendly • Deli • Open daily 11am to 5pm

The smell of soup entices you in when you come in the store. There is a pleasant sit-down eating area where a wide range of food choices are available including vegan, wheat free, dairy free and sugar free items. Organic ingredients are used whenever possible.

PORTLAND

Abou Karim
221 SW Pine St • Portland • (503) 223-5058

VeryVegFriendly • Middle Eastern • Lunch Mon-Fri & dinner Fri-Sat
Closed Sun • Full service • Entrees $5-10

Their vegetarian specialties are at the top of the menu but much of this authentic Lebanese cuisine is actually vegan. Try a whole plate full of appetizers called the Mezza, spoon up some Lentil Soup and make a main dish of Falafel, those crispy deep fried (vegetable oil) patties of herbed and spiced garbanzo and fava flour. Vegans can skip the yogurt sauce. Friendly, cozy.

Assaggio
7742 SE 13th Ave • Portland • (503) 232-6151 • www.assaggiorestaurant.com

VeryVegFriendly • Italian trattoria • Dinner Tues-Sat • Full service
Entrees $10-20 • Reservations highly recommended

Assaggio is a quintessential neighborhood trattoria, nestled in an old brick store-front, on a cozy corner. It is consistently rated one of Portland's best restaurants and with vegan and vegetarian options for most dishes, you can dive into the menu with 'gusto'. The Penne al ragu (minus the salsicce or sausage) is simple and peppy.

Spaghetti Alla Matriciana, served without the customary ham, is a fresh delight, while the fusilli with capers and gorgonzola round out the selection with a lush and creamy finish. Unless, of course, you elect to round out your meal with some homemade gelato.

Bibo Juice
1445 NE Weidler • Portland • (503) 288-5932
622 SW Broadway • Portland • (503) 227-2334
432 NW 11th • Portland • (503) 226-2995

Vegetarian • Juice bar-café • Take out • Entrees below $5

Easily mistaken for a national chain (it's local) with its colorful juice menu splashed across large black boards, uniformed, perky staff and slick, edgy, modern design. It is a perfect spot to grab a non-dairy smoothie such as "Bombay1912" named for grandfather's world travels. All of Bibo's smoothies come with two "boosters" such as ginseng or soy protein but the Santa Monica 1910 comes with nine boosters to send you out into the streets reinvigorated for local adventure.

Bombay Cricket Club
1925 SE Hawthorne Blvd • Portland • (503) 231-0740

VegFriendly • Indian • Daily for dinner • Full service & take out • Entrees $5-10

Often praised by critics as the best Indian restaurant in Portland, it has earned its reputation by delivering exceptional food and outstanding service in a warm atmosphere. On top of several delicious varieties of naan bread, they also offer a selection of Mediterranean appetizers. The dishes are prepared with delicate attention and will leave you satisfied. Romantic. Make a reservation before the rest of Portland does.

Caffe Mingo
807 NW 21st Ave • Portland • (503) 226-4646

VegFriendly • Italian • Dinner daily • Entrees: $10-20

One of the city's most cherished Italian restaurants. It features outstanding, hearty, meatless entrees and antipasti like penne alla zucca, asparagus or mushroom ravioli with walnut sauce, baked semolina gnocchi and a spinach and roasted beet salad. All wonderful things you can anticipate as you dip chunks of wonderfully chewy bread into a big bowl of juicy olives. Racks of wine bottles climb the walls, for what is Italian food without wine? To finish, try their classic panna cotta "cooked cream" dessert with poached fruit, or a simple dish of gelato.

Chef To Go
Corner of SW Park & Yamhill • Downtown Portland • (503) 730-1469

Vegetarian • Lunch cart • Take out, catering & delivery • Items under $7
Mon-Fri only

The Black Cart of Portland's funky mobile lunch food culture has fresh, cheap, quick, simple but memorable vegetarian soups and sandwiches. A much needed alternative to greasy, meat laden competitors. Stroll down the brick sidewalk, sit at a small table under a tree and dig into a French lentil salad with vegan bacon, a provolone grilled panini, a seitan caesar sandwich or a grilled marinated tofu. Throw in some kettle chips, vegan slaw, fresh iced green tea and enjoy a quick chat with the friendly owners. Don't forget some soy ice cream as you contemplate skipping the afternoon to sunbathe in the nearby park.

Cup & Saucer Café
3566 SE Hawthorne Blvd • Portland • (503) 236-6001

VegFriendly • American • Open daily for three meals • Full service & take out
Entrees $5-10

Traditional lunches and hearty breakfasts are served all day. Vegans can enjoy a few different foods, including cornmeal pancakes, cranberry apple coffee cake, carrot cake and home fried potatoes. Tofu may be substituted for eggs in their scrambles. The atmosphere is laid-back and artsy in this diner/café.

Dahlia Café
3000 NE Killingsworth St • Portland • (503) 287-4398

VegFriendly • American • Full service • Open daily for breakfast & lunch,
Wed-Sun for dinner • Entrées $5-10

This NE Portland neighborhood café has become a huge hit because of its natural motif and wonderful dishes. This means usually having to wait in line if you want to try their famous breakfasts consisting of tofu scrambles with fresh herbs, house potatoes and corn cakes, among others. The lunch and dinner menus are also worth noting, offering such sandwiches as an eggplant mushroom sandwich, grilled vegetable sandwich and a vegan reuben tempeh sandwich. Pastas and couscous dishes are also on the menu, as well as a few delightful soups and salads. Most dishes fall around $5, making it an affordable option for good food that everyone will enjoy.

Divine Café
SW 9th Ave, between Washington & Alder • Portland • (503) 314-9606

Vegetarian • A cart • Lunch & dinner • Take out • Closed Sun

This cart serves vegetarian and vegan meals, such as smoked tofu sandwiches and soba salad in peanut sauce. Vegan desserts are also available.

Dogs Dig Deli

212 NW Davis St • Portland • (503) 223-3362

Vegetarian • Deli • Breakfast to early dinner • Open Mon - Fri • Take out

Delicious vegetarian and vegan versions of traditional sandwiches, salads and desserts. Try the organic tofu sandwich with eggless mayo, or fresh veggies of your choice on your choice of specialty breads.

Dot's Café

2521 SE Clinton St • Portland • (503) 235-0203

VegFriendly • American/Mexican • Daily lunch, dinner & late night • Full service & take out • Entrees $5-10

A unique reinvigorated diner with a hip lounge motif serving diner fare with a unique twist. The funky, dimly lit, eclectic atmosphere is as much of an attraction as the food. A handful of items are labeled as vegan. Vegetarian options include a tasty hummus sandwich containing sautéed spinach and mushrooms, a vegan burrito platter and gardenburgers. They also offer vegan cake by the slice. Full cocktail bar with pool table. No minors after 10pm. Food is served until 2am. Smoking/non-smoking sections.

Garbanzo's

922 NW 21st Ave • Portland • (503) 227-4196
6341 SW Capitol Hwy • Portland • (503) 293-7335

VeryVegFriendly • Middle Eastern • Daily for lunch & dinner • Full service & take out • Entrees $5-10.

The simple décor provides a friendly, easy atmosphere. The food is filling and full of flavor. All the salads are vegan except for the coleslaw. Many of their soup offerings are vegan, in particular the delicious vegan lentil soup. The style of food is more on the fast side, quick service.

Garden Café at Portland Adventist Medical Center

10123 SE Market St • Portland • (503) 251-6125

Vegetarian • Cafeteria • Daily lunch & early dinner • Entrees under $5

Vegetarian meals have been served here for more than 100 years. Enjoy a wide variety of foods in a comfortable dining area with indoor and outdoor seating. Choose from vegetarian entrées such as chili macaroni, Singapore curry or cashew loaf. There's an extensive salad bar, a fresh fruit bar and a fast-food grill with vegetarian sandwiches and Boca burgers. The wide selection of beverages are all caffeine free.

Horn of Africa

3939 NE Martin Luther King Jr Blvd • Portland • (503) 331-9844
www.hornofafrica.net

VegFriendly • East African • Lunch buffet and dinner • Closed Sun • Full service
Entrees $5-10

Authentic dishes from the Ethiopian region, using ingredients of exceptional quality many of which are organic. Several vegan options available. Try their veggie combo: fresh collard greens, mixed vegetables, creamy navy beans and organic red lentils, served with a salad, saffron rice and biddeena (home made organic Horn of Africa style spongy bread). The environment is casual and the service is friendly. You can also find a Horn of Africa food cart at the Portland Saturday (& Sunday) Market.

India Grill

2924 E Burnside St • Portland • (503) 236-1790

VegFriendly • Indian • Daily lunch & dinner • Full service & take out • Entrees $8-10

India Grill has an eclectic range of delicious dishes, with part of its menu being vegetarian specials. Favorites include Navratan curry (mixed vegetables), okra with onions and vegetable biryani.

Iron Horse Restaurant

6034 SE Milwaukee Ave • Portland • (503) 232-1826 • www.portlandironhorse.com

VegFriendly • Mexican • Lunch & dinner • Closed Mon • Full service & take out
Entrees $5-10

This large restaurant is both a vegetarian and Mexican lover's delight. Standard southwestern and Mexican dishes are prepared to a scrumptious perfection, making them anything but standard. As soon as you get to your table you are greeted with a smile, chips and some of the best salsa in Portland. The vegetable chimichanga is a treat with zucchini, carrots, mushrooms and guacamole. A vegan menu is available upon request.

It's A Beautiful Pizza

3342 SE Belmont Street • Portland • (503) 233-5444

VegFriendly • Pizza • Daily lunch & dinner • Full service, take out & limited delivery • Entrees $10-20

This popular pizza restaurant offers a wide variety of toppings including artichoke hearts, pine nuts, broccoli, spinach and sundried tomatoes. You may substitute tofu for chicken, and soy cheese may be substituted for cheese on any pizza for the price of an additional topping. Pizzas are named after classic rock legends, including Joni Mitchell and Janis Joplin, and four vegetarian specialty pizzas are offered. The atmosphere has a 1960's feel with decorations of unique murals and large wall hangings. Live music can be heard on certain days of the week.

Jam On Hawthorne

2239 SE Hawthorne • Portland • (503) 234-4790

VeryVegFriendly • American style café • Breakfast/brunch • Full service & take out
Entrees $5-10 • Closed Mon

This classic brunch joint honors the eclectic countercultural spirit of Hawthorne
Boulevard, serving organic coffee, homemade jam, a vegan tofu scramble and tasty
specialties such as lemon ricotta pancakes and a brie and mustard scramble, all
served to the tunes of the Grateful Dead and Phish.

Kalga Kafé

4147 SE Division St • Portland • (503) 236-4770

Vegetarian • International • Lunch & dinner • Closed Tues • Full service &
take out • Entrees $5-10

A recent blessing to Portland's vegetarian scene with creative yet tasteful food served
until midnight. Many of their dishes are naturally vegan and almost all can be made
so. The cuisine ranges from Japanese to Mexican to Indian but don't rule out the pizza
with a vegan cheese option. An eclectic and intimate setting where late night diners
will enjoy DJ music under dim lights, and sip vegan chai served in a golden chalice.

Khun Pic's Bahn Thai

3429 SE Belmont St • Portland • (503) 235-1610

VeryVegFriendly • Thai • Open for dinner Tues-Sat • Full service • Entrees $10-20
No credit cards accepted

This is gourmet Thai with a short but powerful menu, virtually all of which is or
can be vegetarian. The food is reported to be "fantastic" with the specialty here
being that all the orders are prepared solely by Chef Khun Pic. Guests are urged to
ask about the time so that you can enjoy the leisure of conversation as your meal is
custom cooked.

Laughing Planet Café

3320 SE Belmont Ave • Portland • (503) 235-6472

VeryVegFriendly • Juice Bar/Mexican • Daily for lunch & dinner • Counter service
& take out • Entrees around $5

This juice bar/café offers many vegetarian and vegan options including fresh soups,
veggie burgers and quesadillas. Their build-your-own-burritos include tofu, spinach, broccoli, brown rice and other sustainable local farm products. All sauces are
vegan and homemade. They offer vegan soy cheese and sour cream. Vegan desserts
are available, including cookies and brownies. The atmosphere is fun and colorful
and the Café claims a healthy community conscience that supports non-corporate
local events and organizations.

Leaf & Bean Café

4936 NE Fremont St • Portland • (503) 281-1090

VeryVegFriendly • American/International • Open daily for lunch & dinner, Sat-Sun breakfast • Full service • Entrées $7-10

The Leaf & Bean is a quaint little eatery in NE Portland that offers a plentiful selection of vegetarian meals. They specialize in sandwiches, salads and soups, but also serve an impressive dinner menu as well. The friendly staff is happy to provide you with their African peanut stew with carrots, potatoes, tofu and spicy tomato peanut sauce. Some other favorites are their Thai coconut curry, Spinach ravioli and shepherds pie. They are also known for their delectable homemade soups and vegan chili. Don't let the casual atmosphere fool you: the dishes are made with fine culinary experience, and are presented in a surprisingly artful manner.

Nicholas Restaurant

318 SE Grand Ave • Portland • (503) 235-5123 • www.nicholasrestaurant.com

VegFriendly • Lebanese/Middle East • Lunch & dinner • Full service and take out Entrees $5-10.

With a vast array of vegetarian options, this is a Portland mainstay for good reason. Set in a quaint old-world café, the food is as authentic as the rustic Lebanese décor. Veggie kabobs, falafel and mannakish, a pizza with oregano, thyme, sumac, olive oil and sesame seeds, are all made deliciously. If you want to it all, try the mezza platter. Specify either vegetarian or vegan and you will be awarded with a generous assortment of their mouthwatering dishes. Their freshly baked pita bread is wonderful. High chairs for kids.

Oasis Café

3701 SE Hawthorne Blvd • Portland • (503) 231-0901

VegFriendly • Café • Daily lunch & dinner • Entrees $5-10

Oasis' specialty is pizza, with every possible combination of toppings. Try the veggie combo or the Hawthorne special, or design your own with your choice of toppings. An array of sandwiches, soups, salads, focaccia and desserts are also available.

Old Wives' Tales

1300 E Burnside St • Portland • (503) 238-0470

VeryVegFriendly • Inventive • Daily for three meals • Full service & take out Entrees $5-$10

Large, family style restaurant, with breakfast options served all day, plus extensive lunch and dinner choices. The menu is very helpful in explaining vegetarian or vegan dishes. Choices include Tofu Rancheros, Spicy Adobo Roasted Vegetables, Spanokopita and delicious daily soups. Notable salad bar with unique dressings. Vegan dessert options. The service is friendly, with the feeling that the meals are home cooked. Very child friendly.

Omega Gardens

4026 SE Hawthorne Blvd • Portland • (503) 235-2551

Vegetarian • Deli • Open Mon-Sat for lunch and Thurs-Sat for dinner/buffet
Full service & take out • Entrees $5-10

Home to the "Best Salad Bar in Portland," a generous burrito bar, and what they call a "Six Pack." The salad bar alone is worth the visit, and the burrito bar sports a plethora of natural, hearty ingredients all for $4.95. Their crown jewel, however, is the Six Pack: for $5.95 you get a tofu walnut loaf with ginger, and your choice of six side salads that include everything from citrus spinach and soul greens to Asian pasta, Kashi, fruit, vegan potato salad, hijiki, curried garbanzos and more. The portions are generous and the quality of their deli-style salads excellent.

Paradox Palace Café

3439 SE Belmont St • Portland • (503) 232-7508

VeryVegFriendly • American • Daily three meals • Full service & take out
Entrees $5-10

This popular diner style café boasts an extensive variety of eclectic vegetarian/vegan dishes. Sharing the same owners as Vita Café across town, they specialize in meat, dairy and egg-free versions of classic dishes. Try their Tofurky Sandwich, Tempeh Broccoli Surprise and Vegan Sloppy Joes. Breakfast items are available throughout the day and all breads and desserts are vegan.

Plainfields' Mayur

852 SW 21st St • Portland • (503) 223-2995 • www.plainfields.com

VeryVegFriendly • Indian • Open daily for dinner • Full service & take out
Entrees $10-20

Formal, upscale and elegant for a special dinner with exceptional food. Set in an opulent Victorian mansion where black-tie career waiters serve tables set with fine crystal, china and full silver service. There is a glassed-in Tandoori show kitchen. The menu includes a delectable variety of traditional and original Indian cuisine, with about half the menu devoted to vegetarian or vegan dishes. Noted by many critics as one of the best Indian restaurants in the country. Reservations recommended.

The Purple Parlor

3560 N Mississippi Ave • Portland • (503) 281-3560 • www.thepurpleparlor.com

Vegetarian • American/International • Breakfast & lunch • Closed Mon
Full service • Entrees around $5

Situated in a renovated Victorian home in North Portland is a vegetarian café where fresh flavors, healthful cooking and ecological sustainability come together. They serve traditional American fare for breakfast and multiethnic offerings for lunch. The menu includes reasonably priced items such as Greek Scramble, Squash

Chickpea Curry, Eggplant Veggenini and a zesty homemade soy sausage. They also offer vegan housemade breads, scones and desserts. The coffeehouse atmosphere proves casual and inviting with quaint, second-hand furnishings throughout and an eating counter with five old-fashioned barstools. Two patios in front of the house provide seasonal outdoor seating.

Queen of Sheba

2413 NE Martin Luther King Jr Blvd • Portland • (503) 287-6302

VegFriendly • Ethiopian • Lunch Tues-Sat & dinner daily • Full service & take out
Entrees $5-10

Tasty Ethiopian delights including an excellent array of vegetarian dishes. If you feel there are just too many options, try their vegetarian sampler which includes 10 vegetarian dishes and a salad. You will be amazed how so many wonderful flavors can reside on one large piece of bread or injara. Authentic North African style with a broad assortment of unique dishes.

Small World Café

722 N Sumner St • Portland • (503) 546-3183

VegFriendly • American • Open daily three meals • Counter service & take out
Entrees around $5

Located in the back of Big City Produce, an independent grocery store in North Portland, this small, vegan-friendly café serves breakfast and lunch all day using quality organic and fresh ingredients. Try their vegan muffuletta sandwich, vegan black bean cakes or their hummus sandwich. If you don't see what you want on their menu, just ask. If they can accommodate you they'll gladly do so. Small World Café offers a mellow, friendly, casual environment.

Swagat Indian Cuisine

2074 NW Lovejoy • Portland • (503) 227-4300
See review - Beaverton

Sweet Basil Thai Cuisine

3135 NE Broadway St • Portland • (503) 281-8337

VegFriendly • Thai • Daily lunch & dinner, Sat-Sun brunch • Full service &
take out • Entrees $5-10

The food here is well thought out and artfully presented using fresh ingredients. Let your server know you are vegetarian as tofu is an option on many dishes. Try their Lovely Ginger with Tofu or their House Special Curry. Be sure to specify your spicy tolerance: very mild to extremely wild. This charming converted bungalow features outdoor seating during warmer months. Reservations recommended due to space and popularity.

Taco Del Mar

3106 SE Hawthorne Blvd • Portland • (503) 232-7763 • www.tacodelmar.com
433 SW 4th Ave • Portland • (503) 226-0507
438 SE MLK Blvd • Portland • (503) 232-7695
736 SW Taylor • Portland • (503) 827-8311
12122 SE Division • Portland • (503) 761-3120
See review - Beaverton

Thai Orchid Restaurant

2231 W Burnside St • Portland • (503) 226-4542
10075 SW Barbur Blvd • Portland • (503) 452-2544
www.thaiorchid.citysearch.com
See review - Beaverton

Thanh Thai

4005 SE Hawthorne Blvd • Portland • (503) 238-6232

VegFriendly • Thai/Vietnamese • Lunch & dinner • Closed Tues • Full service & take out • Entrees $5-10

This popular restaurant located in the Hawthorne district serves seventeen vegetarian entrees including quite a few mock chicken dishes. For only $6-$7 an entree, you will get generous, filling portions. The atmosphere is casual and the service is fast.

The Tao of Tea

3430 SE Belmont St • Portland • (503) 736-0119

Vegetarian • International • Open Wed-Mon lunch & dinner, Tues dinner only Full service • Entrees $5-10

Known primarily for their extensive tea varieties, this Asian-esque tea house should not be overlooked as a place to dine as well. The completely vegetarian selection ranges from Indian to Japanese, with appetizers such as samosas and edamame. There are Greek, Lebanese and Italian flatbreads, each with their own distinctive flavor and style. They also serve scrumptious desserts. With a soothing water fountain, tranquil background music and walls adorned with eastern art, it offers a very relaxing atmosphere for an intimate meal.

Vita Café

3024 NE Alberta St • Portland • (503) 335-8233

VeryVegfriendly • American/International • Open Thurs-Mon for three meals, Tues-Wed for dinner only • Full service & take out • Entrees $5-10

Considered one of the most vegetarian/vegan friendly food spots in Portland, their menu includes such dishes as Vegan Chicken Fried Steak, Mushroom-Tempeh Paté, Vegan Lasagna and other dishes which range in cultural influence from American to Asian, and Mediterranean to Mexican. Breakfast is served all day and includes such notable treats as Vegan Biscuits and Gravy, Vegan French Toast, and an array of different geographically categorized corn cakes. To top it all off, all of their breads and desserts are egg and dairy-free. This restaurant is located in the Alberta Arts section of town and has an eclectic atmosphere.

SALEM

Thai Orchid Restaurant
285 Liberty St NE, Salem • (503) 391-2930 • www.thaiorchid.citysearch.com
See review - Beaverton

WEST LINN

Thai Orchid Restaurant
18740 Willamette Dr • West Linn • (503) 699-4195
www.thaiorchid.citysearch.com
See review - Beaverton

"Much of what we want for our children - healthy bodies with less illness, ability to concentrate, better study skills, adept physical ability — can be aided with a wholesome diet."
— see page 145

"Start by getting to know your local co-op, natural food store, supermarket natural food section or farmer's market. Take a stroll up and down the aisles and see how many of the products there are familiar to you. Keep an eye out for new varieties and flavors of old favorites."

PART TWO

Shopping for the Vegetarian Kitchen

Shopping for the vegetarian kitchen is easy and fun. We are fortunate, here in the Northwest, to have a wide variety of choices. All you need is information about where to shop, which you'll find in this chapter, and ideas on what to buy and how to prepare it (see the articles on "The Well Stocked Kitchen" and "Cookbooks and other Resources" later in this book). There are four broad categories of stores offering vegetarian options: food co-ops, natural food stores, farmer's markets and mainstream supermarkets.

You may be surprised to learn that the Northwest has many food co-ops both large and small. The odds are excellent that there is one within easy driving distance from your home. Food co-ops sell their memberships to the public. By purchasing one you will become a part owner of the store, with voting rights that give you a say in how the co-op is run, if you wish. The food co-ops became involved in the natural food business very early on and so they have lots of experience. Often they have policies regarding quality and variety that make them an especially good place to shop. Many also offer educational programs to help you learn more about your food choices. Try one out. You don't need to be a member to shop there. However, if you do decide to join, you'll soon find that the co-op discounts are well worth the small joining fee.

Natural food stores, both large and small, abound in the Northwest. You'll find everything from small local mom and pop stores to larger supermarket style stores. The small stores offer well chosen stock and the staff can usually spend time offering advice and making special orders. These smaller stores know their clientele well and will usually have just what you're looking for. The larger natural food stores offer the advantage of a wide variety of items and convenience sections such as a deli, bakery and cafeteria. They are also usually open with extended hours and feature many in store demos so that you can sample some of the latest product lines.

Farmers' markets are a great way to obtain local produce. The farmers often keep their best and freshest produce to sell at these markets. Buying food at a farmer's market is a lot of fun as there is usually something of a festival atmosphere. You'll find produce you might not see in stores, and meet face-to-face with the actual people who planted, nurtured and harvested the fruits and vegetables you'll be enjoying.

Look to buy organic food whenever possible and affordable. Organic food has the advantage of being grown without pesticides and herbicides. You can often save money by buying organic produce that is in season and grown locally.

Not to be overlooked are the mainstream supermarket chains. While they do not offer nearly the same level of choices, they are carrying an increasing amount of vegetarian options these days. In some of today's supermarkets, one can often find a couple of brands of soy milk and tofu, along with some other healthy products. Supermarkets are beginning to recognize that vegetarian food choices are becoming increasingly popular. Beyond specialty items, they also carry a good line of both fresh and frozen produce. Don't overlook the frozen produce. Picked at just the right time, freshness is well preserved and just waiting to be cooked.

Start by getting to know your local co-op, natural food store, supermarket natural food section or farmer's market. Take a stroll up and down the aisles and see how many of the products there are familiar to you. Keep an eye out for new varieties and flavors of old favorites. Use the article "The Well Stocked Kitchen" in this book. When you come upon an unfamiliar item try to learn something about it. Be willing to experiment. Most stores will be happy to make a special order for you if you can't find what you want. Make shopping an adventure in good health!

Shopping in Washington

ABERDEEN

The Market Place
822 E Wishkah St • Aberdeen • (360) 538-1521

Antique and contemporary fixtures greet the eye in this clean, neat, well lit store. The focus on health includes top quality supplements and personal care products. An extensive bulk food, herb and spice section is available as well as conveniently packaged foods, refrigerated and freezer items, and a large low carb section. Open Mon-Fri 9:30am-5:30pm, Sat 9:30am-5pm.

ANACORTES

Anacortes Health & Nutrition
1020 Seventh St • Anacortes • (360) 293-8849

Old fashioned health and nutrition store on beautiful Fidalgo Island with fresh organic produce and healthy foods. Open Mon-Fri 9am-6pm, Sat-Sun 10am-6pm.

AUBURN

Adventist Book Center
5000 Auburn Way • Auburn • (253) 833-6707

Very popular with the vegetarian community. A large selection of vegetarian foods, including very wide choice of meat substitutes such as hot dogs, chicken, etc. Dried fruits, healthy snack foods, cereals, soy milks, soups, etc. are also available. Extensive selection of books on health and nutrition, and cookbooks. Open Mon-Thurs 11am-6pm, Sun 11am-5pm, closed Fri-Sat.

BELLEVUE

Nature's Pantry
10201 NE 10th • Bellevue • (425) 454-0170
15600 NE 8th • Bellevue • (425) 957-0090

For 33 years, a family run natural/organic store carrying fresh organic produce, bulk items, fresh juices, vitamin and body care lines. There is a deli with very reasonable prices in spite of a high end appearance. Excellent customer service from knowledgeable employees. Open Mon-Fri 9am-7pm, Sat 9am-6pm, Sun 11am-5pm at downtown store, Crossroads store stays open later Fri-Sun.

Trader Joe's
15400 NE 20th St • Bellevue • (425) 643-6885 • www.traderjoes.com
See description - Seattle

Uwajimaya
15555 NE 24th St • Bellevue • (425) 747-9012 • www.uwajimaya.com

A smaller version of the Seattle store, it is an excellent source for Asian specialties, spices, and vegetarian and vegan items. Gifts, household items and cookware also available. Restaurant, bakery and deli with some vegetarian and vegan items. Open daily 9am-10pm.

BELLINGHAM

Bargainica
929-B N State St • Bellingham • (360) 715-8020

Bellingham's only discount organic and natural food store. By taking advantage of manufacturer's deals and volume purchases, buying odd lots and cosmetically damaged products, every product offered is 20%-80% below retail price. A fun place to shop and the best place to save on quality food. Open daily 9am-9pm.

Community Food Co-op
1220 N Forest • Bellingham • (360) 734-8151 • www.communityfoodcoop.com

The local premier full service, natural foods grocery store with Whatcom County's only certified organic produce department. Vegan and vegetarian items available across departments. A comfortable and relaxed atmosphere. The café area has nice sunny exposure. Open daily 8am-9pm.

Terra Organica
929-A N State St • Bellingham • 360-715-8020

Terra Organica is the dream store for anyone who loves organic food. Over 99% of the products are organic or wild crafted. All products are thoroughly researched to ensure they are ethically produced and the purest available. Every Sunday 25% off all produce. Open daily 9am-9pm.

BOTHELL

Adventist Book Center
20015 Bothell Everett Hwy • Bothell • (425) 481-3131

Very popular with the vegetarian community. A large selection of vegetarian foods, including very wide choice of meat substitutes such as hot dogs, chicken, etc. Dried fruits, healthy snack foods, cereals, soy milks, soups, etc. are also available. Extensive selection of books on health and nutrition, and cookbooks. Open Mon-Thurs 9am-6pm, Fri 9am-1pm, Sun 10am-5pm, closed Sat.

BURIEN

The Grainery
13629 1st Ave S • Burien • (206) 244-5015

Refrigerated and frozen vegetarian foods including tempeh and tofu, bulk herbs, fresh nuts and grains and a selection of packaged foods. Open Mon-Fri 9am-6pm, Sat 9:30am-5pm, closed Sun.

Trader Joe's
15868 1st Ave S • Burien • (206) 901-9339 • www.traderjoes.com
See description - Seattle

CHEHALIS

Healthy Harvest Natural Foods
576-A W Main St • Chehalis • (360) 748-9399

Organic vegetables and bulk foods. Outdoor fruit market in the summer. Their deli makes mostly vegetarian foods from scratch daily, including soups, sandwiches, pizza, home baked cookies and scones. In and outdoor seating available. Open Mon-Fri 8am-6pm, Sat 9am-5pm.

COLLEGE PLACE

His Garden & Bakery
28 SE 12th • College Place • (509) 525-1040

Small store offering a selection of healthy vegetarian and vegan foods, bulk herbs, bakery and deli items. Lots of fresh whole grain breads baked on premises. Soups, sandwiches and prepared dips with in-store seating area. Open Mon-Thurs 7am-7pm, Fri 7am-3pm, Sun 7am-2pm. Closed Sat.

COLVILLE

Mt Sunflower Natural Market
358 N Main St • Colville • (509) 684-4211

For your nutritional needs from organic foods and bulk items to books and healthy snacks. Fresh juice and smoothies and a staff ready answer your questions. Open Mon-Fri 9am-6pm, Sat 9am-4pm.

EVERETT

Sno Isle Natural Foods Co-op
2804 Grand Ave • Everett • (425) 259-3798 • www.snoislefoods.coop

A full service natural, organic and vegetarian grocery foods store with an extensive variety of vegan options as well as wheat free and gluten free foods. Excellent customer service. Deli and juice bar too! Open Mon-Sat 8am-8pm, Sun 12-6pm.

Trader Joe's
811 SE Everett Mall Way • Everett • (425) 513-2210 • www.traderjoes.com
See description - Seattle

FEDERAL WAY

Marlene's Market & Deli
31839 Gateway Center Blvd S • Federal Way • (253) 839-0933
www.marlenesmarket-deli.com

Conveniently close to I-5 with all the best natural products available and organic produce departments, groceries, herbs, vitamins and supplements. The deli offers customers a sit-down area in a comfortable atmosphere within the store. Open Mon-Fri 9am-9pm, Sat 9am-8pm, Sun 10:30am-6pm.

Trader Joe's
32073 Pacific Highway S • Federal Way • (253) 529-9242 • www.traderjoes.com
See description - Seattle

ISSAQUAH

PCC Natural Markets
1810 - 12th Ave NW • Issaquah • (425) 369-1222 • www.pccnaturalmarkets.com
Open daily 6am -10pm
See description - Seattle

Trader Joe's
1495 11th Ave NW • Issaquah • (425) 837-8088 • www.traderjoes.com
See description - Seattle

KIRKLAND

PCC Natural Markets
10718 NE 68th • Kirkland • (425) 828-4622 • www.pccnaturalmarkets.com
Open daily 7am- 11pm
See description - Seattle

Trader Joe's
12632 120th Ave NE • Kirkland • (425) 823-1685 • www.traderjoes.com
See description - Seattle

LANGLEY

The Star Store & Star Store Basics
201 First St & 199 2nd St • Langley • (360) 221-5222 • www.startstorewhidbey.com

A small full service supermarket committed to quality and customer service. Their store just across the street is stocked with supplements, homeopathy, health and beauty and non-food, earth-friendly products. Many meat alternatives, good frozen selection. Outstanding quality organic produce. Open Mon-Sat 8am-8pm, Sun 8am-7pm.

LYNNWOOD

Trader Joe's
19500 Highway 99 • Lynnwood • (425) 744-1346 • www.traderjoes.com
See description - Seattle

MOUNTLAKE TERRACE

Manna Mills Natural Foods
21705 66th Ave W • Mountlake Terrace • (425) 775-3479

Pleasantly providing 100% organic produce and lots of dairy alternatives. Groceries are all natural and mostly organic. They carry no commercial brands. Freezer section has a wide range of ready-to-cook meals. Open Mon-Fri 9am-8pm, Sat 9am-6pm, closed Sun.

MOUNT VERNON

Skagit Valley Co-op
202 S First St • Mt Vernon • 360 336-9777

One of the friendliest, all product natural food stores in this agricultural area. Highly community centered. Great in-store deli. Open Mon-Sat 8am-9pm, Sun 9am-8pm.

OLYMPIA

Olympia Food Co-op
3111 Pacific Ave SE • Olympia • (360) 956-3870
921 Rogers St NW • Olympia • (360) 754-7666 • www.olympiafood.coop

The Olympia Food Co-op is a member owned, collectively run natural food grocery store in two locations. Extensive volunteer working-member program. Support for local farmers and local production. Organic foods and fresh organic produce, bulk and deli items available. Open daily 9am-9pm east store, 9am-8pm west store.

PORT TOWNSEND

Food Co-op of Port Townsend
414 Kearney • Port Townsend • (360) 385-2883

In 2001 this small co-op was elevated to a large store with many additional goods and services. A full service deli was introduced which features freshly made organic salads and live foods as well as daily hot foods and soups. Additionally there is a wonderful juice bar. The produce department is alive with colors and textures. The health and beauty aids section is well stocked. Open Mon-Sat 8am-9pm, Sun 9am-7pm.

POULSBO

Central Market
20148 10th Ave E • Poulsbo • (206) 522-4588 • www.central-market.com

A major market which consciously caters to all dietary lifestyles: vegan, vegetarian, allergies, macrobiotic and conventional. The produce department comprises 20% of the store and offers a huge selection of organic along with local, Asian and conventional produce. The bulk foods area has over 500 different items. The natural resources department has a full line of dietary supplements, herbs, tea and natural body care including a large selection of bulk bar soaps. Open 24 hrs daily.

RENTON

Minkler's Green Earth
125 Airport Way • Renton • (425) 226-7757

Serving south King County since 1971 with quality natural foods and supplements at the lowest possible prices. They carry a huge selection of supplements, herbs, bulk foods, health and beauty aids and books. Open Mon-Fri 9am-7pm, Sat 9:30am-6pm, closed Sun.

SAMMAMISH

Good Health
3050 Issaquah-Pine Lake Rd • Sammamish • (425) 391-6044

A small, long established store with a staff of professional educators and advisors to help in the selection of organic fruits and vegetables, bulk foods, hypoallergenic skin care, and health and beauty aids. Open Mon-Fri 10am-7pm, Sat 10am-6pm, Sun 11am-5pm.

SEATTLE

Madison Market
1600 E Madison • Seattle • (206) 329-1545 • www.madisonmarket.com

One of the newer, super-natural food stores. Friendly, upbeat and community-based in a modern setting. A member-based co-op open to the public. Broad selection of natural foods, meat substitutes, soy products, frozen and packaged goods, bulk products and of course a huge selection of organic produce. Very responsive to customers' requests. In-store deli with fresh kitchen delights daily. Animal friendly health and beauty aids. Wide selection of vegetarian books and magazines. Open daily 7am-midnight

Mother Nature's Nutrition

516 Queen Ann Ave N • Seattle • (206) 284-4422

In small print the sign says "Vitamins/Cosmetics" but once inside you find herbs, sports supplements, and a small bar for smoothies and juices, home-cooked take-out soups and sandwiches. A small friendly store. No fresh veggies, but some frozen "natural" foods and of course soy milks. Open Mon-Fri 9:30-7pm, Sat 9:30-6pm, closed Sun.

New Roots Organics

Seattle • (206) 261-2500 • www.newrootsorganics.com

They will deliver a bin of 12 to 15 fruits and veggies to your door weekly in Seattle, Bellevue and Kirkland. First source suppliers seasonally are from Washington organic growers.

PCC Natural Market - Fremont

600 N 34th • Seattle • (206) 632-6811 • www.pccnaturalmarkets.com
Daily 6am-midnight

PCC Natural Market - Greenlake

7504 Aurora Ave N • Seattle • (206) 525-3586 • Daily 7am-11pm

PCC Natural Market - Seward Park

5041 Wilson Ave S •Seattle • (206) 723-2720 • Daily 7am-10pm

PCC Natural Market - View Ridge

6514 40th Ave NE • Seattle • (206) 526-7661 • Daily 7am-11pm

PCC Natural Market - West Seattle

2749 California Ave SW • Seattle • (206) 937-8481 • Daily 7am-11pm

PCC is the leader of the natural/organic food movement in the Puget Sound region. From its roots 50 years ago, this co-op has grown to seven locations in the greater Seattle area. PCC pioneered many of the policies in the natural/organic food grocery movement that are now recognized as standards.

In all departments, you can find products that were produced without synthetic chemicals, additives or genetically modified ingredients. Effort is made to select sustainable crops, fairly traded and humanely grown or manufactured foods or products. All stores offer the finest Northwest farm fresh produce with many locally grown organic fruits and vegetables. Every store's deli has delicious made-from-scratch salads and entrees ready to take home or have catered. The bulk food area offers all manner of beans, grains, flours, oils, sweeteners, herbs and teas. The body care products are based on natural botanical ingredients.

As a co-op, PCC addresses various consumer food or industry concerns to legislators and other decision makers with the collective voice of its 40,000 members. Member benefits include special 10 percent off days for members, home delivery of the monthly paper with articles on consumer food concerns and co-op education, and discounts on Foodworks classes, PCC's cooking and nutrition program. PCC's community programs include a Kids Club and is the largest corporate sponsor of the PCC Farmland Fund, a non-profit land trust that preserves endangered farmland for organic production.

Pioneer Organics

901 NW 49th St • Seattle • (206) 632-3424 • www.pioneerorganics.com

From Tacoma to Everett and east to the Sammamish Plateau, Pioneer can deliver various sized boxes of fresh certified organic fruits and vegetables to your door. They will also deliver a wide range of breads and groceries and welcome special orders.

Rainbow Grocery

417 15th Ave E • Seattle • (206) 329-8440

Rainbow has survived for over 12 years in the heart of "alternative" Capital Hill by offering the kind of select products that aren't found at the large high-profile food store chain directly across the street. They offer alternative brands and "ahead of the curve" food items, fresh organic fruits and veggies and a wheat grass juice bar for healthy refreshment. One bin offers ground hemp seeds. Rainbow fits the image of the earlier days of the natural food store movement and it still exists for that reason. Open daily in winter 8am-9pm, summer till 10pm.

Trader Joe's

112 W Galer St • Seattle • (206) 378-5536
4555 Roosevelt Way NE • Seattle • (206) 547-6299 • www.traderjoes.com

VeryVeg and kosher friendly. "TJ's" is a unique chain of medium sized grocery stores often in tucked-away locations. You'll find a treasure of interesting products, mostly packaged, canned or bottled. There is a small but well stocked fresh vegetable section and plenty of faux meats in the cooler or freezer. The kosher label will be found on an extensive number of products in virtually all categories. Many of the foods are private labeled with their own "angle," i.e., vegetarian, organic or just plain decadent. All have minimally processed ingredients from a variety of suppliers, many international, who make interesting products often exclusive to this chain. Known for generally low prices, there is a whole underground of wine aficionados who set price/value standards by TJ's bargain bottles. Open daily 9am-9pm.

Uwajimaya Village

600 5th Ave S • Seattle • (206) 624-6248 • www.uwajimaya.com

The new Uwajimaya Village is a shopping experience that must be seen to be believed. The store is enormous and chock full of the Asian specialties, teas and spices that vegetarians and vegans love. The produce section is large and well stocked with many otherwise hard to find fruits and vegetables. Asian meat analogs as well as some brand name food items. The food court has 7 restaurants and a store deli, each with several vegetarian and vegan options. Open daily 9am-10pm.

Vegan Mercantile

1203 N 41st St • Seattle • (206) 632-5633 • www.veganmercantile.com

Warehouse and online store selling a variety of vegan products including packaged foods, veg pet foods, personal care items, clothing and more. Owned and operated by devoted animal rights activists. Call for hours and more information.

Whole Foods Market

1026 NE 64th • Seattle • (206) 985-1500 • www.wholefoods.com

Whole Foods presents natural foods in a big, clean, contemporary, brightly lit, one-stop environment. The vegetable/fruit section is like walking into a large, colorful, mostly organic garden, glistening with dew. There is a large selection of healthy faux meats. All products sold are free of trans-fat containing hydrogenated oils. There are quality alternative brands of non-food products. Extensive and tempting presentation of ready-to-eat hot foods and salad bar with seating area. Great wine selection. Prices tend to be high, but so is the quality and selection. The employees here are upbeat and helpful. Open daily 8am-10pm.

SHORELINE

Central Market Shoreline

15505 Westminster Way N • Shoreline • (206) 363-9226 • www.central-market.com

A major market which consciously caters to all dietary lifestyles: vegan, vegetarian, allergies, macrobiotic and conventional. The produce department comprises 20% of the store and offers a huge selection of organic along with local, Asian and conventional produce. The bulk foods area has over 500 different items. Full line of dietary supplements, herbs, tea and natural body care including a large selection of bulk bar soaps. Open daily 7am-11pm.

SPOKANE

Adventist Book Center

3715 S Grove Rd • Spokane • (800) 286-0161

Very popular with the vegetarian community. A large selection of vegetarian foods, including very wide choice of meat substitutes such as hot dogs, chicken etc. Dried fruits, healthy snack foods, cereals, soy milks, soups, etc. are also available. Extensive selection of books on health and nutrition, and cookbooks. Open Mon-Thurs 9am-6pm, Fri 9am-1pm, Sun 10am-5pm, closed Sat.

Huckleberry's Natural Market

926 S Monroe St • Spokane • (509) 624-1349 • www.huckleberrysnaturalmarket.com

A large store with a large range of high quality organic foods and a wide selection of organic produce. The Bistro has many freshly prepared soups, sandwiches, salads and hot off the line foods. The bakery has pastries, breads, muffins, pies and cakes. Welcoming ambience, friendly and knowledgeable staff. Open daily 7am-10pm.

Lorien Herbs and Natural Foods

414 E Trent Ave • Spokane • (509) 456-0702

Twenty five years ago, Lorien became Spokane's first natural food store. It carries the largest selection of bulk herbs in the Inland Empire and quality supplements, remedies, books and beauty products. All produce is certified organic. There is an experienced staff for personal help in selection. Open Mon-Fri 10am-6pm, Sat 10am-5pm, Sun 12-4pm

Mt Sunflower Natural Market

10117 N Division St • Spokane • (509)-467-4998

For your nutritional needs from organic foods and bulk items to books and healthy snacks. They have fresh juice and smoothies and a staff ready to answer your questions. Open Mon-Fri 10am-7pm, Sat 10am-5pm.

Pilgrim's Nutrition

210 N Howard St • Spokane • (509) 747-5622

Foods offered include refrigerated and frozen items such as tofu, tempeh, frozen fruit and sprouted breads. Packaged goods, cereals, bulk nuts and other grocery items for vegetarians and vegans. Open Mon-Fri 10am-6pm, Sat 10am-5pm, Sun 12-5pm.

TACOMA

Marlene's Market & Deli

2951 S 38th St • Tacoma • (253) 472 4080 • www.marlenesmarket-deli.com

Conveniently close to I-5 with all the best natural products available, including faux meats, organic produce, vegetarian foods, groceries, herbs, vitamins and supplements. The deli offers customers a sit-down area in a comfortable atmosphere within the store. Open Mon-Fri 9am-8pm, Sat 9am-7pm, Sun 11am-6pm.

Metropolitan Market

2420 N Proctor St • Tacoma • (253) 761-FOOD

A large, beautiful upscale market with a great selection of vegan and vegetarian products. You'll find a salad bar, bulk bins, meat and cheese analogs, nut butters, baby foods and frozen vegan and vegetarian foods as well as health and beauty aids and organics. Open 24 hrs daily.

TONASKET

Okanogan River Natural Foods Co-op

21 W 4th St • Tonasket • (509) 486-4188 • www.planettonasket.com

A unique store in this rural area. The deli regularly prepares vegetarian soups, hot entrees, sandwiches and salads. The produce cooler looks like a garden of organic vegetables. A large percentage is grown locally. They also carry organic foods, bulk items, health and beauty aids. Lunch in the garden gazebo. Open Mon-Sat 9am-6pm (7pm in summer), Sun 12-4pm.

VANCOUVER

Trader Joe's
305 SE Chkalov St • Vancouver • (360) 883-9000 • www.traderjoes.com
See description - Seattle

Wild Oats Natural Marketplace
8024 E Mill Plain Blvd • Vancouver • (360) 695-8878 • www.wildoats.com

Attractive store offering a wide range of natural and organic foods, recycled paper products, fresh flowers, unique gift items and a large selection of supplements and body care items. There is a full-service deli with vegetarian and vegan offerings. Open daily 8am-9pm.

VASHON ISLAND

Minglement
20316 Vashon Highway SW • Vashon Island • (206) 463 9672

A great little natural food store in the heart of Vashon, offering organic produce, bulk products, refrigerated and frozen items, and snack items. Open Mon-Fri 10am-6pm, Sat 10am-5pm, Sun 11am-4pm.

"The key to success is to shop for ingredients that give you the best nutrition and flavor for your money and are convenient to use."

"Although you use them in small amounts, herbs and spices make a big contribution to your meals."
— see page 107

Farmers Markets in Washington

City	Location	Months	Day(s)	Hours
Anacortes	7th St & R Ave	May - Oct	Sat	9am - 2pm
Bainbridge Island	Downtown Winslow, between City Hall & the BPA Playhouse, off Winslow Way	April - Oct	Sat	9am - 1pm
Belfair	Highway 3 at Belfair Elementary School playshed near the Community Center	May - Oct	Sat	9am - 3pm
Bellingham	Railroad & Chestnut Avenues	April - Oct	Sat	10am - 3pm
	10th & Mills St, Fairhaven Village Green	June - Sept	Wed	3pm - 7pm
	Barkley Village	July - Sept	Tues	3pm - 7pm
Bridgeport	Quickie Mart parking lot- Hwy 17 & 173	June - Oct	Fri	9am - Noon
Brinnon	80 Brinnon Land near Highway 101	June - Sept	Sat	9am - 1pm
Burien	4th Ave between SW 152nd & SW 150th Burien	May - Oct	Thurs	11am - 6pm
Burlington	600 East Victoria at Cherry	May - Sept	Fri	3pm - 7pm
Cashmere	Division St & Sunset Hwy	June - Sept	Fri	9am - Noon
Centralia	Pine St between Pearl & Depot Rd	April - Oct	Fri & Sat	8am - 5pm
Chelan	Johnson St & Columbia opposite Chelan Chamber parking lot	June - Oct	Sat	8:30am - Noon
Clinton	Hwy 525 at Thompson Rd	May - Oct	Sat	10am - 2pm
Colville	Public Works parking lot corner Hawthorne & Elm St	May - Oct	Wed & Fri	Noon - 6pm
	Astor & Main	May - Oct	Sat	8:30am - 1pm
Coupeville	8th & Main	Apr - Oct	Sat	10am - 2pm
Eastsound	Eastsound Village Square	May - Sept	Sat	10am - 3pm
Edmonds	Bell St between 5th & 6th Ave	May - Oct	Sat	9am - 3pm
Ellensburg	Wells Fargo parking lot at 4th & Pearl	May - Oct	Sat	9am - 1pm
Ephrata	35 C St NW at the Courthouse	June - Oct	Sat	8am - Noon

Farmers Markets in Washington

City	Location	Months	Day(s)	Hours
Everett	Everett Marina at Port Gartner landing	June - Sept	Sun	11am - 4pm
Forks	Forks Ave N & Campbell St	May - Oct	Fri & Sat	10am - 2pm
Fox Island	1017 9th St	June - Sept	Wed	2pm - 6:30pm
Friday Harbour	County Courthouse parking lot	Apr - Oct	Sat	10am - 1pm
Gig Harbor	5502 Pt Fosdick Dr NW	End of Apr - Oct	Sat	9am - 2pm
	118th St NW & State Rd 302 at Ravensara	June - Sept	Fri	2pm - 6:30pm
	Strohs Field	May - Oct	Sat	8:30am - 3pm
	Bonneville Gardens downtown	May - Sept	Wed	4pm - 8pm
	Park-N-Ride Kimbal Dr	May - Oct	Sun	11am - 3pm
Greenbank	Greenbank Farm off State Rd 525	May - Oct	Sun	10am - 3pm
Hoqiam	1958 Riverside Dr	Year Round	Wed - Sat	9am - 6pm
Ilwaco	Waterfront Way	May - Sept	Sat	10am - 3pm
Issaquah	The Pickering Barn, opposite Costco at 1730 10th Ave NW	Apr - Oct	Sat	9am - 2pm
Kelso	Allen St & Pacific Ave	Apr - Sept	Sun	10am - 3pm
Kenmore	238th & Bothell-Everett Highway (State Road 527)	May - Oct	Fri	10am - 3pm
Kingston	Port of Kingston Marina at Washington & Central	May - Oct	Sat	9am - 2:30pm
Kirkland	Park Lane E between 3rd & Main	Apr - Oct	Wed	Noon - 7pm
Lake Stevens	Rockefeller & Wall St	June - Nov	Wed	10am - 2pm
	Comford Park, 5th St & State Ave	May - Oct	Sat	10am - 3pm
Lakebay	Volunteer Park	May - Sept	Tues	Noon - 6pm
Lakewood	Lakewood Mall parking lot	May - Sept	Tues	Noon - 6pm
Langley	Bayview Rd & State Rd 525 next to Bayview Farm & Garden	Mar - Dec	Sat	10am - 2pm
Leavenworth	City Pool parking lot Hwy 2	June - Oct	Tues	8am - 1 pm

Farmers Markets in Washington

City	Location	Months	Day(s)	Hours
Longview	Cowlitz County Expo Center at 7th & New York	Apr – Oct	Tues & Sat	8am – 1pm
	Downtown on Broadway between 12th & 14th Ave	June – Sept	Wed	3pm – 7pm
Lummi Island	Islander Store parking lot	April – Sept	Sat	10am – 1pm
Moses Lake	Civic Park on 5th & Balsam behind the library & Chamber of Commerce	June – Oct	Sat	7:30am – 1pm
	Civic Park on 5th & Balsam behind the library & Chamber of Commerce	June – Sept	Wed	3pm – 7pm
Mount Vernon	Revetment on the river at Gates & Main	June – Sept	Sat	9am – 1pm
Newport	Hwys 2 & 4 at Washington Ave	May – Oct	Sat	9am – 1pm
North Bend	Mount Si Senior Center Main & Park at State Rd 202	May – Oct	Sat	9am – 1pm
Oak Harbour	Highway 20 next to Visitor Center	June – Sept	Thurs	4pm – 7pm
	Old Town	June – Sept	Tues	4pm – 6pm
Okanogan	American Legion Park	May – Oct	Tues	4pm – 7pm
	American Legion Park	May – Oct	Sat	9am – Noon
Olympia	700 N Capitol Way	Apr – Oct	Thurs – Sun	10am – 3pm
Othello	Pioneer Park, 3rd & Main	May – Oct	Sat	7am – 1pm
Pasco	4th & Columbia	May – Mid November	Wed & Sat	8am – Noon
Port Angeles	1016 E 1st	All year round	Sat	9am – 4pm
	Clallam County Courthouse E parking lot	All year Round	Sat	9am – 1pm
Port Ludlow	Village Center, Port Ludlow	May – Sept	Fri	9am – 2pm
Port Orchard	Marina Park, on waterfront at Bethel & Harris, behind Peninsula Feed Store	Apr – Oct	Sat	9am – 3pm
	Kitsap Community Park, corner Jackson & Lund	May – early Oct	Wed	11am – 4pm
Port Townsend	Madison & Washington	May – Oct	Sat	9am – 1:30pm
	Polk St & Courtyard	June – Sept	Wed	3:30pm – 6pm

Farmers Markets in Washington

City	Location	Months	Day(s)	Hours
Prosser	Prosser City Park	May - Oct	Sat	8am - Noon
Puyallup	Pioneer Park, Meridien & 2nd St SW	May - Sept	Sat	9am - 2pm
Raymond	4th & Heath	Apr - Dec	Wed - Sat	10am - 5pm
Redmond	7730 Leary Way, NW corner of Redmond Town Center	May - Oct	Sat	9am - 3pm
Renton	S 3rd St between Logan & Burnett	June - Sept	Tues	3pm - 7pm
Seattle	N 34th St & Phiney Ave N	Year Round	Sun	10am - 5pm
	22nd Ave NW & Ballard Ave NW	Apr - Nov	Sun	11am - 5pm
	4801 Rainier Ave S at S Edmonds St	May - Oct	Wed	3pm - 7pm
	NE 127th & 30th NE behind the fire station	End of May - Oct	Thurs	3pm - 7pm
	Magnolia Community Center	Mid June - Oct	Sat	10am - 2pm
	Pike Place between Pike & Virginia Sts	All year round	Daily	9am - 6pm
	Corner 50th St NE & University Way	May - Nov	Sat	9am - 2pm
	Corner California Ave SW & SW Alaska	June - Oct	Sun	10am - 2pm
	SW Roxbury Blvd & 15th Ave SW, south of the Bartell Drug Store	June - Oct	Sat	10am - 2pm
Sedro Wooley	State St & Eastern at Feed Barn	June - Oct	Wed	3pm - 7pm
Selah	Naches Ave W & 1st St	June - Nov	Sat	9am - 1:30pm
Sequim	Clallam County Courthouse East parking lot	All year round	Wed	4pm - 6pm
Sequim	2nd & Cedar	May - Oct	Sat	9am - 3pm
Shelton	Wallace-Kneeland Blvd at Sears	May - Sept	Sat	10am - 3pm
Snohomish	1st St, 2 blocks W of Ave D bridge	May - Sept	Thurs	5pm - Sunset
Spokane	Division & 2nd Ave	May - Oct	Wed & Sat	8am - 1pm

Farmers Markets in Washington

City	Location	Months	Day(s)	Hours
Stanwood	1123 Highway 532	May - Aug	Sat	10am - 2pm
	Stanwood Cinema Pavillion 4 miles W of I-5, Exit 212	April - Dec	Wed & Sat	11am - 5pm
Tacoma	North 27th St at Proctor	June - Sept	Sat	9am - 2pm
	Broadway between 9th & 11th	June - Oct	Thurs	9am - 2pm
	(University Place) 35th & E Road	June - Sept	Fri	3pm - 7pm
Tonasket	Triangle Park, Western Ave & Hwy 97	June - Oct	Thurs	3pm - 6pm
Tracyton near Silverdale	Bucklin Hill at Silverdale Hotel	April - Sept	Tues	11am - 4pm
Vancouver	Downtown at Easter St between 8th & 6th	Apr - Oct	Sat & Sun	9am - 3pm
Vashon	1/2 block north of Bank Rd	Mar - Oct	Sat	9am - 2pm
Walla Walla	4th & Main	May - Oct	Sat	8am - Noon
	1st & Main	May - Oct	Thurs	5pm - 7pm
Wapato	Wapato Community Center, 3 miles south of State Road 97	July - Sept	Sat	9am - 2pm
Wenatchee	Riverfront Park, base of 5th St	May - Dec	Wed, Sat & Sun	8am - 1pm
	Riverfront Park, base of 5th St	May - Dec	Thurs	4pm - 8pm
West Richland	Flat Top Park; Bombing Range Rd & Van Giesen	May - Oct	Sat	9am - 1pm
Woodinville	City Hall-Sorenson School at 175th, next to Woodinville Community Center, 13205 NE 175th St	Apr - Oct	Sat	9am - 4pm
Yakima	S 3rd St at Yakima Ave in front of Capitol Theater	May - Oct	Sun	9:30am - 2:30pm

Shopping in Oregon

ASHLAND

Ashland Food Co-op
237 N 1st St • Ashland • (541) 482-2237 • www.acfs.org

Ashland Community Food Store, located 3 blocks from Ashland's main drag in the heart of the Historic District, has a full-service deli, bakery and juice bar, along with indoor and outdoor seating to provide the perfect place for breakfast, lunch or dinner. There are vegan, vegetarian and omnivore selections. Most notable are the supremely beautiful produce section and the extremely friendly and knowledgeable customer service. Also features many wheat and/or dairy-free products. Open Mon-Sat 8am-9pm, Sun 9am-9pm.

PC Market of Choice
1475 Siskiyou Blvd • Ashland • (541) 488-2773

Upscale, carrying natural items next to conventional items, makes it easy to shop for all your food needs. Well organized and customer friendly. In-store deli and bakery. Large produce area with organic and conventional produce. Small eating area. Catering for parties. Open daily 7am-11pm.

Shop 'n Kart
2268 Ashland St • Ashland • (541) 488-1579

Warehouse-type store featuring organic and conventional products with many deals and deep discounts. Customers bag their own purchases. Open daily 7am-midnight.

ASTORIA

Astoria Health Foods
1255 Commercial St • Astoria • (503) 325-6688

This small store located in the heart of downtown Astoria, carries a large variety of supplements, homeopathic remedies, bulk herbs and foods, teas, snacks, books and beauty aids. Plentiful selection of packaged, frozen and refrigerated foods for the vegan/vegetarian palate. Friendly, approachable staff willing to research information and accommodate special orders. Open Mon-Fri 9am-6pm, Sat 9am-5:30pm.

The Community Store
1389 Duane St • Astoria • (503) 325-0027 • www.thecommunitystore.org

The Community Store is a small natural foods cooperative grocery. Provides a wide selection of sustainably produced, fairly traded and organically grown products, with emphasis on the locally grown. The store is open to the public and provides discounts to co-op members. Open Mon-Sat 9am-7pm, Sun 10am-3pm.

BEAVERTON

Manic Organic

20300 SW Clarion St • Beaverton • (503) 430-2500 • www.manic-organic.com

This organic home delivery service delivers the freshest organic produce, eggs and breads right to your door each week. A family run and community based business, they offer a choice of several sized bins customized to your family type and budget.

Trader Joe's

11753 SW Beaverton Hillsdale Hwy • Beaverton • (503) 626-3794
www.traderjoes.com
See description - Portland

Uwajimaya

10500 SW Beaverton Hillsdale Hwy • Beaverton • (503) 643-4512

An excellent source for Asian specialties, spices, vegetarian and vegan items. Large produce section includes organic produce. Gifts, household items, cookware. Restaurant, bakery items and deli items too. Open 9am-10pm daily.

Wild Oats Natural Marketplace

4000 SW 117th Ave • Beaverton • (503) 646-3824 • www.wildoats.com

Attractive store offering a wide range of natural and organic foods, recycled paper products, fresh flowers, unique gift items and a large selection of supplements and body care items. There is a full service deli with vegetarian and vegan offerings. Open daily 9am-9pm.

BEND

Devore's Good Food Store

1124 NW Newport Ave • Bend • (541) 389-6588

A locally owned store and deli for over 27 years featuring all organic produce, natural and ethnic groceries, fine wines and micro-brews. The deli has incredible take-out foods including soups, salads, meat analogs, wraps, dips and desserts all with vegetarian or vegan options. Open Mon-Sat 8am-7pm, Sun 9am-6pm.

Wild Oats Natural Marketplace

2610 NE Hwy 20 • Bend • (541) 389-0151 • www.wildoats.com
See description - Beaverton

CANYONVILLE

Promise Natural Foods & Bakery

503 S Main St • Canyonville • (541) 839-4167

This old country style natural foods store has bulk foods, a large bulk herb section as well as a full grocery line. The produce is from two certified organic farms in the area. Fresh organic breads and pastries baked Mon, Wed, Fri. Sip organic free trade coffee during your visit. Open Mon-Fri 9:30am-6pm, Sat 10am-5pm, Closed Sun.

CLACKAMAS

Adventist Book Center

13455 SE 97th Ave • Clackamas • (503) 653-0978

Very popular with the vegetarian community. A large selection of vegetarian foods, including a very wide choice of vegetarian meat replacement foods such as analogs for chili, hot dogs, burgers, etc. Organic foods, dried fruits, healthy snack foods, cereals, soy milks, soups, etc. Books on health and nutrition, and cookbooks. Open Mon-Thurs 8:30am-6pm, Fri 8:30am-1pm, Sun 11am-4pm.

CORVALLIS

First Alternative Co-op

1007 SE 3rd St • Corvallis • (541) 753-3115
2855 NW Grant Ave • Corvallis • (541) 452 3115 • www.firstalt.coop

Both stores offer a large variety of natural, organic foods, body care products, supplements and general merchandise. Options for vegans, vegetarians and people with allergies and special diet requirements. The kitchen makes delicious dishes for their Feast Alternative deli. Easy meals and salad bar with in and outdoor seating at the 3rd St store. Open daily 9am-9pm.

COTTAGE GROVE

PC Market of Choice

1405 Pacific Hwy N • Cottage Grove • (541) 942-1273
See description - Ashland

EUGENE

Friendly Street Market

2757 Friendly St • Eugene • (541) 683-2079

A small, locally owned and operated neighborhood natural food store featuring local, seasonal and organic foods including a wide variety of vegetarian, vegan and specialty packaged and frozen foods as well as health and beauty aids, gifts, beer and wine. Open Mon-Sat 8am-10pm, Sun 9am-10pm.

PC Market of Choice
1060 Green Acres Rd • Eugene • (541) 344-1901
2858 Willamette St • Eugene • (541) 338-8455
1960 Franklin Blvd • Eugene • (541) 687-1188
See description - Ashland

Sundance Natural Market
748 E 24th Ave • Eugene • (541) 343-9142

A well organized friendly market with a great selection of local, 100% organic produce, a nice bulk foods section and a great organic vegetarian deli featuring a hot
food buffet, green and prepared salad bar, grab and go items and pastries. There are
vegan offerings daily and vegetarian pizzas. Restaurant quality food at deli prices.
Open daily 7am-11pm.

Trader Joe's
85 Oakway Center • Eugene • (541) 485-1744 • www.traderjoes.com
See description - Portland

Wild Oats Natural Marketplace
2580 Willakenzie Rd • Eugene • (541) 334-6382 • www.wildoats.com
2489 Willamette St • Eugene • (541) 345-1014
See description - Beaverton

FLORENCE

Salmonberry Naturals
812 Quince St • Florence • (541) 997-3345 • www.salmonberrynaturals.com

Small and well stocked country store in business for 12 years. Friendly and knowledgeable staff. Focus on local and organic foods. Over 300 bulk herbs and spices
and over 250 bulk food, nuts, seeds and dried fruits. Some raw food items available.
Mon-Fri 9:30am-6pm, Sat 9:30am-5:30pm, Sun 1pm-5pm.

GOLD BEACH

Savory Natural Foods
29441 Ellensburg Ave • Gold Beach • (541) 247-0297

An "oasis" with the largest selection of natural and organic foods on the south
Oregon coast. A welcome café is located in the market (see Restaurants for review).
Opens at 9am Mon-Fri, 11am Sat, closed Sun.

GRANTS PASS

PC Market of Choice
1555 Williams Hwy • Grants Pass • (541) 479-4075
1427 NE 7th • Grants Pass • (541) 474-3067
See description - Ashland

Shopping in Oregon

Sunshine Natural Foods
128 SW H St • Grants Pass • (541) 474-5044

Organic foods, bulk items, health and beauty aids and a place to sit and eat. The deli has prepared foods, excellent soups, sandwiches, plus a salad and juice bar. They bake many vegan pastries. Award winning vitamin selection, including food-based vitamins. Open Mon-Fri 9am-6pm, Sat 9am-5pm, closed Sun.

GRESHAM

Wild Oats Natural Marketplace
2077 NE Burnside Rd • Gresham • (503) 674-2827 • www.wildoats.com
See description - Beaverton

HILLSBORO

New Seasons Market
1453 NE 61st Ave • Hillsboro • (503) 648-6968

Locally owned and operated grocery stores are fun, easy to shop and have everything you need - from thousands of natural and organic selections to the best of grocery basics. The bountiful produce department emphasizes organic and local products. In-store certified organic bakery offers 21 varieties of freshly baked organic bread and the delis make soups, salads and entrees daily. Open daily 8am-10pm.

LAKE OSWEGO

Trader Joe's
15391 SW Bangy Rd • Lake Oswego • (503) 639-3238 • www.traderjoes.com
See description - Portland

Wild Oats Natural Marketplace
17711 Jean Way • Lake Oswego • (503) 635-8950 • www.wildoats.com
See description - Beaverton

LINCOLN CITY

Trillium Natural Foods
1026 SE Jetty Ave • Lincoln City • (541) 994-5665

Trillium's primary focus is fresh, organically grown whole foods. It is a small store yet has one of the best selections on the Oregon coast, including a large bulk products section. Prices are good too. Mon-Sat 9:30am-7pm, Sun 11am-6pm.

MANZANITA

Mother Nature's Natural Foods
298 Laneda Ave • Manzanita • (503) 368-5316
www.neahkahnie.net/mothernatures/index.html

Three blocks from the beach, this progressive little natural food store has a creative floor plan and unique product selection that will delight you! Packed with stunning organic produce, a mighty bulk selection, wine/beer, books and specialty grocery. There's an organic juice bar and deli to go, spelt fruit muffins made daily, fair trade chocolate and coffee, and a welcoming down to earth staff. Open Mon-Sat 10am-7pm, closed Sun.

MEDFORD

Adventist Book Center & Veg Foods
632 Crater Lake Ave • Medford • (541) 734 0567

Very popular with the vegetarian community. A large selection of vegetarian foods, including a very wide selection of vegetarian meat replacement foods such as ana-logs for chili, hot dogs, burgers, etc. Organic foods, bulk products, healthy snack foods, soy milks, soups, etc. Books on health and nutrition, cookbooks. Open Mon-Thurs 11am-6pm, Sun 11am-3pm. Closed Fri-Sat.

NEWPORT

Oceana Natural Foods Cooperative
159 SE 2nd St • Newport • (541) 265-3893 • www.oceanafoods.org

The emphasis is organic products from bulk foods to wine, beer, spices and herbs, cheese and other dairy products. They carry organic socks(!), organic coffee, tea, tortillas, meat, juice and chips. The friendly staff can assist with information on dietary needs, supplements and other health related subjects. There is a pleasant sit-down eating area where a wide range of food choices is available including vegan, wheat free, dairy free and sugar free items. Open Mon-Fri 8am-7pm, Sat 8am-6pm, Sun 10am-6pm.

PORTLAND

Alberta Cooperative Grocery
1500 NE Alberta St • Portland • (503) 287 4333 • www.albertafoodcoop.org

A member owned cooperative where all are welcome to shop. They carry natural foods and a wide variety of organic or sustainably grown produce. As a community resource they provide information about food and other products. Neighbors meet here and a community bulletin board advertises neighborhood goods and services. Open daily 9am-10pm.

The Daily Grind

4026 SE Hawthorne • Portland • (503) 233-5521

This large store has been family owned for 15 years. Exceptional, all-organic fresh produce. Fresh salad bar. Fresh-made daily soups and casseroles for take-out. Large bulk department, including bulk herbs. This is the only store in Portland stocking Loma Linda and Worthington foods. In-store bakery with fresh-made specialty breads, scones, muffins, etc. Extensive selection of quality vitamins and supplements. Open daily 9am-9pm.

Food Fight Grocery

4179 SE Division • Portland • (503) 233-3910 • www.foodfightgrocery.com

"A vegan 7-11" this all vegan convenience store carries mostly "junk food" and hard-to-find items, faux meats, frozen foods, T-shirts and comics. Vegan comfort food. One of a kind! Open weekdays 9am-8pm, Sat-Sun 10am-8pm, closed Tues.

Food Front Co-op

2375 NW Thurman • Portland • (503) 222-5658

Established over 30 years ago, this medium to large sized store is conveniently located. It offers an excellent selection of local produce, bulk items, natural food items and non food items. It has a vegetarian and vegan deli offering a fabulous selection of eclectic choices, snacks, coffee, pastries, juices and fresh fruits. There's a small indoor/outdoor eating space. Open daily 8am-9pm.

New Seasons Market

5320 NE 33rd Ave • Portland • (503) 288-3838 • www.newseasonsmarket.com
7300 SW Beaverton-Hillsdale Hwy • Portland • (503) 292-6838
1214 SE Tacoma St • Portland • (503) 230-4949

Locally owned and operated grocery stores are fun, easy to shop and have everything you need - from thousands of natural and organic selections to the best of grocery basics. The bountiful produce department emphasizes organic and local products. In-store certified organic bakery offers 21 varieties of freshly baked organic bread and the delis make soups, salads and entrees daily. Open daily 8am-10pm.

Organics to You

309 SE Pine St • Portland • (503) 236-6496 • www.organicstoyou.org

Fresh, 100% certified organic produce and groceries, including breads, soy products, coffee and dog treats, are delivered directly from local farmers and cooperatives to homes in Portland and most surrounding areas. A selection of different bin choices is offered.

PC Market of Choice

8502 Terwilliger Blvd • Portland • (503) 892-7331
See description - Ashland

People's Food Co-op
3029 SE 21st Ave • Portland • (503) 232-9051 • www.peoples.coop

An all vegetarian (except pet food) natural foods co-op carrying a full line of fresh and packaged natural foods. Even the cheese is rennet-free. Vegan options as well as alternatives for allergies or nutritional preferences. Large selection of bulk food items. Fresh produce emphasizes seasonal organics purchased locally where possible. Bicycle delivery for area residents. Open daily 9am-9pm. Hosts a weekly farmer's market on Wednesdays, 2-7pm all year round.

Pioneer Organics
4530 NE 42nd • Portland • (503) 460-2729 • (877) 632-3424
www.pioneerorganics.com

Throughout the Portland area, Pioneer delivers various sized boxes of fresh certified organic fruits and vegetables to your door. They will also deliver a wide range of breads and groceries, and welcome special orders.

Trader Joe's
2122 NW Glisan • Portland • (971) 544-0788 • www.traderjoes.com
4715 SE 39th Ave • Portland • (503) 777-1601
4218 NE Sandy Blvd • Portland • (503) 284-1694

VeryVeg and kosher friendly. "TJ's" is a unique chain of medium sized grocery stores often in tucked-away locations. You'll find a treasure of interesting products, mostly packaged, canned or bottled. There is a small but well stocked fresh vegetable section and plenty of faux meats in the cooler or freezer. The kosher label will be found on an extensive number of products in virtually all categories. Many of the foods are private labeled with their own "angle," i.e., vegetarian, organic or just plain decadent. All have minimally processed ingredients from a variety of suppliers, many international, who make interesting products often exclusive to this chain. Known for generally low prices, there is a whole underground of wine aficionados who set price/value standards by TJ's bargain bottles. Open daily 9am-9pm.

Whole Foods Market
1210 NW Couch St • Portland • (503) 525-4343 • www.wholefoods.com

Located in the historic downtown Pearl District, this new store is designed to give urbanites the opportunity to celebrate quality-conscious natural foods, organic fruits and vegetables that are found in this local region. There is a good selection of faux meats and a selection of some of the world's best products. The staff is passionate about providing customers with a high standard of quality products and services, sharing information and educating. Open daily 8am-10pm.

Wild Oats Natural Marketplace

3016 SE Division St • Portland • (503) 233-7374 • www.wildoats.com
3535 NE 15th Ave • Portland • (503) 288-3414
6344 SW Capitol Hwy • Portland • (503) 244-3110
2825 East Burnside St • Portland • (503) 232-6601

Attractive stores offering a wide range of natural and organic foods, recycled paper products, fresh flowers, unique gift items and a large selection of supplements and body care items. There is a full-service deli with vegetarian and vegan offerings. Open daily 9am-10pm.

ROGUE RIVER

Rogue River Natural Foods

510 E Main St • Rogue River • (541) 582-3075

Groceries for all types of diets: low carb, wheat-free, sugar-free, vegan and vegetarian, in a small country owner/operator setting. Being rural they carry a wide line of items as books, tapes, organic wines and natural skin care products with custom scenting. Open Mon-Sat 10am-5:30pm.

ROSEBURG

New Day Quality Grocery

210 SE Jackson St • Roseburg • (541) 672-0275

A 100% meat-free store carrying fresh organic produce, organic foods, bulk items and non food items including books, clothing, kitchenware, health information, nutrition center and beauty aids. Open Mon-Fri 9:30am-6:30pm, Sat 9:30am-5:00pm.

SALEM

LifeSource Natural Foods

2649 Commercial St SE • Salem • (503) 361-7973
www.lifesourcenaturalfoods.com

LifeSource has a great selection of natural and organic foods with a large produce department. Their deli and almost all their foods are vegetarian. Their knowledgeable staff excel at friendly, helpful service. Open Mon-Fri 9am-9pm, Sat 9am-8pm, Sun 10am-6pm.

SEASIDE

Seaside Health Foods

144 N Roosevelt • Seaside • (503) 738 3088

Offers a plentiful selection of packaged, frozen and refrigerated foods suitable for vegetarians and vegans. They carry a large variety of bulk herbs and foods, teas, snacks, books and beauty aids. An added bonus is the juice bar and fresh organic produce case. Helpful staff will research information and accommodate special orders. Open Mon-Fri 9:30am-5:30pm, Sat 9:30am-5pm, closed Sun.

WALDPORT

Health 101

185 Arrow St (Hwy 101) • Waldport • (541) 563-6101

Largest combined inventory of top-quality, name-brand nutritional supplements and natural foods on the coast. Also carrying a complete department of natural products for pets. Open Mon-Sat 9am-5pm, Sun 10am-5pm.

"Vegetarian cooking is easy, fun and the results are usually delicious....
A good vegetarian cookbook or two is an excellent way to start."
— see page 113

Shopping in Oregon

Farmers Markets in Oregon

City	Location	Months	Day(s)	Hours
Ashland	Central Ave at 9th St	May - Oct	Sat	8:30am - 1:30pm
	The Armory on East Main Street	Jun - Nov	Tues	8:30am - 1:30pm
Astoria	12th Street at Marine Drive	May - Oct	Sun	10am - 3pm
Baker City	Klamath Bank parking lot, Main & Church St	June - Sept	Sat	9 - 11am
Bandon	350 2nd St, Old Town	July - Sept	Sat	10am - 2pm
Beaverton	Hall Blvd between 3rd & 5th St	July - Sept	Sat	8am - 1:30pm
	Hall Blvd between 3rd & 5th St	July - Sept	Wed	3pm - 7pm
Bend	Mirror Pond-Brooks St, Riverfront Plaza	June - Oct	Wed	3pm - 7pm
Canby	1st Ave between Elm & Holly	May - Oct	Sat	9am - 1pm
Coos Bay	Hwy 101 & Commercial Ave	June - Oct	Wed	9am - 3pm
Corvallis	Water Ave between Broadalbin & Ferry St	April - Nov	Sat	8am - Noon
	1st & Jackson (North end of River Front)	Apr - Nov	Sat	9am - 1pm
	Benton County Fair-grounds, 110 SW 53rd St	Apr - Nov	Wed	8am - 1:30pm
	Polk County Farmers Market	May - Nov	Sun	9am - 2pm
Cottage Grove	Coiner Park	May - Nov	Sat	9am - 4pm
Dundee	Parking lot, Dundee Bistro/Ponzi Wine Bar, 7th & Hwy 99	June - Oct	Sun	9am - 1pm
Elgin	790 Division	June - Oct	Sat	8am - 4pm
Estacada	4th & Broadway St	May - Early Nov	Sat	10am - 3pm
Eugene	East 8th & Oak St	May - Oct	Tues	10am - 3pm
	East 8th & Oak St	Apr - Nov	Sat	9am - 4pm
	Lane Country Fairgrounds, Auditorium Bldg, 796 W 13th Ave	Nov - Dec	Weekends	10am - 6pm
Florence	Hwy 126 & Quince St	June - Oct	Sat	9:30am - Noon
Forest Grove	Pacific Ave & Cedar St	May - Oct	Sat	8:30am - 1pm

Farmers Markets in Oregon

City	Location	Months	Day(s)	Hours
Grants Pass	4th & F St	Mar - Nov	Sat	9am - 1pm
	Valley View Road at I-5	May - Oct	Fri	9am - 2pm
Gresham	Miller St between 2nd & 3rd	May - Oct	Sat	8:30am - 2pm
Harrisburg	Downtown - 4th & Smith	May -Sept	Alternate Sat	9am - 1pm
Hermiston	McKenzie Park, 1st & Orchard	May - Oct	2nd Sat	8am - Noon
Hillsboro	Courthouse Square, 2nd & E Main	May - Oct	Sat	8am - 1pm
	Couthouse Square, Main St, 1st to 3rd Ave	June - Aug	Tues	5pm - 8:30pm
	NW Cornell Rd & Orenco Station	May - Oct	Sun	11am - 3pm
Hood River	5th & Cascade Ave, down-town	May - Oct	Sat	9am - 3pm
Independence	Sterling Bank, 302 S Main St	May - Nov	Sat	9am -1pm
Jacksonville	C Street, next to the museum	May - Oct	Sat	9am - 3pm
Jefferson	Main & Ferry St	June - Oct	Sat	9am - 1pm
Joseph	Wildflower Bakery & Café on Main St	June - Sept	Sat	9am - 1pm
Kings Valley	Corner of Hwy 223 & Maxfield Creek Rd	June - Oct	Sun	1pm - 4pm
Klamath Falls	9th St between Klamath Ave & Main St	June - Oct	Sun	10am - 1pm
La Grande	Sunflower Book Store lawn	June - Oct	Sun	10am -Noon
	4th & Adams	June - Oct	Sun	10am - Noon
Lake Oswego	First St between A & B Ave	May - Oct	Sun	8am - 1pm
McMinnville	Wilco Farm parking lot	Aug - Sept	Sat	8am - 11am
	Cowls St between 3rd & 2nd	June - Oct	Thurs	3am - 6pm
Medford	Medford Center, Royal Ave & Stevens St	Mar - Nov	Thurs	8:30am - 1:30pm
Milwaukie	SE Main between Harrison & Jackson, across from City Hall	May - Oct	Sun	9:30am - 2pm
Newport	North of Newport Chamber of Commerce, Hwy 101	May - Oct	Sat	9am - 1pm
Pendleton	Main St between Emigrant & Frazer St	May - Oct	Fri	4:30pm - 8pm

Shopping in Oregon

Farmers Markets in Oregon

City	Location	Months	Day(s)	Hours
Portland	Safeway parking lot at Sunset Mall, NW Cornell & Murray	June - Sept	Sat	8am - 1pm
	SE 20th & SE Salmon	July - Sept	Thurs	4pm - 8pm
	SW Capitol Hwy & Sunset, across from Nature's	May - Oct	Sun	10am - 2pm
	NE Hancock between 44th & 45th, one block S of Sandy	May - Oct	Sat	8am - 1pm
	NW Corner SE 92nd & Foster Rd	June - Oct	Sat	9am - 1pm
	3029 SE 21st Ave	All Year	Wed	2pm - 7pm
	Park Blocks at PSU Campus, 1800 SW at Montgomery	May - Nov	Sat	8:30am - 2pm
	South Park Blocks at Portland State	May - Oct	Wed	10am - 2pm
	Jamison Square, NW 10th & Johnson	June - Aug	Thurs	4pm - 8pm
	7007 NE Martin Luther King Blvd at Bryant	July - Sept	Sat	10am - 2pm
Rogue River	E Evans Valley Rd & Covered Bridge	May - Oct	Sun	9am - 1pm
	Wilmer Enterprise Grange, 8700 E Evans Creek Rd	April - Oct	Sun	9am - 3pm
Roseburg	Roseburg Valley Mall, Stewart Pkwy & Garden Valley Blvd	April - Oct	Sat	9am - 1pm
	500 block of Jackson St	May - Sept	Thurs	5pm - 8pm
Salem	1917 Lancaster Drive NE	All Year	Tues, Thurs & Sat	Noon - 6 pm
	Green State parking lot, Summer St & Marion St NE	May - Oct	Sat	9am - 3pm
	Salem Transit Mall, Chekemeta between High NE & Liberty NE	May - Oct	Wed	10am - 3pm
Sherwood	Oldtown Veteran's Park	May - Sept	Sat	8am - 1pm
Silverton	Town Square Park, Main & Fiske	May - Oct	Sat	9am - 2pm
Stayton	Wilco Farm parking lot	June - Oct	Sat	9am - 1:30pm

Shopping in Oregon

95

Farmers Markets in Oregon

City	Location	Months	Day(s)	Hours
Tigard	9250 SW Hall Bvd & Oleson Rd, NE corner	May - Oct	Sat	8am - 1pm
Tillamook	Laurel Ave between 2nd & 3rd	June - Oct	Sat	9am - 2pm
Vale	Main St between A & B	June-Aug	Sat	10am - 2:30pm
Williams	1240 Rural SE	All Year	Sat	8:30am - 1pm
Woodburn	Woodburn Library, 1st St at Garfield	May - Oct	Sat	9am - 3pm
	Warzynski Plaza	May - Oct	Sat	9am - 3pm
Yachats	Yachats Commons (Old School on Hwy 101)	May - Oct	Sun	9am - 1pm

"Whole foods are foods as they are found in nature, foods that contain flavors and ingredients nature intended."
see page 101

Shopping in Oregon

PART THREE

Living

The Vegetarian Way

We encourage you to learn as much as you can about the many benefits vegetarian food has to offer and the steps you can take to improve your diet. To help, we have arranged for a panel of experts to share their opinions and knowledge. Naturally each of our experts differs slightly in their opinions and recommendations. However, they all strongly agree that a vegetarian diet is best both for us and the world we live in.

Our experts have provided articles covering the most important aspects of a vegetarian diet. They will show you how to get started, and how a healthy vegetarian diet can help you to prevent or recover from some common diseases. They will explain about nutrition at every stage of life and present four good reasons why a vegetarian diet benefits so much more than just our health. If you're already a vegetarian, you'll find all kinds of information on how to improve your diet even further.

Getting Started

We'll help you get started on your way to a healthy vegetarian diet. Begin with the article on *Basic Vegetarian Nutrition* by Karen Lamphere, certified nutritionist. This article explains the fundamentals of good nutrition and will also serve as the background to reading some of the other articles.

Once you've had a mini course in nutrition, you'll be ready to restock your kitchen. In *The Well-Stocked Kitchen* by food writer Cheryl Redmond, you'll find an invaluable guide to selecting and using foods that are both healthy and delicious. Look at the store reviews for the location of a store near you where you can find everything on your shopping list.

At Vegetarians of Washington we love to eat. We love great tasting food and we'll accept nothing less. The *Cookbooks and Other Resources* article by Amanda Strombom, President of Vegetarians of Washington, will help steer you toward excellent cookbooks with delicious recipes. You will also find other books where you can learn more about the wide-ranging benefits of vegetarian diet.

Staying Healthy

As time goes on, more and more research shows the benefits of a vegetarian diet in the prevention and treatment of many diseases. In this section you'll learn just how valuable a vegetarian diet can be in improving your health. Dr. Patricia Gross will explain how to avoid heart disease and cancer and how a vegetarian diet can help those of us with these diseases to get well again.

Diabetes is on the rise in our country in both adults and children. Dr. Gregory Scribner explains how a vegetarian diet is invaluable in getting a handle on this disease.

Osteoporosis has gone from a relatively rare disease to a household word. Dr. Ray Foster explains how animal products in our diet have led to an increase in osteoporosis and shows how a vegetarian diet plays a key role in keeping our bones healthy.

They say that every journey begins with a single step and the switch to a vegetarian diet is no exception. Marilyn Joyce, a registered dietician and international speaker, explains how small changes in your diet can make a big difference in your health, especially if you are recovering from an illness.

A Diet For All Ages

If you have a family to feed, you may need to put in some extra effort to encourage them all to follow a healthy vegetarian diet. Sometimes one member will start first. Other times, the whole family dives right in. Every family is different. The key to remember is that it's OK if everyone at the table is eating different food, especially in the beginning. While it may be a little extra work at first to prepare some different meals, in time it will get easier and faster, and it's definitely worth the results.

In this section you'll find information for every stage of life. We start with babies and their moms. Your baby's nutrition starts even before it's born. Reed Mangels, a registered dietician and nutrition advisor, will show you how to have a healthy pregnancy on a vegetarian diet, and how your baby can achieve optimal health after it's born.

They grow up so fast. Cynthia Lair, a lecturer at Bastyr University, will show you how to attract your children to eating healthier foods, even if they are picky eaters.

In no time at all they will be teenagers, and perhaps aspiring athletes. A vegetarian diet is the diet of champions. So we asked ultrathon champion Scott Jurek to explain how a vegetarian diet gives an athlete an edge on the way to a gold medal.

Susan Gins, a certified nutritionist, shows how certain foods can help to ease the experience of menopause.

Finally, Heather Woods, a naturopathic doctor, explains how a vegetarian diet plays a key role in keeping us healthy as we move through our senior years.

Four Good Reasons Why

One of the reasons for following a vegetarian diet is to promote our health. Most of us are aware of the problems caused by saturated fat and cholesterol in our diet, but this is just the beginning of the health problems associated with meat and other animal products. In his article, Dr. Neal Barnard talks about a broad range of health problems associated with animal products.

The days of Old MacDonald's farm are now long gone. Today's farming is known as factory farming. The advent of factory farming has led to increasingly inhumane conditions for farm animals. These animals do not have the legal protection that other animals have and therefore really need our help. Jennifer Hillman, Campaign and Legislative Coordinator for the Progressive Animal Welfare Society, explains how following a vegetarian diet can make a substantial contribution to animal welfare. As it turns out, a vegetarian diet is another win-win situation, benefiting both us and our animal friends!

Many people are surprised to learn how animal agriculture wastes vast amounts of energy, water, natural habitat and other natural resources. While many environmentalists were slow to recognize the value of a vegetarian diet in saving the environment, mounting evidence and continuing research have made the environmental reason for changing to a vegetarian diet as strong as any other. In these days of continuing stress on the environment, we all need to look for ways to help. Environmentalists Tim Fargo and Anne Johnson, explain the impact of animal agriculture and how we can all improve our environment by following an earth-friendly diet.

A vegetarian diet is a perfect fit with whatever religious faith you happen to follow. Stewart Rose, Vice President of Vegetarians of Washington, shows how, beginning in ancient times and continuing to the present day, many religious and spiritual leaders have advocated following a vegetarian diet. Today a growing number of people, from a wide range of religions, consider a vegetarian diet an important part of their beliefs and practices.

A vegetarian diet is an adventure in both learning and eating. Let these articles be the starting point for further learning. In no time at all, you'll find that you're "Veg-Feasting" and loving it.

"To incorporate the best aspects of a vegetarian diet, create meals that combine elements of all the food groups - whole grains, legumes, fruits, vegetables and healthy fats (in moderation)."

Getting Started

Basic Vegetarian Nutrition

by Karen Lamphere, MS, CN

People choose to become vegetarian for many reasons, one being the immediate relationship between vegetarianism and good health. The health benefits associated with eating a vegetarian diet are many. Studies show that vegetarians have less risk than non-vegetarians of developing coronary heart disease, hypertension, type II diabetes and some cancers. Vegetarians also have less incidence of obesity. But just because a diet is vegetarian doesn't automatically mean it's healthy. A diet high in processed, refined foods is undesirable whether it contains animal products or not. The healthiest diet is based on whole foods.

Whole foods are foods as they are found in nature, foods that contain the flavors and ingredients nature intended. They are free of artificial flavors, colors and chemicals added to increase shelf-life. Minimally processed, they have not lost their vitamins, minerals and fiber.

In a whole-foods vegetarian diet, the bulk of the calories comes from legumes, grains, vegetables, fruits, nuts and seeds.

Protein

The question of adequate protein intake is the one people most often raise, although studies consistently show that even strict vegetarians have satisfactory protein intake. Dietary proteins contain amino acids that are the body's building blocks. One of our most important nutrients, they make up our muscles, organs, bones and skin. Protein is found in both animal and plant foods, but plant sources alone can easily provide adequate amounts of amino acids as long as a variety of plant foods are consumed and caloric intake is sufficient.

How Much Protein?

No other area of nutritional need has been the subject of so much controversy as the daily protein requirement. The average adult Recommended Dietary Allowance (RDA) for protein is 0.8 grams per kilogram of body weight. Protein requirements for vegetarians may be slightly higher due to plant protein digestibility differences, so 1 gram per kilogram of body weight is a good rule of thumb. To determine your daily protein need, multiply your body weight (in pounds) x 0.45. That translates to 67.5 grams for a 150-pound adult, an amount easy to obtain from a vegetarian diet.

Vegetarian Protein Sources

The foods that supply the most protein in a vegetarian diet are legumes (beans, dried peas, soy products), grains, vegetables, nuts and seeds. Legumes have the highest concentrated protein and are a great source of fiber, complex carbohydrates, vitamins and minerals. A vegetarian diet should include two or more legume servings a day. A serving is typically 1/2 cup cooked beans, 1 cup soymilk, 4 ounces tofu.

Living

Plant protein is much healthier than animal protein because it is lower in fat content and has a higher fiber, vitamin and mineral content.

Protein Content of Selected Food Items

Food Item	Serving Size	Grams Protein
Tempeh	½ cup	16 grams
Tofu	½ cup	10 grams
Peanut butter	2 Tbsp	8 grams
Lentils	½ cup, cooked	8 grams
Black Beans	½ cup, cooked	7.5 grams
Chickpeas	½ cup, cooked	7.5 grams
Soymilk	1 cup	7 grams
Broccoli	1 cup, cooked	5 grams
Quinoa	½ cup, cooked	5 grams

Carbohydrates

Carbohydrates are the body's primary source of energy. During digestion they're converted into glucose and provide fuel for our cells. It's recommended that 60 percent of total daily calories come from carbohydrates. Carbohydrate sources include fruits, vegetables, legumes, grains and concentrated sweeteners. When choosing carbohydrate-rich foods, select unrefined foods such as fruits, vegetables, peas, beans and whole grains, rather than refined, processed foods such as soft drinks, desserts, candy and sugar.

Whole Grains

Whole grains, an essential part of the vegetarian diet, are the edible parts of seeds with the germ, endosperm and bran layers intact. They include whole wheat, brown rice, oats, corn, rye, millet and quinoa. Whole grains contain some protein, and are an excellent source of fiber, vitamins, minerals, complex carbohydrates and phytonutrients. They are also low on the glycemic index and cause a slower rise in blood sugar than refined grains, helping maintain normal insulin and blood sugar levels. When whole grains are refined, the bran and germ are removed along with most vitamins and minerals. Only a few of these lost vitamins and minerals - B1, B2, B3, iron and folic acid - are added back. So it's important to emphasize whole rather than refined grains in the diet. Five or more servings per day should be included. One serving is typically 1/2 cup of cooked grain, 1 ounce of cereal, or 1 slice of bread. Each serving contains about 3 grams protein and 15 grams carbohydrate.

Quinoa, a grain that merits special mention, has been hailed as a "supergrain." It contains more protein than any other grain (5 grams per 1/2 cup, cooked). It's a great substitute for rice or other grains in almost any dish.

Vegetables and Fruits

Vegetables and fruits are nutritional powerhouses rich in fiber, vitamins, minerals and antioxidants and should be eaten in abundance. Special emphasis should be given to dark green and yellow-orange fruits and vegetables to ensure adequate intake of vitamin A. Sweet potatoes, carrots, kale and cantaloupe are great sources. These deeply colored fruits and vegetables are high in carotenoids, the metabolic precursors to the biologically active form of vitamin A, important for optimal vision and immune function. Choose seasonal, organically raised vegetables and fruits. Aim for at least five vegetable servings per day: 1 cup raw, or 1/2 cup cooked. Fruit is best limited to 2-4 daily servings due to its higher sugar content. A standard serving is one medium size fruit, 1/2 cup raw, cooked or canned fruit, or 3/4 cup fruit juice.

Fats and Oils

The healthiest sources of fats and oils come from foods like avocados, olives, nuts and seeds. Fats are an essential part of the diet. They supply energy and help our bodies absorb certain vitamins and phytonutrients. Two important types of fats are omega-3 and omega-6, also known as essential fats because our bodies can't make them. These fats are important for reducing inflammation, and promoting cardiovascular health, fetal and infant brain development and visual acuity. Omega-6 fats are plentiful in the vegetarian diet, coming primarily from corn, safflower and sunflower oils, and nuts and seeds. Omega-3 fats are more difficult to obtain; the richest sources are flax oil and flaxseed, followed by canola and soybean oil, walnuts, hemp and pumpkin seeds. Since most diets, including vegetarian, contain too many omega-6 fats, it's wise to limit omega-6 fats by substituting olive or canola oil in cooking and baking, and increase omega-3s by including a daily intake of ground flaxseed or flax oil, soy products, walnuts or pumpkin seeds. Overall fat intake should be about 20% of total calories.

Trans-fats, also known as partially hydrogenated oils, raise cholesterol and heart disease risk and should be entirely eliminated from the diet. They are found in fried foods, crackers, cookies, pastries, and many convenience and fast foods. Read ingredient labels - if you see the words _hydrogenated, partially hydrogenated,_ or _vegetable shortening_ - don't eat it!

Improperly stored fats and oils can oxidize and become rancid. It's best to buy organic, cold-pressed oils and store them in the refrigerator, along with shelled nuts and seeds. Flax oil should be reserved for cold uses, like salad dressings - not for cooking.

Vitamins and Minerals

A vegetarian diet rich in legumes, whole grains, vegetables and fruits will easily satisfy nutritional requirements. However, a few specific nutrients are needed to ensure adequate amounts for optimal health. These include vitamins B12 and D, and the minerals calcium, iron and zinc.

Living

Vitamin B12

Vitamin B12 is an essential nutrient important for the nervous system, red blood cell production and cardiovascular health. B12 is made by the bacteria that live in the soil. Much of the B12 found in plant foods in lost through modern methods of hygiene. Reliable vegetarian sources of vitamin B12 are fortified foods such as Red Star Vegetarian Support Formula Nutritional Yeast, soymilks, cereals and B12 supplements. The RDA for vitamin B12 is 3 micrograms.

Vitamin D

Vitamin D is a fat-soluble vitamin that acts like a hormone, regulating formation of bone and absorption of calcium. Vitamin D is usually obtained from the action of sunlight on the skin, but studies show that in areas such as the Pacific Northwest where sunlight is scarce in winter, vitamin D deficiency is possible. Deficiency can cause osteomalacia (softening of the bones), rickets and osteoporosis. Vegetarian sources of vitamin D include fortified soymilk, fortified rice or almond milk, some fortified breakfast cereals and supplements. The RDA for vitamin D for children, pregnant and lactating women is 10 micrograms per day. For other adults it is 5 micrograms per day.

Calcium

Calcium, the most abundant mineral in the body, is essential for maintaining healthy bones and teeth. It is also required for normal nerve function, muscle contraction, blood clotting and the prevention of osteoporosis. Recent studies indicate that dietary calcium may reduce the risk of colon cancer. Inadequate calcium intake can lead to poor bone formation, weak bones, osteoporosis and poor dental health.

Calcium in green vegetables like kale, broccoli, collard greens, mustard greens and Chinese cabbage is well absorbed. The recommended intake of calcium for adults age 19 through 50 is 1000 milligrams per day. An intake of 1200 milligrams of calcium is recommended for those 51 and older.

Calcium Content of Non-Dairy Foods in Milligrams (mg)

Food Item	Serving Size	Grams Calcium
Calcium-fortified orange juice	1 cup	300 mg
Edamame	1 cup	261 mg
Tofu (made with calcium sulfate)	1/2 cup	204 mg
Broccoli	1 cup	178 mg
Okra	1 cup	176 mg
Blackstrap molasses	1 Tbsp	172 mg
Collards	1 cup	150 mg

Living

Figs, dried	5	150 mg
Refried beans	1 cup	141 mg
Tahini	2 Tbsp	128 mg
Kale	1 cup raw	100 mg
Almonds	1 oz	70 mg

Iron

A trace mineral found in every cell of the body, iron plays an important role in transporting oxygen from the lungs to the tissues. It's used in the manufacture of hemoglobin, the pigment that gives blood its red color. Iron is important for normal immune function, energy production and cognitive function. Iron deficiency is one of the most common nutritional deficiencies worldwide, highest among children and women of childbearing age. Lack of iron leads to iron deficiency and, ultimately, anemia.

Eating foods high in vitamin C at the same meal can greatly enhance iron absorption. For example: brown rice and tofu served with vitamin C-rich foods such as tomato sauce and broccoli can double or triple iron absorption. Using cast-iron cookware, particularly when cooking acidic foods like tomato sauce, also contributes to dietary intake. The recommended daily intake of iron for adult men and women is 10 mg and 15 mg, respectively.

Iron Content of Plant Foods

Food Item	Serving Size	Grams Iron
Lentils, cooked	1 cup	6.5 mg
Chickpeas, cooked	1 cup	4.7 mg
Lima beans, cooked	1 cup	4.5 mg
Blackstrap molasses	1 Tbsp	3.5 mg
Tahini	2 Tbsp	2.7 mg
Tempeh	3 ½ oz	2.1 mg
Figs, dried	5	2.1 mg
Chinese cabbage, cooked	1 cup	1.8 mg
Broccoli, cooked	1 cup	1.8 mg
Almonds	1 oz	1.2 mg
Kale, raw	1 cup	1.2 mg
Sunflower Seeds	1 oz	1 mg

Living

Tips for increasing iron intake and absorption

• Toast nuts and seeds; add to oatmeal, salads and stir-fries.
• Sprout beans and lentils, add to salads and sandwiches.
• Use fermented soy foods like tempeh and miso.
• Add dried fruits to salads, trail mixes and desserts.
• Include vitamin C-rich foods such as kale, red bell peppers and
  citrus fruits with each meal.
• Use iron-fortified foods such as cereals.
• Use cast-iron cookware for cooking.

Zinc

Zinc, a trace mineral needed for cell reproduction and tissue growth and repair, is essential for the proper function of the immune system and maintaining a sense of taste. Vegetarian sources of zinc include nuts, pumpkin and sunflower seeds, whole-grain yeast breads, wheat germ, legumes and fermented soy products like tempeh and miso. Calcium and iron supplements interfere with zinc absorption. The RDA for zinc is 15 mg per day.

Summing it all up

To incorporate the best aspects of a vegetarian diet, create meals that combine elements of all the food groups - legumes, whole grains, vegetables, fruits and healthy fats (in moderation). Limit refined sweeteners and refined grains. Consider supplements to fill nutrient gaps. A multivitamin will meet B12, D, zinc and iron needs. Take calcium supplements separately. Health-oriented cookbooks and magazines contain many ideas for whole foods vegetarian meals. Try some of the following simple combinations:

• A seasoned vegetable stir-fry with cashews or toasted walnuts over a bed of grains.

• A corn tostada layered with refried beans, sliced avocado and salsa, topped with shredded carrot, lettuce and soy cheese.

• A whole-wheat pita-bread sandwich stuffed with hummus (a dish made from pureed chickpeas and sesame butter available at most natural foods stores), sliced black olives, lettuce and sprouts.

• A large raw salad with assorted veggies and marinated tofu (available in natural foods stores) tossed with Dijon vinaigrette dressing made with flax and olive oil.

• For dessert, try a bowl of fresh fruit topped with a few raisins and toasted coconut, or a fruit smoothie made with frozen organic strawberries, soy or almond milk, vanilla extract and sweetener to taste. Bon Appetit!

To find out about the author, please see "About the Contributors" on pages 181-183.

Living

The Well-Stocked Kitchen

by Cheryl Redmond, freelance writer, columnist and food editor

The first step to creating healthy meals is to make sure you've got wholesome ingredients on hand. But the choices can seem overwhelming, and simply having a pantry full of food doesn't mean you'll be inspired to cook. The key to success is to shop for ingredients that give you the best nutrition and flavor for your money and are convenient to use. Here are some of these must-have foods, along with tips for choosing and using them.

Beans and Legumes

Star Qualities: Beans are tiny bundles of energy, providing abundant protein as well as soluble fiber, calcium, iron, and B vitamins, particularly folate. They come in such a variety of colors and flavors and can be transformed into so many different dishes (from patties to purées, from stews to salads) that you could eat beans every day and not get bored.

At the Market: Choose canned beans when you're in a hurry. Black beans, chickpeas, white beans, and kidney beans are particularly versatile for last-minute meals. It's worth purchasing organic brands because they usually have less sodium. Frozen beans, such as lima beans and shelled edamame (green soybeans), are another nutritious option. Among dried legumes, lentils are most suitable for weeknight dinners; they don't need soaking and they cook in 15 to 30 minutes.

In Your Kitchen: Make storebought soup more nutritious by adding a can of beans. Add white beans to tomato sauce for pasta, or purée them with garlic, lemon juice, salt, and pepper and spread on toasted country bread. Sauté lima beans or edamame with corn kernels, diced tomatoes, and onions for a quick succotash.

Whole Grains

Star Qualities: Whole grains have their nutritious bran and germ intact. They're a good source of protein, B vitamins, and minerals like iron and zinc. Unlike refined grain products, whole grains are rich in beneficial fiber, are filling and have a satisfying texture.

At the Market: When you're pressed for time, turn to quick-cooking grains like bulgur (cracked wheat), instant polenta (corn), and quick-cooking barley. If the thought of cooking with whole grains intimidates you, try quinoa. This ancient grain from the Andes has an appealing nutty taste and a delicately crunchy texture. It cooks quickly, is suitable for everything from hot breakfast cereal to pilaf and is an excellent source of protein. Other nutrient-dense whole grains include amaranth and tef.

In Your Kitchen: Many grains, including quinoa, benefit from this cooking method: Sauté grains in a little oil for a minute or two before adding cooking water.

Bring to a boil, cover, and simmer. When the grains are completely cooked, remove from heat, leave the lid on and let the grains steam for about 5 minutes. Fluff with a fork before serving.

Brown Rice

Star Qualities: This whole grain is so nutritious and versatile it deserves a category of its own. Rice is a good source of iron, protein, and B vitamins. White rice is milled and polished to remove its bran and germ. Brown rice (like other whole grains) retains these nutritious components, yielding twice as much fiber as well as a good supply of vitamin E. Brown rice has a wonderfully chewy texture and slightly nutty flavor.

At the Market: Quick-cooking brown rice is a good choice when you don't want to give up convenience for nutrition. When you have a little more time to spare, try whole-grain versions of your favorite white rices, like fragrant basmati and jasmine, and creamy arborio. Whole-grain rice comes in many shades besides brown and each variety has its own unique flavor. Experiment with these delicious, exotic-sounding varieties of rice such as Black Japonica, Camargue Red, Bhutanese Red, Forbidden Black, or Wehani.

In Your Kitchen: Try brown rice as a hot breakfast cereal. You can make it sweet with honey and dried fruit or savory with tamari, sesame seeds and shredded carrots. Use earthy, sweet red rice in pilafs and stuffings. Make great risottos, desserts, and side dishes with nutty, soft-textured black rice. It's important to keep whole-grain rice in a cool, dark place so it won't go rancid. Buying in bulk is fine, but don't purchase more than you can use in a month or two.

Nuts

Star Qualities: Most nuts are rich in monounsaturated fat, which helps to lower levels of LDL ("bad") cholesterol while maintaining levels of HDL ("good") cholesterol in the blood. (Walnuts are high in polyunsaturated fat, which is also heart-healthy.) Nuts contain arginine, an amino acid that helps keep arteries clear, and magnesium and potassium, which have been associated with lowering blood pressure. Nuts also provide other important nutrients like fiber, calcium, and vitamin E. Because nuts have a high satiety value, adding a modest amount to your diet can help you feel full so you don't overeat.

At the Market: Because they have so much oil, it's crucial to buy fresh nuts. Shop at a market that has a rapid turnover. If you buy from bulk bins, use your sense of smell to determine freshness; don't buy if you detect any unpleasant odors. Buy whole nuts and chop them yourself; small chopped pieces are more vulnerable to oxidation (exposure to air, which can make them stale).

In Your Kitchen: Add chopped almonds to pilafs and homemade veggie burgers. Sprinkle walnuts or pine nuts on salads instead of croutons. Blend cashews and water to make a thick purée and use it to add a creamy richness to soups and pasta sauces. Although nuts are good for you, there's no denying that they're calorie-dense, so portion control is important. One ounce, or about a quarter-cup, is one serving of nuts. In recipes, make the most of a modest amount of nuts by lightly toasting them first to intensify their flavor. Stir them in a dry skillet over medium heat or bake them at 350 degrees just until they turn golden brown and fragrant. Store nuts in a sealed container in the fridge or freezer to help keep them fresh.

Dried Fruit

Star Qualities: Dried fruit provides vitamins, minerals, and fiber like fresh fruit, but in a concentrated and convenient-to-store form. It's a quick, naturally sweet source of energy. A handful of chopped, dried fruit adds flavor, texture, and antioxidants to a wide range of dishes, from cereals to stews.

At the Market: Choose plump dried fruit with a uniform color and without signs of sugar crystallization. Be aware that many dried fruits are treated with sulfur dioxide to retain their color. This is why golden raisins are light-colored, not brown. Sulfur dioxide aids the retention of certain vitamins, like beta carotene, but diminishes others, like thiamin, and it can trigger headaches and asthma in people sensitive to it. Check the label if you have concerns.

In Your Kitchen: You can toss just about any kind of dried fruit into hot or cold cereal or yogurt, but breakfast isn't the only meal that gets a boost from dried fruit. Dried cranberries make a nice addition to spinach or arugula salad. Currants, dried cherries, and golden raisins go well with couscous and other grain dishes. Dried plums and apricots are delicious with beans and lentils, especially in stews.

Tofu and Tempeh

Star Qualities: Soyfoods are a valuable source of protein as well as plant chemicals called isoflavones which are being studied for their cancer-fighting, heart-protecting, and bone-building abilities. Tofu and tempeh offer the benefits of soy in traditional, minimally processed forms. Tofu's smooth texture and mild flavor make it endlessly versatile. Tempeh has a hearty flavor and chewy texture.

At the Market: The two basic kinds of tofu are silken tofu and regular tofu. Both varieties are available in different firmnesses, though regular tofu is generally firmer. Many stores also carry tofu that has already been baked and seasoned. Tofu can be high in fat but you can buy reduced-fat tofu (sometimes called enriched). Also check the label for the calcium content; some tofu is processed with calcium, making it a good source of this bone-building mineral. Avoid genetically modified soybeans by choosing organic tofu.

Tempeh is made from cooked soybeans to which a culture has been added. It's extremely high in protein and has a somewhat nutty and yeasty taste. For a robust flavor choose all-soy tempeh. For a milder flavor, purchase tempeh made with a mixture of soy and grains.

Living

In Your Kitchen: Silken tofu blends well into sauces, smoothies and dressings. Firm or extra firm tofu is good for scrambles and stir-fries. Use slices of baked tofu in sandwiches or dice it into salads. Crumble tempeh into chili or slice and marinate it in barbecue sauce and heat, and then serve in a sandwich.

Try pressing tofu to make it firmer and give it a pleasantly chewy texture. Cut a block of tofu in two equally thick slices, put them in a large dish, cover them with a piece of plastic wrap, and place a couple of pounds of weight on top. Cast-iron skillets or a cutting board with some heavy pantry items work well. Let tofu drain for half an hour while you prepare the rest of your meal.

Whole-Grain Pastas

Star Qualities: Whole-grain pastas bring you the goodness of whole grains, protein, vitamins, and fiber in a convenient, familiar form. Hearty whole-grain pasta and sauce is a quick and easy meal that satisfies vegans and meat eaters alike.

At the Market: Japanese soba noodles, found in the international aisle at many supermarkets, are made with buckwheat flour. Spelt pasta is made from an ancient relative of wheat that's high in protein and easy on the digestive system. Other healthy pasta varieties blend durum semolina with corn, quinoa, amaranth, or kamut.

In Your Kitchen: Pair whole-grain pastas with robust tomato, mushroom, or other vegetable sauces. Roasted vegetables go especially well with whole-wheat pasta. Corn and quinoa pastas taste best with lighter sauces. Try corn pasta with fresh diced tomatoes, fresh chopped cilantro, and minced jalapeño to taste. Be sure not to overcook whole-grain pastas. Their lower gluten content means they're apt to fall apart unless served al dente (slightly firm).

Olive Oil

Star Qualities: Olive oil is high in heart-healthy monounsaturated fat and contains the antioxidant vitamin E. Extra-virgin olive oil is minimally processed, for optimal flavor and health benefits. It's not subjected to heat or cleaned with chemical solvents like bland, colorless cooking oils are. A drizzle of oil is a nice finishing touch for many dishes, and it's a healthy alternative to butter (or margarine) on vegetables, bread, and rice.

At the Market: Extra-virgin olive oils come in a wide range of prices. Buy a moderately priced oil for everyday use and splurge on a spicy, fruity, good-quality oil for salads and dipping. It makes sense to buy organic if you can afford it, because extra-virgin oil isn't cleaned before bottling. You can also purchase olive oils that have been infused with citrus, herbs, or spices.

In Your Kitchen: Naturally flavorful extra-virgin olive oil needs only a splash of vinegar and a sprinkling of salt and pepper to make the perfect dressing for green salads. Infused oils quickly add layers of flavor, making a simple meal taste like you spent hours in the kitchen. Try lemon-infused oil on steamed vegetables, drizzle basil oil on beans or pizza, or brush garlic oil on bruschetta.

Unless they contain ascorbic acid or another preservative, oils with herbs or other ingredients added to them should be stored in your refrigerator and used within a couple of weeks. All oils should be stored away from light and heat.

Vinegar

Star Qualities: Vinegar is a low-sodium, low-calorie flavor builder that can enhance a wide range of vegetarian dishes.

At the Market: Try rice wine, sherry, and Champagne vinegars. Look for full-strength vinegars; you can always dilute them yourself. If you find yourself using vinegar more, invest in a couple of good-quality vinegars like traditional balsamics and wine vinegars made by the Orleans method (the label will say so). Stay away from flavorless distilled white vinegar.

In Your Kitchen: Drizzle a few drops of high-quality balsamic vinegar on vanilla ice cream or strawberries. Splash sherry vinegar into black bean soup or gazpacho. Perk up steamed vegetables with wine vinegar. Use rice vinegar in vinaigrette—its mild flavor means you can use less oil. Add vinegars, especially better-quality ones, at the end of cooking so their flavor isn't dissipated by high heat.

Miso

Star Qualities: This fermented soybean paste is a rich source of the isoflavones, genistein and daidzen, believed to have a protective effect against cancer. Unpasteurized miso contains beneficial enzymes that aid digestion. Miso has a savory quality (called umami in Japan), which is valuable for meatless cooking. It provides depth of flavor to soups, sauces, and dressings.

At the Market: There are many varieties of miso, including barley, rice, soy, and chickpea, but there aren't any rules about which one to use. Just remember that, generally speaking, dark misos have been aged longer and have a more assertive, saltier taste than lighter ones. Look for unpasteurized miso in tubs in the refrigerated aisle.

In Your Kitchen: Use light miso in a savory salad dressing or spread it sparingly on sandwiches. Try dark miso in split pea soup or a casserole with mushrooms. Miso is very salty, so add a little at a time, tasting as you go. If you're using unpasteurized miso in soups or stews, add it at the end of cooking to preserve its healthful qualities.

Garlic and Ginger

Star Qualities: Garlic promotes circulation and lowers cholesterol. It also contains sulfur compounds like allicin, that may prevent cancer cell growth. Ginger is famous for its ability to quell nausea and contains a compound called gingerol that may lower blood pressure and improve circulation.

At the Market: If you have access to an Asian market, look for young ginger. The skin is translucent and almost pink instead of papery beige, and the root itself is less fibrous, so it's easier to chop. If you buy mature ginger, choose specimens that look smooth, not wrinkled, and watch out for mold. When buying garlic, look for heads with firm, plump cloves and no green shoots.

In Your Kitchen: Braise or roast garlic cloves until soft to give dishes a mellow richness rather than a sharp garlic flavor. Add fresh grated ginger to gingerbread. Chopped crystallized ginger puts zip into fruit salads. Minced garlic and ginger are classic aromatic stir-fry ingredients. To preserve their health benefits and flavor, wait until your other stir-fry ingredients are nearly cooked, then clear a space in the middle of the pan and add the aromatics. Allicin develops upon exposure to air, when garlic is chopped. To maximize its effect, peel and mince garlic ahead of time and let it sit about 10 minutes before cooking with it.

Herbs and Spices

Star Qualities: Although you use them in small amounts, herbs and spices make a big contribution to your meals. For example, quercetin in oregano, carnosol in rosemary, and curcumin in turmeric are all antioxidants that have been studied for their cancer protective effects. In any form, herbs and spices add flavor without adding calories.

At the Market: If you're an occasional cook, stick to a small selection of herbs and spices so you'll use them up more quickly. Whole spices stay fresh longer, but if you're not likely to grind them yourself, it's better to buy them in a form that's easier to use.

While soft herbs like basil, cilantro, and parsley taste better fresh, tougher herbs like oregano and rosemary hold up well when dried. It's handy to have a spice blend like garam masala or curry powder on hand; they provide a quick and easy way to liven up meals.

In Your Kitchen: Mix up sweet and savory flavors: Try a pinch of cinnamon in couscous or a smidgeon of black pepper in gingerbread. Nutmeg and cayenne both go well with greens like spinach and chard. Thyme has an affinity for mushrooms, basil is a nice addition to salads, while oregano makes a wonderful accent for beans, eggplant, and olives. Be adventurous; the possibilities are endless.

Remember, even dried herbs have a shelf life. If you have to look at the label (rather than relying on your nose) to tell you what's in that herb or spice jar, it's time to replace it.

To find out about the author, please see "About the Contributors" on pages 181-183.

Living

Cookbooks and other helpful resources

by Amanda Strombom, MA, President, Vegetarians of Washington

The question I hear most often when people are thinking of going vegetarian is, "What can I cook at home?" A good vegetarian cookbook or two is an excellent way to start. In this article, I have reviewed many cookbooks from my favorite vegetarian authors and a selection of other books you might find interesting too. There are many more available than can be listed here. Choose any book by any of the authors below and you won't go wrong. Many of these cookbooks use the word vegan in the title. Don't worry if you're not vegan, vegetarians will find them delicious too.

Vegetarian cooking is easy and fun, and the results are usually delicious. It is easy to keep many of the most useful ingredients stored in your pantry or refrigerator, ready for whenever you might need them. It's fun to experiment with a variety of ingredients, to create familiar flavors using some new ingredients, and to try some flavors that are new to you too. As you experiment, you will discover new recipes which will delight your taste buds and those of whomever you cook for. Some recipes will become your new favorites, to be cooked regularly. Others will be sampled and saved for a special occasion. And there will no doubt be a few which you decide are not for you, but you will have learned from the experience, and you will know which ingredients suit your palate and cooking style the best. At Vegetarians of Washington, we ask only that you are willing to experiment and willing to learn, and that you do the best you can. Every step you take towards a vegetarian diet is a step towards better health, fewer animals being harmed and less destruction to the environment.

Cookbooks

The Accidental Vegan, by Devra Gartenstein, Crossing Press, 2000
This compact cookbook, which fits on a small handy shelf in your kitchen, is extremely useful for those already familiar with typical vegan foods. It is packed full of recipes, including appetizers, soups, main dishes, sides, sauces, lots of salads and dressings, and a few desserts. The instructions for each recipe are very clear and concise—often saying simply "mix the ingredients." The section on seitan is particularly helpful if you want to create a meaty texture in main dishes, perhaps to make your meat-eating friends feel comfortable when they come for dinner. My favorite dessert is the vegan baklava.

The Bold Vegetarian Chef, by Ken Charney, Wiley, 2002
Here is a forthright and determined approach to creating bold and generously spiced dishes. In this book Chef Ken Charney has shared many of his secrets, including what you should buy to equip your kitchen and those extra special techniques and tricks that make the difference between a good meal and a great one. There are chapters on everything from breakfast to dessert. Especially welcome is a complete explanation of how to prepare tofu and tempeh, thus transforming these healthy soy foods into dishes with an exciting and satisfying taste.

Living

113

The Everyday Vegan, by Dreena Burton, Arsenal Pulp Press, 2001
This book is a great "all-rounder" with ideas and recipes to meet every need. In addition to the entrees and side dishes, there are recipes for many appetizers and munchies, sauces, gravies and salad dressings. Sweets lovers are especially well catered for with over 24 recipes for puddings, cookies, cakes and pies. The sections on basic ingredients, cooking and preparation techniques are useful for anyone new to preparing healthy vegan food. There are seven different menu plans, quick meal ideas and ideas for potlucks, picnics and kids' birthday parties.

Fabulous Beans, by Barb Bloomfield, Book Publishing Company, 1994
Beans are an excellent source of protein and fiber in the vegetarian diet. With 12 different varieties of beans, and over 100 recipes to choose from, the choices presented in this book are almost unlimited. Learn how to store, prepare and cook each type of bean into all kinds of recipes, including salads and dips, soups and entrees, and even a couple of desserts. There are recipes from every corner of the Earth, from Mexico to Spain, and Brazil to India. I never knew there were so many possibilities.

Feeding the Whole Family, by Cynthia Lair, Moon Smile Press, 1997
Cooking with whole foods, and preparing food for children of all ages form the focus of this book. It's packed with helpful information about how to motivate children to eat more healthily, with whole chapters on breakfasts and on lunchboxes. The recipes are nearly all vegan, although a small number of fish recipes and one chicken recipe are included. The chapter on cooking whole grains and beans of all kinds is particularly useful. I love the recipes in this book, particularly the ones for tempeh meals. They are quick and easy, but enable you to create wholesome meals to feed everyone in the family.

Meatless Meals for Working People, by Debra Wasserman and Charles Stahler, The Vegetarian Resource Group, 2001
This book is perfect for people who don't have the time or the inclination to cook meals from scratch. The true-life stories about how real working people make good vegetarian choices and the nutrition charts in the back of the book add interest and make this book special. The lists of convenience foods are useful to stock your pantry, and lots of very simple recipes use these ingredients to recreate familiar foods, including breakfasts, side dishes, soups, soy dishes, meals from Mexico and Chinese favorites. A large portion of the book gives hints on how to make good vegetarian and vegan choices at fast food restaurants, including lots of details on which company's pizza crusts are vegan, etc.

The Native Foods Restaurant Cookbook, by Tanya Petrovna, Shambhala Publications, 2003
The Native Foods Restaurant in Palm Springs serves up delicious creative vegan meals. This cookbook enables us all to share in some of these creations in the comfort of our own homes. The entrees recreate many traditional meat-based dishes such as Hungarian Goulash, but there are plenty of new ideas too. Seitan is a

particular specialty of this restaurant, and its preparation from the basic ingredients is described. Chestnut Yam Pudding Cream makes a delicious creative dessert. A comprehensive glossary of the ingredients used, along with hints for equipping the kitchen, preparing and cooking the food, with special mention of how to work with all kinds of grains, beans, tofu and tempeh, is invaluable if whole foods cooking is new to you.

Nonna's Italian Kitchen, by Bryanna Clark Grogan, Book Publishing Company, 1998
To discover real Italian ingredients and techniques while staying with vegan principles, delve into this delightful cookbook, packed with delicious recipes from all parts of Italy. Learn how to prepare your own pasta, use nuts or soy products to prepare creamy sauces, and use lentils, other beans and a wide variety of vegetables to prepare nutritious entrees. With lots of interesting information provided in introductions and side-bars, this book is a pleasure to read even if you don't plan to cook a meal.

The Prostate Diet Cookbook, by Buffy Sanders, Harbor Press, 2002
There is much evidence to suggest that diet has a big impact on cancer treatment and prevention, and in particular on those cancers such as prostate cancer which are hormone driven. Buffy Sanders explains which foods feed cancer and which inhibit its growth. She provides delicious recipes for every meal. incorporating all the best cancer-fighting foods, making this a must-have cookbook for anyone fighting cancer.

Tofu, Quick and Easy, by Louise Hagler, Book Publishing Company, 1986
This handy little book will fit onto any kitchen shelf. It is packed with all kinds of recipes based on tofu, from breakfast to supper, with soups, light lunches and desserts too. My favorite recipe is the Hawaiian Stir Fry, using water chestnuts and pineapple chunks. The use of readily available convenience foods, the short lists of ingredients and the clear format of the recipes make it very easy to put great tofu dishes together in no time.

The Uncheese Cookbook, by Joanne Stepaniak, Book Publishing Company, 1994
If you love cheese, but know it's not good for you to eat, you will love the opportunity to create cheese-flavored dishes of all kinds without using dairy products. Using ingredients such as tofu, nuts and nutritional yeast, Joanne creates "cheezes"— spreads, dips and sauces that look and taste incredibly similar to the traditional dishes and products we're familiar with. She provides recipes to make every kind of cheeze, including Parmazano, Havarti and even a round of Brie. Then there are the soups, the fondues, sauces, pizzas, quiches and casseroles, followed by the cheesecakes and creamy desserts. This is a complete cookbook for every cheese recipe you've ever wanted, with zero cholesterol.

Vegan in Volume by Nancy Berkoff, RD, Vegetarian Resource Group, 2000
When you need to cook for large numbers of people for a party or special event, or

Living

115

perhaps year-round in a school, hospital or in a deli for example, you need to estimate quantities in a different way from regular recipe books. This·book is a really useful resource in those situations, with most recipes designed for 25 servings and easily scalable. Chapters are arranged around the types of events you might be catering for - kids' lunches, dinner parties, college students, weddings and hospitals for example. The recipes are clear and simple, but delicious, with nutritional information per serving provided.

Vegan Microwave Cookbook by Nancy Berkoff, RD, Vegetarian Resource Group, 2003
For someone living in a dorm or small apartment, with no stove or oven available, for the office worker who wants to prepare a quick lunch, or for the person new to cooking, who wants to prepare their own meals keeping it as simple as possible, this book is just what you need. The tips on what works in a microwave and what doesn't will prove invaluable. You'll be amazed at the bread and muffin creations you can make, and there are great ideas for using leftovers, canned and convenience foods to create a wide variety of tasty meals.

Vegan Planet by Robin Robertson, Harvard Common Press, 2003
For a really comprehensive vegan cookbook, you can't beat Vegan Planet. With chapters on salads and slaws, pasta, beans, grains, etc, there are over 400 tasty recipes to choose from. I particularly like the idea of having some chapters based on particular cooking methods, such as "Food that sizzles—Grilling, sautéing and stir-frying" or "The Global Oven" which includes a variety of lasagnes, pies and other baked dishes. Interesting notes, personal experiences and historical tidbits are scattered throughout to add color to this warm and appetizing cookbook.

The Vegetarian 5 Ingredient Gourmet, by Nava Atlas, Broadway Books, 2001
How to simplify meal preparation down to the essentials, using just a few high-quality ingredients in each delicious dish. Focusing on whole foods and fresh produce, enhanced with a few natural convenience foods, Nava Atlas recommends a variety of choices for everyday meals, with dozens of menu suggestions to make meal planning easy. There are 250 flavorful recipes, including a wide variety of pizza toppings and ingredients to make delicious wraps, along with soups, salads, pasta and grain dishes. This is an ideal family recipe book focusing on easily prepared tasty meals for a typical family.

The Vegetarian Way by Virgina Messina, MPH,RD and Mark Messina, PhD, Three Rivers Press, 1996
This comprehensive book covers every aspect of vegetarianism with lots of useful details. The many important reasons for going meatless are explained. All the dietary facts you might be concerned about are discussed, including meeting your protein, calcium and other mineral requirements. Each stage of the lifecycle from infancy to growing old is considered, along with special dietary needs such as for athletes or diabetics. When you're ready to makeover your kitchen and start cooking vegetarian meals, everything you need to know is covered with a number of useful recipes thrown in for good measure.

Living

The Veggie Book by Ray Foster, MD and Frances Foster, RN, NEWSTART Healthcare, 2003

This is a great little starter book for changing to a healthy way of eating and going vegetarian. The principle of a hearty breakfast, a good lunch and maybe just a light supper, without snacking in between, provides a foundation for giving your body all the energy and nutrients it needs, without feeling bloated, gaining weight or losing sleep. One chapter is devoted to describing many different fruits, vegetables, grains and beans which form the basis of the vegetarian diet. There are answers to many of the common questions about a vegetarian diet, tips on how to eat away from home, and a selection of recipes to try.

Books Which Focus on Health

Dr Dean Ornish's Program for Reversing Heart Disease, Ballantine Books, 1991

Dr Dean Ornish was the first clinician to offer documented proof that heart disease can be halted or even reversed simply by changing your lifestyle. His program has yielded amazing results. Participants have reduced or discontinued medications; their chest pain diminished or disappeared; they felt more energetic, happy and calm; they lost weight while eating more; and blockages in coronary arteries were actually reversed. This book presents the evidence and guides you step by step through the program, including the foods you should eat, exercise you need and how to look after your psychological and spiritual well-being. This book has become a classic, and a must-read for anyone suffering from heart disease.

Eat Right, Live Longer by Neal Barnard, MD, Crown Trade Paperbacks, 1997

If you want to learn what to eat to enjoy a long and healthy life, this is the book for you. Neal Barnard, a recognized expert on the impact of diet on health, details the many aspects of your health that are affected by diet. With strategies to boost immunity, strengthen bones and joints, and protect every cell in your body, the way to minimize aging and maximize your well-being again and again is to eat a low-fat vegan diet. To aid you in making the transition to this diet, there are menu plans, lists of ingredients to stock in your pantry, and lots of simple, straightforward recipes.

Eat More, Weigh Less by Dean Ornish, MD, HarperCollins, 1993, 2001

How to lose weight is a challenge that many people in the US face today. The low-fat vegan diet has consistently proved to be the diet that over the long term enabled the majority of the participants to lose weight and keep that weight off permanently. Dr Dean Ornish looks at many of the psychological factors that impact our feelings about food, what we choose to eat and how much we weigh. More than two thirds of the book is packed with suggested menus and delicious recipes for you to follow, making it a snap to lose weight and gain a new lease on life.

The Healthiest Diet in the World by Nikki and David Goldbeck, Dutton, 1998

"Goldbecks Golden Guidelines" outlines ways to live a healthy life, focused around the basics of fats, carbohydrates, protein and super-foods, with basic steps to start

Living

you on your way. These guidelines are expanded upon in more detail later in the book, with a chapter devoted to each guideline, and extensive footnotes relating to the scientific studies on which this information is based. The comprehensive recipe section covers many different types of vegetarian meals, along with many whole-food cooking tips and techniques. This book gives a comprehensive lifestyle plan, which you can modify to fit your needs.

The Wider Implications of Dietary Choices

Fast Food Nation by Eric Schlosser, Perennial, 2002

Eric Schlosser really helps us understand how America's dietary habits and food industries have become what they are today, and the impact of those habits on our health, our environment and on workers in the food industry. The growth of the fast food companies, the development of the meat packing industry and the conditions of workers in those industries are described in graphic detail. The effect on ranchers and the environment is also uncovered. Particularly unnerving are the standards of hygiene typical in the meat packing industry and the impact of super-bugs such as E. Coli on our health. I was appalled to learn what is going on in these industries, and very glad to be a vegetarian.

Recommended Informational Resources

International Vegetarian Union – www.ivu.org

This site provides all kinds of information about vegetarianism, including history, frequently asked questions and thousands of recipes from around the world.

Natural Choice Directory – www.naturalchoice.net

Listings and links to all kinds of resources in the Puget Sound area including holistic health, fitness and body work, natural remedies and products, bookstores, restaurants and natural food stores, counseling, and education and spiritual resources. A free printed version of the directory is available at many stores and other locations.

Vegetarian Resource Group – www.vrg.org

A fantastic range of information on vegetarian and vegan recipes, vegetarian and vegan nutrition, vegetarian and vegan cookbooks, Vegetarian Journal excerpts, vegetarian travel information, vegetarian and vegan brochures, and even a vegetarian game. Enjoy!

To find out about the author, please see "About the Contributors" on pages 181-183.

Living

Staying Healthy

Food for a Healthy Heart

by F. Patricia McEachrane Gross, MD

What Is Cardiovascular Disease?

Cardiovascular disease (CVD) includes any disease that affects the heart or the blood vessels. Coronary (heart) artery disease, hypertension, and carotid (neck) artery disease are the ones that do the most damage here in the United States. But there are other diseases, such as aortic aneurysm and peripheral arterial disease, that we may be aware of but don't always remember when we talk about cardiovascular disease.

Two of the top three killer diseases in the U.S. are heart disease and stroke. When we talk about someone having a heart attack, we are referring to an acute event that damages the muscle of that person's heart-one that may or may not cause permanent injury or death. Although the event is sudden in onset, the process that leads to a heart attack is a very gradual one. A stroke is a sudden event that can be as devastating as a heart attack, and as with a heart attack, the process within the arteries usually takes a while to get to the point of causing damage—in this case, to the brain.

This is very important information to have as early as possible in life, because the process begins in childhood. Of course, young children are not expected to make lifestyle decisions based on knowledge about cardiovascular risk, but the adults who take care of them are. More than likely, some people who have suffered heart attacks and strokes could have been spared if wise choices had been taught and modeled to them.

Risk Factors for CVD

Several lifestyle habits increase your risk for CVD. There are also some risk factors that you cannot control. The more risk factors you have, the higher your risk for developing CVD. Therefore, it's very important to reduce as many risk factors as you can.

First, let us look at the risk factors that you cannot control: age, sex, race and heredity. The older you get, the greater your chance of developing a heart attack or stroke. Statistically, males have heart attacks and strokes at an earlier age than females. African-Americans have higher rates of heart attacks and strokes than Caucasians. You have a higher risk of heart attack or stroke if a first-degree relative (a parent, a sibling, or a child) has had one.

The good news is that you can lower your risk by quitting smoking if you do smoke, lowering your cholesterol, lowering your blood pressure, increasing your physical activity, avoiding obesity and controlling your blood sugar if you are diabetic. Alcohol, drugs such as cocaine, and an unhealthy response to stress have also been associated with an increased risk of CVD.

Dietary Recommendations for Prevention of CVD

Let's look specifically at the recommendations made in 2002 by the American Heart Association (AHA). The goal for dietary intake outlined in the AHA Scientific Statement is an overall healthy eating pattern. It specifically advocates consuming fruits, vegetables, grains, and legumes, as well as reducing saturated fats to less than 10% of caloric intake, reducing cholesterol to less than 300 mg/day, and reducing transfatty acids by substituting grains and unsaturated fatty acids from fish, vegetables, legumes, and nuts. In addition, it recommends limiting salt to less than 6 grams/day. Although the AHA's recommendations are not strictly vegetarian, it's clear that these leading scientists are moving more and more in the direction of a greater understanding of the major benefits of a vegetarian diet in terms of cardiovascular health.

Another interesting fact about this guide is that it emphasizes a family-centered approach to primary prevention of CVD, in recognition of both genetics and behavior as causes of the "well-established familial aggregation of heart disease and stroke." In other words, the family is a strong influence on how healthy or unhealthy we are, not only in terms of genetics but also in terms of lifestyle. What we learn at home (by words and example) about diet and exercise is what we will grow up to practice. Let us now take a closer look at some of the specifics of the AHA guidelines.

Is There Any Cholesterol in a Vegetarian Diet?

Cholesterol is found only in animal foods such as meat, eggs, milk, cheese, and other dairy products. In the new guidelines, the recommendation is less than 300 mg/day. (Note that a single egg yolk contains 275 mg.) The ideal for anyone who is at increased cardiovascular risk is to consume less than 150 mg/day. The strictest kind of vegetarian diet, a vegan diet, contains no eggs or dairy products and can significantly reduce serum cholesterol levels in a period as short as one month.

Although cholesterol is one of the most valuable substances in the human body, we do not need to get it from our diets. The liver makes up to 2000 mg/day. Only in certain chronic illnesses where the liver is impaired is cholesterol deficient. In fact, we would do well not to consume any cholesterol at all, because it's very easy to absorb and very difficult to eliminate.

What About Saturated Fats?

The recommendations say that saturated fats should make up less than 10% of our calories. Saturated fats, which are the primary determinants of serum cholesterol levels, are not essential for human metabolic processes. They do provide some energy, but very often they are deposited in fat depots instead, and they act to increase cholesterol levels. They are very highly concentrated in meats such as beef, veal, pork, ham, and lamb, and in dairy products such as milk, butter, ice cream, hard cheeses, cottage cheese, and yogurt. Coconut oil, palm oil, palm kernel oil, and other tropical oils are saturated vegetable oils.

The higher the ratio of unsaturated fat in the food the better. That may seem a little confusing at first, but it's important to remember that both types of fat exist in most foods. So choose foods that are higher in unsaturated fats, especially mono-unsaturated foods such as olives and olive oil, and many kinds of nuts including walnuts, pecans, almonds and cashews. Foods that are high in monounsaturated fats decrease the risk of CVD by increasing the "good" cholesterol (HDL) and decreasing the "bad" (LDL) cholesterol.

What About Transfatty Acids?

The food industry uses hydrogenation as a way of preventing unsaturated oils from spoiling. Unfortunately, this process alters the way the body handles such fats. They are handled as saturated fats and thus increase the level of blood cholesterol. In addition, transfatty acids reduce HDL levels. If you read the label on your bag of potato chips, you will probably see that it says "partially hydrogenated." Even though the oil used may be a vegetable oil, it has virtually been changed to a saturated fat. Margarine, crackers, cookies, and other snack foods tend to be high in transfatty acids. The less processed and more natural the food, the better off you are. Read all labels carefully.

Do Fruits, Vegetables, Grains, Legumes, and Nuts Affect CVD?

As you can tell by looking at the list of these staples of a vegetarian diet, they are all high in fiber. "Fiber" is the word used to describe the components of plant cell walls and their indigestible carbohydrate residues. There is no fiber in animal-based foods. Fiber has been shown to have several positive cardiovascular effects, such as reducing LDL, raising HDL, reducing blood pressure, and reducing total cholesterol.

Vegetarian diets also tend to have higher concentrations of folic acid, which reduces homocysteine levels in the blood. Homocysteine is an amino acid that, when found in excess in the blood, has been strongly associated with injury to the inner lining of arteries and promotion of blood clots. Levels are strongly influenced by dietary and genetic factors. Folic acid and B vitamins help break down homocysteine and therefore lower its levels in the body. Citrus fruits, tomatoes, vegetables, and grains are good sources of these nutrients.

Fruits and vegetables have been shown to act as preventive factors against strokes. Vegetable proteins have balanced quantities of arginine, an amino acid that dilates blood vessels. Antioxidants such as Vitamin C and E, carotenoids, and other phytochemicals contribute to vegetarians having lower mortality from CVD than omnivores. Vegetarian diets have also been successful in arresting coronary artery disease.

A dietary intervention study performed in Australia followed subjects who were similar in most respects; it found that blood pressure and serum cholesterol fell significantly during the period when the participants were consuming a vegetarian diet. This effect was unrelated to changes in other lifestyle factors. Dietary analysis showed that the vegetarian diet provided more polyunsaturated fat, fiber, vitamin C, vitamin E, magnesium, calcium, and potassium, along with significantly less fat, saturated fat, and cholesterol, than an omnivore diet.

Living

What Do I Do About Salt?

Because salt is one of the least expensive ways to add flavor to food, we tend to find this ingredient in almost every item on the grocery shelves, including baby food. Millions of people get far too much salt in their diet. The more salt in the diet, the greater the risk of high blood pressure, which is the major controllable risk factor for stroke. People with hypertension (high blood pressure) have up to seven times greater risk of stroke than those who have normal blood pressure. We should be eating only about the equivalent of one teaspoon of salt per day, but many people are getting at least twice that amount. Bread, breakfast cereals, soups, and prepackaged meals tend to have large amounts of salt.

Try to cut back on salt by using herbs for seasoning. Avoid flavor enhancers such as soy sauce and soup stock cubes. Fresh fruits and vegetables are low in salt, so use them in abundance and cut down on added salt from canned vegetables, ketchup, sauces, and other processed foods.

A well-balanced vegetarian diet, with a variety of fruits, vegetables, whole grains, nuts, and seeds, and a minimum of fatty and highly processed foods, will go a long way in the prevention of coronary artery disease, stroke, and other types of CVD. If you know people who are at risk for these serious illnesses, let them in on what you know about dietary habits. After all, their lives depend on it.

To find out about the author, please see "About the Contributors" on pages 181-183.

"Lower levels of environmental contaminants such as DDT, DDE and PCBs are seen in the breast milk of vegetarians compared to the breast milk of women in the general population."
— see page 141

Living

Avoiding Cancer

by F. Patricia McEachrane Gross, MD

When asked what illness they fear the most, the majority of Americans say cancer. It certainly is the number two killer in America (heart disease is number one), claiming the lives of more than half a million people each year and affecting the health of over three times that many in the same period of time. Most of us have had this dreaded disease come close to home, and it is not unreasonable to believe that someone reading this article has had firsthand experience of it.

In the year 2001, according to estimates from the National Institutes of Health, the overall cost of cancer in the United States was about $156.7 billion: $56.4 billion in direct medical costs, $15.6 billion in lost productivity due to illness, and $84.7 billion in lost productivity due to premature death. The estimated number of new cases in the state of Washington in the year 2002 was 25,600. This excludes basal and squamous cell skin cancer and all in situ carcinomas except urinary bladder.

What is cancer?

The American Cancer Society (ACS) defines cancer as "a group of diseases characterized by uncontrolled growth and spread of abnormal cells." It has also been described as anarchy in a city where police have lost control, and everybody is out for himself. Every cell is controlled by definite laws which tell it when to do its thing, when to divide, or even when to die. A cancer cell is one that has gone berserk and no longer responds to the laws that it should obey.

When cancer cells begin to divide without control, they create an enlarging mass that encroaches on nearby cells, tissues, vessels, and organs. Some types of cancer divide faster than others, but when there is enough division, multiplication, and spread of cancer cells throughout the body so that the body cannot function, death occurs.

What causes cancer?

Many internal and external factors may act together to convert normal cells into malignant (cancerous) ones. We are familiar with many of the external causes such as tobacco, asbestos, radiation, and viruses, but it has taken some time for us to understand how internal factors such as mutations, hormones, and an impaired immune system can work together with the external ones to produce cancer. It may seem unusual that many more people do not get cancer, since we are all exposed to carcinogens (cancer-causing agents) on a daily basis. This is where our immune systems play a vital role.

The immune system is a complex, intricately designed network of cells and organs that works to protect the body from foreign invaders such as bacteria, fungi, and carcinogens. Through a series of mechanisms that are too complicated to explain in this article, the immune system puts up a constant, awe-inspiring defense on the body's behalf. For example, do you know that your tonsils and adenoids, your appendix and your spleen are all part of this defensive system? Also, are you

123

aware that large white cells called phagocytes, which can engulf and digest foreign invaders, are found in organs all over your body, including your brain, lungs, liver, spleen, and kidneys? If you are interested in learning more about this powerful military system that resides within your body, a good place to start is the National Cancer Institute's "Science Behind the News" Web page.

It is not difficult to understand that when any part of this complex network is injured, removed or neglected, the network becomes weaker. When the immune system breaks down or is weakened by poor nutrition, lack of sleep, other negative health behaviors, prolonged stress, depression and even aging, a number of health disorders, including cancer, can occur. We all therefore have individual and collective responsibilities to implement and maintain good health habits and to encourage others to do the same.

But is cancer really preventable?

All cancers caused by tobacco and heavy alcohol use are completely preventable. ACS also estimated, based on scientific evidence, that about one-third of the 555,000 cancers that were expected to occur in the U.S. in the year 2002 could also have been prevented because they were related to nutrition, physical inactivity, obesity, and other lifestyle factors.

What role does nutrition play in cancer?

As with cardiovascular disease, we can tell what leading scientists think about the role of a specific behavior, according to the recommendations that they make regarding that behavior in the prevention of illness. Although ACS admits to the complexity of the scientific study of nutrition and cancer and cautions that more information is needed about the specific dietary components that influence cancer risk, their recommendations are surprisingly radical for such a large, nationally recognized organization. According to them, "the best advice is to emphasize whole foods and the consumption of a mostly plant-based diet."

One must recognize how significant this statement is when other cultural information is taken into consideration—information such as the prevailing messages received by the public from the highly influential media. These messages consistently and overwhelmingly promote the consumption of meat, fats, sugar, and alcohol. In the midst of this blatant commercialism, ACS has been able to clearly state: "Studies have shown that populations that eat a diet high in vegetables and fruit and low in animal fat, meat and/or calories have reduced risk of some of the more common cancers." Here are the Society's specific recommendations for individual dietary choices: 1) eat five or more servings of vegetables and fruit each day, 2) choose whole grains in preference to processed (refined) grains and sugar, 3) limit consumption of red meats, especially high-fat and processed meats, and 4) choose foods that help maintain a healthful weight.

Why should I believe the American Cancer Society?

The scientific evidence is firmly on the side of ACS. A study of 88,757 American nurses was found that colon cancer was closely associated with eating high amounts of animal fat, processed meats, and liver. Women who ate red meat every day had 2½ times the risk of colon cancer when compared with those who ate it less than once per month. Major reviews undertaken by the Harvard Center for Cancer Prevention, the World Cancer Research Fund, and the American Institute for Cancer Research have demonstrated convincing evidence for the relationship between certain dietary elements and cancer risk. Here is a summary of some of the findings on fruits, vegetables, red meat and alcohol.

Fruits: The current data is convincing that fruits reduce the risk of cancers of the oral cavity, esophagus, and stomach. There is no evidence that fruits increase the risk of any type of cancer.

Vegetables: The current data is convincing that vegetables reduce the risk of cancers of the esophagus, stomach, larynx, lung, and urinary bladder. There is no evidence that vegetables increase the risk of any type of cancer.

Red meat: The current data is convincing that red meat increases cancer of the large bowel. There is no evidence that red meat reduces the risk of any type of cancer.

Alcohol: The current data is convincing that alcohol increases the risk of cancers of the oral cavity, esophagus, liver, larynx, and breast. There is no evidence that alcohol reduces the risk of any type of cancer.

What are some of the specific benefits of a vegetarian diet in terms of cancer risk reduction?

One very important benefit is the abundance of antioxidants in a vegetarian diet. Antioxidants neutralize harmful chemicals called free radicals that are generated by the body's metabolic processes as a result of toxic effects such as poor nutrition, smoking, alcohol, carcinogens, environmental pollutants such as smog, and radiation. Free radicals wreak havoc by attacking vital structures such as cell membranes and causing damage that contributes to the development of cancer as well as arthritis, cataracts, and other degenerative diseases.

A high-fat diet based on animal products increases the fat content of cell membranes and the likelihood of free-radical damage. On the other hand, antioxidants protect cells and tissues by fighting free radicals and the oxidative reaction that is caused by them. Nutrients that have antioxidant activity include beta-carotene, vitamin C, vitamin E, selenium, copper, and zinc, among others. Here is a partial list of food sources for each of these nutrients:

Beta-carotene: dark green leafy vegetables (e.g., collards), apricots, papayas, lemons, oranges, watermelons, apples, peaches, red peppers, tomatoes, corn, squash, sweet potatoes, carrots.

Vitamin C: papayas, guavas, cantaloupes, kiwis, oranges, brussels sprouts, green peppers (raw), cantaloupes, watermelons, strawberries.

Vitamin E: wheat germ oil, sunflower seeds, almonds, pecans, hazelnuts.

Selenium: whole grains, brewer's yeast.

Copper: brazil nuts, cashews, dried fruits, sesame seeds, walnuts, yeast.

Zinc: soy meal, wheat bran, buckwheat, millet, rice bran, oatmeal, brown rice, corn meal, black-eyed peas, green peas, lentils, limas, garbanzos, pumpkins, peanuts, spinach.

Although the relationship between fiber and cancer has come under fire in the last few years, we do know for sure that fiber binds bile acids, cholesterol, toxins, and carcinogens. It also increases the weight and amount of stool formed in the colon, which in effect dilutes carcinogens. Fiber decreases the transit time in the gastrointestinal tract so that carcinogens are excreted more quickly. Also, a high-fiber diet keeps the intestinal flora healthy, so that the bacteria do not die and produce fecapentaenes, which are very potent mutagens (agents that cause mutations). Fecapentaenes have been found in the stools of people who have low-fiber diets and who have developed colon cancer. They have not been found in the stools of fiber-eating populations who are free from colon cancer.

Does a vegetarian diet help my immune system?
A high-quality vegetarian diet with balanced amounts of carbohydrates, protein, vitamins and minerals helps enhance the immune system. A balanced diet should include omega-3 fatty acids. This is because the body uses omega-3 fatty acids to produce prostaglandins that reduce inflammation and activate T-cells, which are a significant component of the immune system Vegetarian sources of omega-3 fatty acids include flaxseeds, flaxseed oil, walnuts, soybeans and other legumes.

Finally
In closing this article, a few words should be said about the relationship between food additives and cancer. Some additives that have been definitely shown to cause cancer have been banned from the food industry, but others are still around, even though they are regarded with suspicion. For example, nitrites are used as meat preservatives to prevent botulism and to add color. When meats that contain them, such as hot dogs, are cooked, the nitrites can react with other compounds to form potent carcinogens called nitrosamines.

Obviously, many other dietary factors (e.g. pesticides in our food) play a role in the development of cancer. It is beyond the scope of this chapter to address all of these issues. However, each one of us should assume responsibility for the gift

Living

of health that we have been given and do all that is within our power to retain that gift. In choosing a vegetarian diet as part of our strategy for healthy living, we can be confident that the scientific evidence gives strong support to our efforts.

To find out about the author, please see "About the Contributors" on pages 181-183.

You're never too young to start watching your cholesterol because the process of clogged arteries begins in childhood.
— see page 119

"The best diet for diabetes control and diabetes reversal is a simple vegetarian diet..."

Diet and Diabetes

by Gregory Scribner, MD

Diabetes is an increasing problem in America. A 2001 report suggests that over 15 million Americans are affected, over 5 million of these not knowing that they have the disease. Doctors believe that changing lifestyle factors, especially diet, are the cause of the dramatic increase in the rate of diabetes. Often diabetics have other health problems such as high cholesterol and high blood pressure and are overweight.

Diabetes (medically referred to as diabetes mellitus) is a disease that results in too much sugar in the blood. A diagnosis of diabetes results if the fasting tests for blood sugar on two occasions reach 126 mg/dl or more. Blood sugar levels are controlled by insulin, a hormone released by the pancreas that helps glucose enter the body's cells. The blood sugar can be elevated due to an insufficient amount of insulin (IDDM or Type 1 diabetes) or to the body's resistance to adequate amounts of insulin (NIDDM or Type 2 diabetes). Diabetes can also be related to pregnancy (gestational diabetes mellitus) or to other causes such as pancreatitis.

Most diabetics appear to have non-insulin dependent diabetes mellitus (NIDDM). NIDDM can be well treated by changes in life style. But even IDDM may improve so that less insulin is needed and health is improved with changes in life-style.

If your diagnosis was made early, you may be able to avoid organ problems that can occur if the disease is untreated: blindness, kidney problems, heart attack, stroke, loss of a limb, susceptibility to infection, nerve damage, and tooth and gum problems. Nearly all diabetic complications can be reduced with blood sugar closer to normal levels.

Treatment options for diabetes include insulin injections or oral medications that lower blood sugar. But many people with NIDDM can control blood sugar by reducing their weight, entering into an exercise program and making dietary changes.

A switch to a healthy vegetarian diet can help reverse many of the complications of diabetes even in advanced cases, and can often prevent the disease from occurring in the first place. These changes will also help the cholesterol, blood pressure and weight problems that are often seen with people who have diabetes, enhancing health even more. While a good lifestyle program is the key to diabetes treatment, some people may also want to consider one or more supplements: chromium, magnesium and vanadium.

Diabetes and the Vegetarian Diet
Fill up on fiber
The best diet for diabetes control and diabetes reversal is a simple vegetarian diet that provides low fat and high fiber, plant foods that are close to the way they grow. For instance, a baked yam without sauce or with baked beans mixed in would be good. Apples are preferred to apple juice since fiber may help moderate blood sugar swings and promote smoother digestion.

129

Living

Avoid fats

It is important to avoid fats. These include butter, margarine, creams, cheese, fried foods, pastries, meat, chicken and fish—even fish oil may worsen diabetic sugar control. This may be new information to some diabetics who are careful to avoid simple sugars but who also are fairly free in eating food with moderate or even high fat content. But check your blood sugar on a regular basis for 10 days on a low-fat diet. Your blood sugar will almost certainly fall, with other things being equal, if you significantly lower your fat intake.

You might ask, "Then why doesn't just about everybody follow a low-fat diet?" The answer in part is that we in America have developed a taste for foods with significant fat content and that taste is very difficult to dismiss. Take courage: after only three to five days on a low-fat diet, you will find that your taste preferences change and that you enjoy lower fat foods much more.

Watch salt intake

If you have elevated blood pressure, start on a low salt diet. Commercially prepared foods often have significant extra salt, so these should be avoided or chosen carefully. Even reduced salt foods may have too much salt. And reduce the amount of salt that you use in cooking.

Follow these steps

It might be difficult for some NIDDM patients to believe that their disease could be regulated by changing diet and lifestyle, especially if they have spent years on insulin or other medication. Making such changes, in consultation with your medical advisor, could lead to significant improvement.

1) Notify your doctor that you intend to make major changes in your lifestyle including diet and exercise. (Your doctor might want to lower your medication dose before you start to prevent serious low blood sugar problems.)

2) Begin a regular walking program of about two miles twice daily. You could work up to this over several days or a couple of weeks.

3) Start eating two or no more than three meals per day (no snacks unless you have a low blood sugar reaction). Let the last meal be at least five hours before bedtime.

4) Let everything that you eat be unrefined and vegetarian. Good choices include whole-wheat bread, oatmeal, vegetables raw or cooked, fresh fruit and small amounts of nuts such as almonds. Avoid processed foods: whole-wheat flour is preferred to white; juice raises blood sugar more easily than whole fruit. Avoid refined sugar and oil - oil has a damaging effect in diabetes. Use no meat or cheese, and avoid dairy products.

5) Check your blood sugar more frequently since it will probably fall significantly.

6) Keep your doctor informed of your falling blood sugar so that your medications can be reduced or stopped. (This is important!)

7) Try to get a friend to exercise with you.

Living

This program often produces dramatic results, eliminating the need for medications. Does this sound too good to be true? How will you really know unless you try? Commit to a ten-day trial to see how it affects your diabetes. Track your changing blood sugar and experience success yourself.

As a tool for encouragement and reinforcement of your new behaviors, write down what you are doing. Make a chart such as the one below to remind you that your lifestyle changes are actually making a difference. Some items do not need to be tracked every day; for example, blood pressure and weight might not be easy to track frequently depending on your equipment at home.

Date	Items of food eaten	Minutes or distance exercised	Blood sugar maximum today	Blood pressure today	Weight today	How I feel (1-10)

Use a new row for each subsequent day recorded.

Column one: record the date.

Column 2: record types of food eaten such as "baked beans and whole wheat bread." It is not necessary to record the quantity. The goal is to eat types of food listed in #4 of the seven-point list above.

Column 3: record time or distance exercised; your goal is 45 minutes or a two-mile walk every day, six days per week, preferably outside.

Columns 4-6: track objective measurements of your improving health.

Column 7: use a number to describe the way you feel. You might choose one as feeling poorly, ten as feeling great. This system allows you to scan over several days and see your improvement.

Make a commitment to yourself to stick with the program for at least ten days. You might find yourself feeling weak and tired around days three to five before the beneficial effects of your new program start to give you that refreshed feeling of health. Hopefully, this will be a life-long adventure.

To find out about the author, please see "About the Contributors" on pages 181-183.

"Experimental data proves the connection between high levels of animal proteins in the diet and high osteoporosis rates."

Nutrition for Healthy Bones

by Ray Foster, MD, FACS

Question: What is a modern disease rarely seen in many countries of the world, caused in part by what is advertised to us as the cure? It is often painless until it has advanced into life-threatening complications.

Answer: Osteoporosis.

Question: What is osteoporosis?

Answer: A simple definition of osteoporosis is porous or soft bones that squash or break too easily. Bones that break too easily cause most of the problems, but bones with microscopic fractures can also be a source of pain. Backache can be caused by fractures of the vertebrae when the bone becomes too soft.

While the disease has been known for over one hundred years, it did not become common enough until recent years to qualify as a household word. What has made the difference? Why was osteoporosis so uncommon even thirty years ago?

Osteoporosis in different populations

The highest incidence of osteoporosis in the world occurs among Eskimos who eat the most meat in their diet. They have by far the highest incidence of osteoporosis and at the youngest age. Countries that have the highest intake of meat and dairy have the highest incidence of osteoporosis, measured in rates of hip fracture.

In the USA the hip fracture rate is 98 per 100,000. The average protein intake in the USA is 106 grams per day. Compare this to the lowest incidence of osteoporosis, 6 hip fractures per 100,000, which occurs among Blacks in South Africa. There, the average mother has ten children, breast feeds all ten and eats an average of 21 grams of protein a day.

Studies show that those populations eating moderate amounts of protein, primarily from plant sources, have little osteoporosis. Those populations that have high amounts of protein, primarily from animal sources, in their diet have high rates of osteoporosis. Experimental data proves the connection between high levels of animal proteins in the diet and high osteoporosis rates.

Experimental Data

In human calcium balance studies, people who ate 48 grams of protein a day could stay in positive calcium balance, which means that more calcium is kept in the body than is excreted in the urine and stools. When 95 grams of protein was eaten each day there was relentless loss of calcium, a negative calcium balance, no matter how much calcium was included in the diet. The body stores calcium in the bones, so a loss of calcium causes weaker bones. This is the real cause of osteoporosis in humans. It should be noted again that the average American eats 106 grams of protein a day and most of that protein is from animal sources.

Which bones are most prone to break from osteoporosis?

There is a fairly consistent pattern in which bones break most often, but there are age and sex differences. Wrist and rib bones tend to break at any age and with little sex difference once the bones are soft enough. Spine compression fractures are much more common at all ages in women than in men, probably because women generally have smaller bones than men.

The hip fracture is the dreaded osteoporotic fracture because it carries with it an elevated risk of death. The 2003 mortality from hip fractures was reported to be 15-20% in the first year after surgery. A hip fracture from weak bones puts you in bed, or severely interferes with your activity, putting you at risk for pneumonia and bladder infections.

What causes osteoporosis?

An acid diet and little physical exercise are the main causes of osteoporosis. Of these two causes, an acid diet is probably the chief cause of osteoporosis.

The body chemistry is very sensitive to what is called pH or the acid/base relationship. The body's chemistry cannot work unless the pH balance is maintained within very strict limits. What this means is that if what you eat is acidic, then the body needs to neutralize it in order to keep the pH balance of the blood where it needs to be. A high-protein diet causes a high-acid diet. Protein is made up of amino acids, and proteins from animal sources are particularly acidic because they are high in Sulfur-containing amino acids. The resulting sulfuric acid must be neutralized. The base needed to neutralize the acid comes from the calcium in your bones. That is why an acid diet softens your bones in time. This is the chief cause of the epidemic of osteoporosis being experienced in this country.

Misunderstandings and misinformation

Many people believe that protein gives strength. Protein does not give strength. It is a body-building material. Muscles are built from proteins, but strength is a measure of the use of the muscle, not a measure of what makes muscle. A car is made of metal but it is the gasoline that powers the car, not the metal. Carbohydrates, not proteins, are the energy foods.

It is also important to understand that every food contains some protein. It is not possible to get too little protein if you are getting enough food to eat, unless you eat a lot of junk food. If you are getting too little protein, you are getting too little food and you are starving for want of enough food.

It must be noted that the American diet averages about 106 grams of protein daily. The average American eats several times as much protein as the body needs. This excess protein in the diet is the cause of osteoporosis, which is of epidemic proportions today. The irony of it is that the protein excess is being eaten in the belief that it is good and even necessary to be strong!

Too much protein in the diet can also place stress on the liver and kidneys. The reason is that the body does not store protein. It has to get rid of the excess protein in the diet, which is done by the liver and the kidneys working together. Because of excess protein in the diet, we have increased the incidence of three epidemics simultaneously: liver disease, kidney failure, and osteoporosis now occurring at younger and younger ages.

What is the solution?

As long as you get enough plant food, it is impossible not to get all the proteins the body needs. You can also get all the calcium you need from greens, grains, vegetables, nuts and seeds, without the excess protein that is found in dairy products. Calcium, along with all the other minerals that our bodies need, comes from the ground. Cows get their calcium from greens. Greens are an excellent source of calcium. In those countries of the world where people live on greens, vegetables and grains, they get all the calcium they need for excellent bones and strong teeth. It is media hype to sell dairy that has led to the belief that we need to eat dairy products to get calcium to make our bones strong.

Meat and dairy products are the two sources of most of the excess protein in the standard American diet. The obvious solution to reverse the epidemic of osteoporosis is for us all to eat less animal protein and get more exercise.

To find out about the author, please see "About the Contributors" on pages 181-183.

"Bill Pearl, Mr. America and champion body builder, along with Edwin Moses, 400 meter hurdle gold medalist, are prime examples that muscular power and strength can be developed on vegetarian fuel."
– see page 147

Living

"You will be surprised at how easily change occurs when you take it one step at a time. Enjoy the journey along the way."

Living

Small Changes Make a Big Difference

by Marilyn Joyce, RD, PhD

Many people are creatures of habit, actually very resistant to change and quite content, on the surface, to continue doing what they have always been doing as long as nothing gets in the way of their habits. However, this situation has been rapidly changing over the very recent years. Many diseases have recently become more common. Children are developing diseases which only older adults used to get a few decades ago. Overweight and obesity affects about 66% of the North American population. Two-year-olds have the beginnings of atherosclerosis already forming in their arteries. Type II Diabetes, once called Adult Onset Diabetes for good reason, is afflicting children 8, 10, and 12 years old today. People constantly bemoan the situation to me, stating that there is nothing they can do. Others look for a simple solution—an instant fix!

Though I have a thousand stories I could share about people making life-altering changes—natural changes—I will tell you about a situation that reminded me of how simple it is to make changes that can impact your life dramatically.

With new clients, I expect a four-month commitment to a new program. This is the time required in order to experience significant benefits from a positive change. That is based on the fact that it takes 90 to 120 days to replace all of the red blood cells in the body, and as these cells are replaced, they are also developing a new cellular memory. Now, if you change nothing, none of your desires or cravings will change. However, what we have seen with individuals who change even just one thing positively in their diet, there is a significant change in what they desire, and generally in the status of their health.

Several years ago I had a patient who had both cancer and multiple sclerosis (MS). His diet was the typical American diet: bacon, eggs and sausage, washed down with lots of coffee, loaded with cream and sugar, for breakfast; coffee and donuts in the AM; Big Mac, fries and large shake for lunch; soda and a candy bar in the late afternoon; small pizza and a six-pack of beer for dinner; and finally, sweets and munchies throughout the evening. My client had no weight issues, so he saw no problem with his diet. He had no concept of healthy food versus unhealthy food. It had not occurred to him that unhealthy food would lead to an unhealthy body.

When I asked this dear man if he had ever heard of the 5-a-day campaign (a government campaign to encourage people to eat five vegetables and fruits each day), he looked at me as though I had lost my marbles. Vegetables had never passed his lips prior to our work together. And the only fruit he had ever recalled tasting was from a can, soaked in a heavy sugar syrup. Grains took the form of white pasty hamburger buns, filled with dead animal meat, pumped full of hormones and antibiotics. And he loved plate-loads of pasta laced with sauce made from the same dead animal flesh, ground up, and cooked in a base of sugar, salt, hydrogenated fats and MSG (monosodium glutamate). And of course, all of this was done in an attempt to add flavor to food that would otherwise have no natural flavor of its own.

Living

When this gentleman came to see me, he was in a wheelchair due to the MS, unable to hold a glass of anything without a lid on it. And his cancer had never gone into remission in 13 years! I had my doubts at the time about any kind of resolution to his condition bar death. However, I have always loved a challenge. So I recommended that my client change just one thing in his diet the first week. He could choose from any of the 25 Rules for the Road (found in *5 Minutes to Health*), which I had developed specifically to help my clients incorporate healthy foods into their lives. He was stunned. He had expected a much more aggressive approach in view of the seriousness of his condition. I reminded him of all of the severe strategies he had already tried, and quit, because they demanded too many radical changes far too quickly.

Each week or two he was to add another change, and then another change, until he had implemented the 25 Rules. Within just a few short months, a whole life of unhealthy habits was changed without a great deal of conscious struggle, versus the all-or-nothing philosophy that predominates today. His cancer went into remission the first year, followed a year later by all symptoms of the MS. Is he unique? Believe it or not, no! Choosing to make the changes was simple. And the changes themselves were simple. However, for the first 4 months, until significant changes began to be felt, or witnessed in his blood tests, it was not easy to keep dropping the unhealthy foods while implementing healthier choices. Is it easy for him now? You bet it is! He's predominantly vegan now—no animal products—and claims he's never felt better in his life.

It all began with the first step. Watch a baby learn to walk. It really is a simple process: sit up, roll over, crawl, attempt to stand up with help, take a step with help, then a few more steps and finally walk successfully without help. The same is true of many changes we make. We simply, but not always easily, take one step after another, with persistence, focus and diligence. And then, like my client, we wake up to renewed vitality, optimum health and a zest for life.

I have consistently found in my practice that very few people are really motivated to quickly shift over to a vegetarian diet from the typical meat-based diet that is so prevalent in developed countries today. Despite all of the research to warrant this shift, it is best achieved by implementing small changes over time. As a person experiences positive changes in their health, they begin to take greater responsibility for their own health. In turn they read more, learn more and develop an awareness of the positive effects of changing to a predominantly, if not completely, vegetarian lifestyle.

No one has to force the person to stay with a program after they have experienced positive results. But it takes time, along with some slipping and sliding along the way. The most important thing to remember is that it is okay to take it a step at a time and to slip once in awhile. It is during the journey that we learn what works for each of us individually. A strong foundation is formed brick by brick. Balance in life, and commitment to maintaining our health, can only occur when there is a solid foundation of understanding, and a system of consistently practicing healthy habits.

History and research prove that a vegetarian diet is a far safer bet than a diet of dead animal flesh and processed foods, processed with animal fats, transfats (hydrogenated and partially hydrogenated fats), salt, sugar and MSG. Just take a look at the health of our children today. Need I say more?

So, I have provided a chart of alternative foods to choose when we face those moments of potential slipping and sliding.

Recommendations for Your Journey to Optimum Health

Instead of:	Use:
Roasted salted nuts	Raw almonds, cashews, Brazil nuts
Roasted salted seeds	Raw sesame, sunflower, and pumpkin seeds
Hydrogenated plant oils	Virgin olive oil, expeller pressed sesame, walnut, flaxseed, almond and safflower oils
White, distilled vinegar	Balsamic, rice and wine vinegars
Regular breads	Sprouted and whole-grain breads
Mayonnaise	Soy mayonnaise
Commercial salad dressings	Homemade dressings
Regular pasta	Whole-wheat or other whole-grain pasta
Regular milk	Soy or almond milk
Regular eggs	Egg replacer
Regular yogurt	Soy yogurt
Regular egg salad	Eggless egg salad made with tofu
Beef or Turkey Burgers	Veggie Burgers
Beef, Pork, Lamb, Chicken	Tempeh, TVP (textured vegetable protein) products, baked tofu and meat substitutes

You will be surprised at how easily change occurs when you take it one step at a time. Enjoy the journey along the way.

To find out about the author, please see "About the Contributors" on pages 181-183.

"Lower levels of environmental contaminants such as DDT, DDE and PCBs are seen in the breast milk of vegetarians compared to the breast milk of women in the general population."

A Diet for All Ages

Nutrition for Babies and Their Moms

by Reed Mangels, RD, PhD, FADA

Pregnancy is a time of increased nutritional needs, both to support the rapid growth of a baby and to allow for all the changes that are taking place in a pregnant woman's body. Infancy, too, is a time when good nutrition is very important to support the rapid growth and development that occurs during this time. A healthy vegetarian or vegan diet can meet the needs of both pregnant women and their infants.

Nutrition for Pregnant Women

Adequate weight gain is important during pregnancy as it represents the growing baby, an increase in the volume of the mother's blood, uterus and breasts, and the weight of the placenta and amniotic fluid. Weight gain should be from a minimum of 15lbs for an overweight woman up to 40lbs for an underweight woman. Teens may need more to support their own needs for growth. In the second and third trimesters, a weight gain of 1-1½ lbs a week is common for all pregnant women.

An increased calorie intake is needed to support this weight gain. Women who were underweight prior to pregnancy or who are having difficulty gaining weight in pregnancy may need to use concentrated sources of calories and nutrients. These foods include milk shakes (soy milk blended with fruit and tofu or soy yogurt), nuts and nut butters, dried fruits, soy products and bean dips. Fatty foods like salad dressings, margarine, and oil are another source of concentrated calories. Small, frequent meals and snacks can help to increase food intake.

Protein recommendations for the second and third trimesters of pregnancy call for an additional 25 grams of protein daily. Attention to good sources of protein such as soy products, dried beans, whole grains, nuts and nut butters makes it possible to meet protein recommendations. As an example, 10-15 grams of protein can be added by adding two cups of soymilk or nine ounces of tofu or three ounces of tempeh to the usual diet.

Because folate is so important in the early development of the baby's nervous system, all women capable of becoming pregnant should consume 400 micrograms of folic acid from supplements or fortified foods in addition to good sources of dietary folate. Good sources include dark green leafy vegetables, orange juice, wheat germ, bran flakes, whole and enriched grains and cereals, and legumes (beans).

Vitamin B12 is a critical nutrient for the baby's development in pregnancy. Some good sources of vitamin B12 are many soymilks, ready-to-eat cereals, and fake meats. Be sure the label indicates, "Fortified with vitamin B12." Vegetarian Support Formula nutritional yeast also is a good source of vitamin B12. If a pregnant woman's diet does not have daily and reliable food sources, a prenatal B12 vitamin should be used.

Iron needs are greatly increased during pregnancy to support tissue growth and the increased blood supply of both the mother and baby. The current RDA for iron for pregnant vegetarians is close to 50 milligrams per day, a level that is difficult to achieve without the use of iron supplements. Even when iron supplements are used, pregnant women should consume foods rich in iron like whole and enriched grains, leafy green vegetables, dried fruit, prune juice, legumes and tofu.

An increase in calcium or vitamin D intake during pregnancy is recommended only if calcium and vitamin D intakes were inadequate prior to pregnancy. To meet calcium needs, eat eight servings per day of calcium-rich foods. This could be a half cup of fortified-soymilk, calcium-set tofu, tempeh, soybeans, or calcium-fortified juice, one cup cooked collard greens, kale, broccoli, Chinese cabbage, mustard greens or okra. Vitamin D fortified foods or supplements are recommended for pregnant women who do not have adequate sun exposure.

Pregnant and breast-feeding vegans should include sources of linolenic acid in their diet. Linolenic acid is a type of fat that is used to make an important fatty acid called DHA (short for docosahexaenoic acid). DHA seems to play a role in the development of the brain and the eye. Sources of linolenic acid include ground flaxseed, flaxseed oil, canola oil and soybean oil. Vegan DHA supplements are also available.

Morning sickness (nausea and vomiting) is a concern of many pregnant women. Aversions to foods that used to make up the bulk of the diet are extremely common in early pregnancy. This is probably due to a heightened sense of smell and hormonal changes. Some coping mechanisms are: eating low-fat, high-carbohydrate foods which are digested more quickly; eating often; avoiding foods with strong smells and eating healthful foods which are tolerated. The healthcare provider should be contacted if a pregnant woman is unable to eat or drink adequate amounts of fluids for 24 hours.

Breast-feeding

The best diet for breast-feeding is very similar to the diet recommended for pregnancy. Calorie and vitamin B12 needs are slightly higher, while the need for iron is reduced. It is a good idea to use a standard prenatal vitamin shortly before, during and after pregnancy, along with eating a well-balanced diet.

The ideal food for a baby's first year of life is breast milk. Benefits to the breast-fed baby include enhancement of the immune system, protection against infection and reduced risk of allergies. Benefits to the mom include reduced risk of premenopausal breast cancer, release of stress-relieving hormones and convenience. Breast-feeding also provides nutritional advantages such as higher bioavailability of iron, zinc and other micronutrients and a better digestibility of fat and protein. Lower levels of environmental contaminants such as DDT, DDE, and PCBs are seen in the breast milk of vegetarians compared to the breast milk of women in the general population.

Nutrition for Infants

Growth and development throughout infancy is normal when vegetarian and vegan infants receive adequate amounts of breast milk or fortified infant formula and their diets are planned in accordance with current dietary recommendations and contain good sources of energy and nutrients like iron, vitamin B12, and vitamin D. Extremely restrictive diets such as fruitarian and raw foods have been associated with growth delays. Such diets are not recommended for infants and children.

Vitamin B12: Vegan moms who are breast-feeding should use vitamin B-12-fortified foods or supplements daily. Breastfed infants should receive supplements of 0.4 micrograms of vitamin B12 for the first six months and 0.5 micrograms for infants aged six months to one year if the mother's diet does not contain reliable sources of vitamin B12.

Vitamin D: Breastfed infants should be supplemented with 5µg (200 IU) of vitamin D daily. Infant formula supplies adequate amounts of vitamin D. Vitamin D deficiency leads to rickets (soft, improperly mineralized bones).

Iron: The breastfed infant should be started on iron supplements or iron-fortified foods (like baby cereal) between four and six months. Formula-fed babies may not need the supplement since infant formula contains iron. Iron-fortified cereals provide additional iron. If you give iron supplements to your baby, ask your pediatrician for the correct dose.

It is important to note that ordinary soymilk, rice milk, and homemade formulas should not be used to replace breast milk or commercial infant formula during the first year. These foods do not contain the right amounts of nutrients for babies.

Solid foods should be introduced between four and six months of age. Try to introduce one food at a time, waiting two to three days before trying another food, to see if the baby has a reaction to the food. If an allergic reaction occurs, the offending food is more easily identified.

A good first food is iron-fortified infant rice cereal. It is an excellent source of iron, and rice cereal is least likely to cause an allergic response. Once the baby eats this cereal well, begin introducing other cereals such as oats, barley, and corn. Vegetables may be introduced next—again, one at a time to check for allergies. Vegetables must be well mashed or puréed. Well-mashed potatoes, carrots, peas, sweet potatoes, and green beans are good first vegetables.

Fruits are usually introduced after vegetables, theoretically in order to allow acceptance of vegetables before the sweet taste of fruits is experienced. Good first fruits are well-mashed bananas, pears, or peaches.

Protein foods are generally introduced around seven to eight months. Some good sources of protein include mashed, cooked legumes (beans); mashed tofu; and soy yogurt. Smooth nut and seed butters spread on bread or crackers can be introduced after the first birthday.

Many parents wish to make their own baby foods. These should be prepared without added sugar, salt, or spices. Foods should be well cooked, mashed or puréed, and handled under clean conditions. It is recommended that parents who choose to use commercial baby foods read the labels carefully.

Living

Fat is important in brain development. Babies under age two need more calories and fat than at any other time in their lives. Some foods used to increase fat in the diet are mashed avocado, vegetable oil, and nut and seed butters. Spread on crackers for children older than one year.

To minimize the risk of choking, avoid foods like nuts, nut butters, vegetarian hot dogs, chunks of hard raw fruits and vegetables, whole grapes, hard candies and popcorn.

In families with a strong history of allergy, foods which contain common allergens such as citrus, egg whites and nuts are generally not introduced in the first year and peanuts and other nuts should not be introduced before three years. Honey and corn syrup should not be given to infants younger than one year because of the risk of botulism.

Commercial, fortified, full-fat soymilk can be added to the diet when an infant is at least a year old and is growing normally and eating a variety of foods. Following introduction of fortified soymilk, parents should continue to offer breast milk or commercial soy-based infant formula as a supplementary beverage until the child is at least two years old or is able to regularly drink 24 ounces of soymilk daily. Since soy milk is relatively low in fat, other foods that provide fat should be added to the diet of vegan infants so that dietary fat is not too low. Rice milk is not recommended as a main beverage for vegan infants and young children because it is low in calories and protein.

Young children have small stomachs and eating a lot of high-fiber foods may not give them enough calories. A diet rich in fresh fruits, vegetables and whole grains is also usually high in fiber. The fiber content of a vegan child's diet can be reduced by offering him or her some refined grain products, fruit juices, and peeled fruits and vegetables. Foods like avocado, nut and seed butters, dried fruits and soy products can pack a lot of calories into small quantities, which is great for the growing child. To promote synthesis of DHA, an important fat, include sources of linolenic acid like canola oil, flaxseed oil and soy products in the child's diet.

To find out about the author, please see "About the Contributors" on pages 181-183.

Attracting Your Child to Healthier Food

by Cynthia Lair, lecturer at Bastyr University

There are some very simple steps that parents can take to assure their child of better nutrition. Much of what we want for our children: healthy bodies with less illness, ability to concentrate, better study skills, adept physical ability, can be aided with a wholesome diet. The first step is to remind ourselves that we are role models. If we are eating vital, wholesome foods such as whole grains, beans, fresh vegetables and fruit, our children will be more likely to follow suit. Sometimes this requires parents to negotiate a united purpose. If one parent offers celery stalks for snacks and the other scoots out to the ice cream store, the children get mixed messages and will lean toward the more stimulating food.

Parents not only need to be in sync, they have to be willing to set boundaries around food and eating habits. Just as you would not let a five-year-old choose when to go to bed, it is inappropriate to expect a young child to make a nutritious decision about what to eat for lunch. Children are affected by happy-looking packaging, entertaining advertisements and artificially colored ingredients in commercial foods. They do not have the knowledge or wisdom to overcome marketing ploys and make healthful choices. Parents need to make the decisions or offer simple, limited choices like offering an apple or an orange.

Assuming you want your child to eat well, what can you do to pave the path toward good eating habits?

Honor mealtimes

Studies show that children who sit down to regular shared family meals have more emotional stability, do better in school and eat a wider variety of foods. With busy schedules you may not be able to get everyone together more than once a day, or even twice a week. Whatever you can manage, find times that work and keep them sacred.

Provide excellent choices

If you don't want your child to eat something, don't buy it. Keep the cupboards and fridge stocked with things you can feel good about your child eating.

Announce that what's served is served

Make only one meal for breakfast, lunch or dinner. Don't fall into being a short-order cook. If every dish of the meal you've prepared is rejected, allow the child to be excused from the table until the next meal. This may sound like tough love but if you keep this one simple rule you can avoid many parent-child battles.

Include a winner with every meal

Most kids like foods like fresh fruit, applesauce, bread and butter, or potatoes. Whatever you choose for the meal, try to make sure there is something on the table that your child will like, even if it is just a side dish.

Living

145

Refrain from using food to bribe, reward or punish

Parents are prone to make desserts and sweets a reward if the child has been good or cooperated. Messages like this can eventually lead to eating disorders. If you must bribe, reward or punish use something other than food to encourage your child to do what you want.

Set clear rules about special treats and favorite "less-nutritious" meals

Say you have a child who loves macaroni and cheese and will only eat macaroni and cheese. Don't deny total access, just set up when and how often you think it's healthy and reasonable to have it. Make it clear that we have macaroni and cheese on Friday nights. After awhile the standard will be set and the pleading will stop.

Create appealing presentations

Some kids don't like their food mixed up or touching. They might try a sauce if it was on the side to dip into rather than smothering the dish. Salad might get an "ugh" but some cut up carrots, cucumbers and radishes will get eaten. Pay attention to how foods are put on the plate. Usually the simpler the better.

Set Boundaries

Most picky eater problems are really about parents not wanting to set up any boundaries about food. As parents we find it difficult to let our children experience disappointment. Yet we know that learning how to face obstacles and adapt is how we learn to be resourceful. This simple truth applies to food. Be willing to set limits. Let your child face the disappointment of not eating ice cream when they are coming down with a cold, or not going to a fast-food restaurant two nights in a row. They will not only survive, they'll grow stronger.

There are many ways to enhance your child's love of good food starting when they are very very young. Serve babies freshly cooked vegetables and fruits that have been run through a blender rather than jarred baby food that is old, processed, and full of fillers. Start a garden in your yard or on your porch and let young children see how food grows. They will love foraging for snacks. Encourage your children to help you in the kitchen. Make them feel needed, useful and creative by involving them with meal preparation. Children will mirror your relationship with food. Let them see you shop, prepare and enjoy eating fabulous whole foods.

To find out about the author, please see "About the Contributors" on pages 181-183.

Living

Winning the Race on a Vegetarian Diet

by Scott Jurek, MA, PT

You don't need to be an champion athlete to utilize the wealth of information in the area of sports nutrition. I consider anyone who exercises regularly to be an athlete. From the casual to the professional athlete, sports nutrition concepts link nutrition and exercise to develop a picture of total health.

The Myth

Haven't you heard that a vegetarian diet is inferior to an meat-based diet? How can you get enough protein to build and support muscle? How can you consume enough calories? How can you have enough endurance? How can a vegetarian athlete receive the necessary amounts and types of vitamins and minerals? All these questions stem from the common myth that a vegetarian diet is inferior and insufficient to match an meat-based diet.

Over the last century, many endurance and strength athletes have excelled on a vegetarian diet. Dave Scott, four-time champion of the Hawaii Ironman Triathlon (2.4 mile ocean swim, 112 mile cycle ride, and 26.2 mile run) is deemed to be the fittest man on the earth. His performances were achieved while on a vegetarian diet. Six-time Ironman champion, Ruth Heidrich, continues to excel into her sixties on a vegetarian diet. Both Billie Jean King and Martina Navratilova have amazed tennis fans with their astounding tennis careers. They too are vegetarian. What about power and strength events? Bill Pearl, Mr. America and champion bodybuilder, and Edwin Moses, 400-meter hurdle gold medalist, are prime examples that muscular power and strength can be developed on vegetarian fuel.

I also have been utilizing a vegetarian diet since 1998. All five of my Western States 100 Mile Endurance Run victories (1999-2003) were fueled by a vegetarian diet. I have noticed improvements in recovery time, stamina, endurance and strength during my demanding training sessions. I've also noticed an improved vitality in my everyday life and a greater appreciation for the consciousness of choosing healthy foods.

Defining a vegetarian diet

Properly and *balanced* are key words to consider when speaking of nutrition in general and this should be a focus in a vegetarian diet as well. Vegetarian diets sometimes get a bad name due to people eating poorly balanced vegetarian diets. It is common for new and experienced vegetarians alike to consume high quantities of heavily processed and low-quality foods such as those high in refined sugar, white flour, and hydrogenated oils. These ingredients are found in almost all processed foods today.

I consider a properly balanced vegetarian diet to be one that consists of whole foods (foods in their unrefined state), is organic (has been grown without the use of pesticides, herbicides, chemical fertilizers and genetically modified organisms) and

Living

147

is sufficient in quantity appropriate to the individual athlete. This diet will enable you to achieve optimal health and performance.

Quantity

The quantity of food for athletes is as important as the quality. With activity, energy needs increase due to a greater number of burned calories. The actual number of calories burned varies with the mode, amount, and intensity of the exercise. Resting metabolism can also increase by up to 30% with regular exercise. With both of these factors increasing an athlete's daily caloric needs, energy requirements of an athlete can soar to as high as 4,000-8,000 calories per day!

The athlete's body needs sufficient quantities of energy (calories), vitamins and minerals for optimal performance, repair and recovery. Exercise places added stress on the body. This stress is necessary for developing endurance, strength, power and coordination. In order for the body to deal with this added load of stress, a sufficient quantity of fuel is paramount for optimal functioning. Many vegetarian athletes complain of decreased energy and often blame this on lack of protein, and more specifically, lack of animal protein. Although these athletes could be lacking protein intake, the more important and more common area they may be falling short is total caloric consumption. If these athletes increased their caloric intake they would see their stamina and energy levels return to normal and possibly increase.

If caloric intake is low, athletes can experience a decrease in metabolic rate. This decrease in metabolic rate causes inefficient fuels such as protein (from muscles) to be used as fuel, and decreases the energy available for the body's use. Therefore an athlete may actually use protein in their muscle mass for fuel rather than building a stronger and healthier body. Many athletes fear that they are going to increase their body weight when they increase their caloric intake. They then avoid obtaining a sufficient caloric intake, at the expense of performance. Optimal performance and health require sufficient caloric intake!

Carbohydrates

A properly balanced vegetarian diet for an athlete should consist of a high percentage of carbohydrates. According to the American Dietetic Association and the American College of Sports Medicine, both vegetarian and nonvegetarian athletic diets should consist of 60-70% carbohydrate.

For decades, research has shown that a high-carbohydrate diet can enhance an athlete's endurance. When an adequate quantity of carbohydrates is consumed on a daily basis, athletes maximize glycogen stores in their muscles. It is these glycogen stores that are accessed quickly for energy and allow the athlete to surge or produce an explosive burst of energy for a sustained amount of time. Daily carbohydrate intake spares protein in the muscle from being used for energy. Both strength and endurance athletes will want to use stored and ingested carbohydrate and stored fat sources for fuel while exercising and recovering. Carbohydrates and fats are the most efficient fuel sources.

Carbohydrate benefits for the athlete
• Improve endurance and speed.
• Maximize glycogen stores in muscles.
• Most efficient fuel to consume during exercise.
• Spares protein in muscle from being used for fuel, thus increasing strength.

Carbohydrate quantity
60-70% of total caloric intake.

Sources of carbohydrates
Whole foods such as fruits, vegetables, whole grains and legumes offer a wide variety of carbohydrate sources. Minimize intake of refined and processed carbohydrates such as those made with "white" flour and "white" sugar. Low glycemic carbohydrates, those that cause a minimal insulin response, are also preferable (see Andrew Weil's *Eating Well for Optimal Health*).

Be creative! Carbohydrate sources do not have to be limited to bread and noodles. Try cooking with different varieties of grains. (See the article "The Well-Stocked Kitchen" for further ideas.)

Fat
Fat is something that many athletes fear. These athletes assume ingested fat will directly increase body fat and minimize performance. This is not the case. Fat is a necessary energy source used to fuel endurance activities and supply the body with energy when not exercising. Athletes who are able to use fat for fuel as much as possible are able to conserve glycogen stores for when they are needed most. Essential fatty acids (a fat that is needed by the body and is only obtained through the diet) are often low in modern-day diets. Some of these essential fatty acids play a role in minimizing the inflammatory process, which may occur during the rigors of training.

Fat Benefits for the Athlete
• Major fuel source for endurance activities and daily life.
• Makes up cell membranes.
• Transports the fat soluble vitamins (A, D, E, and K).
• Essential fatty acids aid in recovery and minimize the inflammatory process.
• Cushions the organs and body tissues.

Fat Quantity
Fat intake will vary from 15% to 30% of calories depending on the level of endurance required.

Sources of fat
High quality fats are those that are mostly monosaturated, less refined, and are not heated excessively. The best sources are cold-pressed, extra virgin olive oil, avocados, almond butter, and canola oil. Essential fatty acids should be a daily priority and

should come from flax seeds and flax seed oil, pumpkin seeds, hemp seeds, walnuts, and sunflower seeds. Omega-3 fatty acids are of particular importance and are most abundant in flax seeds, walnuts and hemp seeds. Avoid saturated fats in your total fat intake.

Protein

Protein intake is essential for construction and repair of tissues in the body. Athletes are constantly stressing the body and stimulating the construction and repair processes. Proteins maintain the structure and function of our body tissues so they can achieve optimal function. A small percentage of protein is occasionally used for fuel, although protein is not an efficient fuel source and the body prefers to use it for rebuilding purposes.

Muscle mass is essential for all athletic pursuits and during basic activities such as walking up stairs and squatting. Contrary to popular belief, muscle mass is not achieved by increasing protein intake. Total caloric intake maintains and allows for increases in muscle mass by sparing the protein within the muscles. Although our bodies can synthesize certain amino acids to build proteins, ten amino acids are termed essential and must be supplied through the diet. Athletes do require a slightly higher amount of protein than sedentary individuals; however protein remains a much smaller percentage of the total caloric intake compared to carbohydrate and fat.

For athletes, most sources recommend 15% to 20% of total caloric intake come from protein depending on the type and amount of activity, size of the athlete and caloric requirements.

Protein Benefits for the Athlete
• Enhances and speeds recovery.
• Maintains structure and function of body tissues.
• Can be used for fuel during ultra long events, although should be minor source.

Protein Quantity
1.0-1.2g/kg* for standard athletes
1.2-1.7 g/kg* for endurance athletes
1.2-2.0 g/kg* for power and speed athletes

High fibrous protein sources such as legumes, nuts and seeds, may require an increase in protein intake by 10-15% due to reduced digestibility of these sources.

Sources of Protein
Despite what many people believe, a vegetarian diet has many options when it comes to protein sources. Vegetarian protein sources are devoid of the many toxins and additives utilized in many animal protein sources. Dense and mildly processed soy foods such as tofu and tempeh are important protein staples for athletes. Legumes are a great protein source and are abundant in low-glycemic carbohydrates as well—excellent fuel for athletes! Although lower in protein than soy products and legumes, nuts and seeds can be included as a protein source and have beneficial

fatty acids. Try to incorporate a variety of protein sources and use soy protein powders as needed if the above sources are not prevalent in your diet.

Vitamins and minerals

Vitamins and minerals are involved in many vital functions and processes within the body. They are especially important for athletes who demand much from the body. If an athlete includes a high percentage and wide variety of whole foods including fruits and vegetables into their diet, the vitamin and mineral content should be sufficient for high performance and health. Actually, an athlete's vegetarian diet can be higher in vitamins and minerals than a non-vegetarian diet. In addition, organic foods have been shown to have higher amounts of vitamins and minerals than their non-organic counterparts. Overall, a vegetarian athlete who incorporates a wide variety of organic whole foods should have minimal supplementation needs.

The following vitamins and minerals are of particular importance to the vegetarian athlete and requirements may be increased due to the demands of exercise and training: Vitamin B12, Vitamin D, iron, calcium, zinc, magnesium, potassium, chromium and copper. For more information on these vitamins and minerals I would recommend consulting additional sources such as vegan sports nutrition texts and registered dieticians.

Due to free radical production during exercise, athletes may want to incorporate antioxidant supplementation. These antioxidants (beta-carotene, Vitamin C, Vitamin E and selenium) help to reverse the damage done by free radicals. Although it is possible for the body to process higher amounts of some of these vitamins and minerals without risk of toxicity, excesses should be avoided.

In summary, a vegetarian athlete's diet should be
• Properly balanced with a variety of organic whole foods.
• Adequate in caloric intake.
• High in quality carbohydrates.
• Abundant in premium protein sources.
• High in quality fats, low in less desirable fats.
• High in vitamin- and mineral-rich foods.
• Delicious and enjoyable.
• Affordable and cost-effective.

To find out about the author, please see "About the Contributors" on pages 181-183.

Soy foods are "especially helpful in lessening hot flashes and night sweats."

Easing Menopause

by Susan Gins, MS, CN

Hot flashes, night sweats, weight gain, mood swings, irritability, depression and memory loss are some signals that a woman's body is undergoing change. Other symptoms that may not individually signal biological transformation include sleep deprivation, decreased vaginal lubrication and thinning vaginal mucosa, insomnia, urinary incontinence, loss of libido and changes in the skin. However, any one or a combination of these symptoms, together with a woman's age, suggest that menopause is at hand.

Most women do not suffer from all of these symptoms and can actively participate in reducing the things that do bother them. Diet, exercise, stress reduction, vitamins, minerals and herbs can all positively affect the transition from child-bearing years to non-child-bearing years. Preparation prior to entering menopause can greatly reduce suffering, and dietary choices are a prime element of control.

Menopause, cessation of the menstrual cycle for one year, consists of four stages: pre-menopausal, peri-menopausal, menopausal and post-menopausal. In the peri-menopausal phase, women first start to notice differences in their cycles, such as shortening or lengthening of periods, and lighter or heavier flow. Caused by sharp drops in the level of the hormone estrogen produced in the body, these and the above mentioned symptoms of menopause diminish as one progresses to the post-menopause stage.

Isoflavones are plant based "phytoestrogens" ("phyto" refers to plants), phyto-chemicals that bind with estrogen receptor cells. They help supply the body with a compound similar to estrogen. Having a reliable plant source of phytoestrogens is especially helpful in lessening hot flashes and night sweats. Soy foods are a major source of isoflavones and by increasing your intake of soy products, your body continues to have a reliable source of these valuable compounds. By providing yourself with food that helps diminish the effect of lower estrogen production in your body, you may help lessen the symptoms caused by less internally produced estrogen.

Flax seeds are another important source of naturally occurring phytoestrogens. Sprinkle ground flax meal on cereal, salads and vegetables to increase your phytoestrogen supply. You can purchase ground flax seeds or grind your own in an inexpensive coffee grinder. Flaxseed oil is a supplement that helps lubricate dry skin and supplies essential fatty acids that can help improve memory. Memory lapses seem to be most acute during the years prior to period cessation and improve when a woman reaches the post-menopausal stage.

Many important vitamins and minerals reduce symptoms and help ensure future good health. These include the antioxidants "A.C.E.S.": beta-carotene, vitamin C, vitamin E and selenium. A variety of fruits and vegetables in your diet assures a steady supply of these important nutrients. Eat from the rainbow and vary your color palate to get everything you need (orange/carrots, green/spinach, blue/berries). Buy organically grown produce to eliminate peripheral substances that can increase symptoms in women sensitive to artificial chemicals used in fertilization, production and preservation of non-organic foods. New testing shows that organic vegetables and fruits are high in many important elements of a healthy diet.

Eliminating or reducing certain lifestyle factors can contribute to an easier menopause. Limit the amount of caffeine, alcohol and soda in the diet to help reduce unpleasant symptoms. Some women find that spicy food increases hot flashes. Caffeine and smoking increase metabolic rates, thereby increasing night sweats and hot flashes. Caffeine intake can diminish sleeping and adrenal function, leading to increased depression and fatigue. Drinking eight glasses of purified water daily can help increase mental sharpness, energy, reduce weight gain and cool the body.

Estrogen is stored in your fat cells, so your body fights to hold onto 10 pounds as a supply of estrogen. Do not be discouraged by this. When you reach the post menopause phase, this weight will be much easier to lose with proper diet and exercise. Remember this is your body's way of supporting you during this time. As long as you don't gain more weight, you can return to your pre-menopausal weight with ease. Exercise remains a crucial component for good mental health, stress management, bone health and weight loss at this time.

To find out about the author, please see "About the Contributors" on pages 181-183.

"*Studies have shown that populations that eat a diet high in vegetables and fruit and low in animal fat and meat... have a reduced risk of some of the more common cancers.*"
— *see pag123*

Nutrition for Seniors

by Heather D. Woods, ND

When it comes to aging, the prevention of age-related illness is just the start. Real rejuvenation is also possible. It is not to be found in any fanciful Shangri-La, nor in the fountain of youth once sought by Ponce de León, nor in any particular drug or magic potion. It is, rather, to be found in the choices we make every day. Depending on how we choose, we can age painfully, losing energy and function with each passing year, or we can maintain our health and vitality, and even, with a little bit of knowledge and attention, reverse many of the losses of age and restore youthful vigor. Retirement can be the time to explore oil painting and hang gliding, or learn a foreign language and travel to a new country to practice it—not just a time to catch up on the articles in those old magazines in your doctor's waiting room.

What is the most troublesome complaint of aging? Although cardiovascular problems are the number one cause of death, they are not necessarily what bother people the most. "Of all the things I've lost, what I miss most is my mind," has become an all too common lament of the baby boomers. The people who made up the youth culture of the '60s are now starting to place huge demands on an already creaky health care system with their age-associated diseases, including Alzheimer's. Like most of the signs of aging, memory loss-whether it takes the forms of senility, Alzheimer's disease, or just garden-variety "senior moments"-is all too often accepted as normal, and neurological problems are threatening to outstrip cardiovascular disease as the leading health problem in this country.

Why does one person continue to be mentally sharp and active into her nineties and another begin to decline in her forties? The reasons can be complex and varied. Certainly genetics plays a role, and there is no one simple solution. And yet, there is much less mystery than most people realize about the way to maintain healthy mental function. One of the first and strongest statistical associations to show up in studies of Alzheimer's disease is that the more sugar consumed, the higher the risk. Diabetes also increases risk of memory problems.

Saturated fats and cholesterol, which come from animal-based foods, have been implicated in carotid artery occlusion. When these arteries, which supply nutrition and oxygen to the brain, get clogged, the brain can't help but lose function. The same saturated fats affect arteries to the heart, causing cardiovascular problems, and gum up the receptor sites for insulin on our cells, a factor in maturity-onset diabetes. Although by now most people know that saturated fat and cholesterol in excess may not be good for them, the American diet is still full of both. Eating more whole foods, emphasizing fresh vegetables, beans and whole grains rather than hamburgers and doughnuts, are simple changes. Combined with a few other commonsense measures, they can have profound effects on the mental and physical health of many people—and could have an equally profound effect on the financial survival of our healthcare system.

Living

Cholesterol is not present in foods of vegetable origin. It is not necessary in the diet, as the liver makes all that we need. Lacto-ovo vegetarians can still get excessive amounts of cholesterol and saturated fat from their diets. Vegans, the strictest vegetarians, get very little saturated fat, and no cholesterol. Not surprisingly, a recent large-scale study in England, comparing the effects of diet on blood pressure, found that vegans have the lowest blood pressure and are also leaner. There was no significant statistical difference between fish eaters and vegetarians; these two groups fell in between the meat eaters, who of course had the highest blood pressure and the most body fat, and the vegans, who clearly came out ahead in reduction of risk for heart disease and stroke. Incidentally, vegans also tend to have a low incidence of osteoporosis, since the excess protein in meat causes the body to excrete calcium. A high-protein diet is also very stressful for the kidneys, and healthy kidneys are essential to maintaining normal blood pressure. American foods, especially processed foods, tend to be excessively high in fat, salt, sugar, and protein. Is it really any mystery why we have the disabilities and illnesses that we do? Having more vegan meals and staying away from most processed foods is an obvious way to improve health.

Excessive inflammation is a common denominator in many diseases of aging, from arthritis to arteriosclerosis to memory lapses. The quality and quantity of dietary fats influences level of inflammation as well as many other aspects of health, down to the composition of our cell membranes. Americans in general eat too much fat, and the wrong kinds. One of the main reasons why the quality and quantity of fats in the diet is important is that the body uses different kinds of fats to make different kinds of prostaglandins. These chemicals mediate the body's inflammatory and immune responses. Some prostaglandins promote inflammation, and some diminish it. Increasing the anti-inflammatory ones tends to promote health, reducing the risk of clogged arteries and arthritis, as well as damage to brain cells that handle short-term memory. By consuming less animal and more vegetable fats, we can ensure that our intake of the essential fatty acids (EFAs) linoleic and alpha-linoleic is adequate, and help our bodies be less prone to excessive inflammation in general.

By consuming some very beneficial oils, such as flax oil, we can increase the omega-3 oil ratio, which will reduce inflammation even further. All of these fatty acids are delicate so they should not be used for cooking and should be kept refrigerated in dark bottles.

In addition to changing the kinds of fats and oils we consume, and making sure that we have adequate vitamin and mineral intake, we need to avoid toxins as much as possible, decreasing the chemicals that can damage and cause inflammation in our bodies and brains.

Continuing to use our brains, to entertain new ideas, to try new activities, both physical and mental, to keep learning and growing, helps keep the mind young. Learning about health and nutrition can serve a double purpose!

Health doesn't just come out of a pill though. Again, it is all of our daily choices that build health or disease. As we age, it becomes more important to follow good basic health guidelines.

Eat fresh whole foods: Many of the best books and articles, the oldest traditions and the newest scientific studies, can be summed up in these simple words! The closer most foods are to their original form, the better they are.

Avoid toxins: Buy organic, or grow your own as much as possible. In addition to lessening your toxic load, you will be increasing your intake of natural minerals, vitamins, and antioxidants. Cook in nontoxic pots and pans—glass or stainless steel, not aluminum, scratched Teflon, or damaged enamel. Never use lead crystal to serve or store foods, especially wine. Avoid baking powder and antacids containing aluminum. Avoid foods that contain rancid, overheated, artificially hydrogenated, or cottonseed oils. Don't use toxic products around your home or place of work.

Remember to drink water: Many people confuse hunger with thirst and eat when they are thirsty. You should be drinking approximately six to eight glasses of pure water per day. Drink a big glass when you first get up in the morning. If your lips are getting chapped easily, you are quite dehydrated. However, you should minimize your consumption of soda pop. Substitute green tea for other caffeinated drinks.

Eat some fresh fruit and vegetables every day: Fruits and vegetables are also a great source of fiber, so important to lowering cholesterol and to maintaining a healthy digestive tract. Raw seeds and nuts are a great source of essential fatty acids.

Chew your food well: Vegans need to take B12 supplements regularly. Try to avoid eating on the run and under stress. Relax and enjoy meals, whether you're alone or with family.

Eat only when you're actually hungry: If you have to ask yourself whether you are hungry, you aren't. Obesity is associated with increased morbidity and mortality from many causes—cardiovascular disease, some cancers, diabetes, and of course, it can make arthritis worse by putting a strain on joints. If you eat the same amount of calories, but in smaller, more frequent portions, you will tend to lose weight! In addition, small frequent meals help control blood sugar. Sometimes people overeat because they are not getting enough other satisfaction from their lives, or enough emotional nourishment. If you are doing all the right things and not getting results, it's time to consider a consultation with a health care professional.

Moderation and a variety of activities are the key to healthy exercise: Don't believe the "no pain, no gain" fanatics. Always listen to your body. It knows even more than the experts. Pain is an important message from the body, one that only the foolish ignore. Exercise should be fun.

Social connections are very important to health, statistically as important as lab values like cholesterol: Satisfying work, satisfying intimate relationships, creative outlets, helping others, and having faith in some benevolent force in the universe have all been shown to enhance health. Practicing some form of prayer or meditation, or learning and practicing a stress-reduction technique, can make a huge difference for people in stressful situations they cannot control, and are ben-

Living

eficial for everyone. Not all techniques are created equal, and some are best learned from a skilled practitioner. But anyone can make it a point to breathe deeply four times when he or she feels stressed, to take vacations, to plan days off and days to do things just for the joy of it, to turn the mind toward positive thoughts.

Although there is much we can do for ourselves, there are times when we all need some expert help. Medical screening tests have become more accurate, and your doctor may be able to help you assess where you are starting from and what you need to focus on to find the best path to health. A naturopathic doctor can help you put together a comprehensive individualized program. In addition to thorough testing to sort out your individual health issues, there are many natural therapies, techniques, and supplements that are useful for seniors.

We all have a lot of power over our own health. We cannot change our basic genetic structure, but the things we do to take care of ourselves can make a huge difference. Exercise, sleep, stress reduction, eating more organic vegetarian foods, and keeping active both mentally and physically all help ensure that our hearts and minds will remain healthy. These daily measures, so much less dramatic than drug effects, are nonetheless far more profound and effective. They are the keys to retaining health into old age.

To find out about the author, please see "About the Contributors" on pages 181-183.

"A well-balanced vegetarian diet…will go a long way in the prevention of coronary artery disease."
— see page 119

Four Good Reasons Why

Beyond Fat and Cholesterol
Further Reasons to Avoid Animal Products

by Neal Barnard, MD, and Kris Kieswer, Editor, "Good Medicine"

Many people adopt a vegetarian diet to prevent heart disease, diabetes, cancer, and obesity. Without question, consuming a vegetarian diet offers significant protection against these and other chronic illnesses prevalent in the United States and other developing countries. But diet-related dangers are not always as conspicuous as the streaks of artery-clogging fat running through a steak. Other hazards lurking in meat and dairy products receive less attention, but they also pose a serious threat to good health.

The Rise of Superbugs

A recent Consumer Reports exposé on contaminated chicken products purchased nationwide offered a grim assessment: infectious salmonella and campylobacter germs are widely present and are often resistant to antibiotics that once could eradicate them. And it mattered little whether the chicken was expensive, free roaming, organic, or processed by well-known companies such as Perdue and Tyson. In all, 42 percent of chickens in Consumer Reports' 25-city test pool harbored campylobacter, while 12 percent carried salmonella. Most other surveys provide even worse assessments.

Why should consumers care? Because these bugs can be dangerous, even fatal. Campylobacter is now the most common cause of diarrhea in the United States and can sometimes lead to a paralysis-inducing disease called Gullian-Barre Syndrome. Salmonella causes severe, sometimes deadly, food poisoning.

A study tracking salmonella outbreaks from 1973 to 1975 and again from 1985 to 1987 found an increase of 130 percent. Currently, about 45,000 salmonella isolates (cultures taken from sick patients) are reported to the Centers for Disease Control (CDC) annually, resulting in about 20,000 hospitalizations, 500 deaths, and medical expenses in excess of $50 million. But the CDC estimates that only one to five percent of infections are reported.

Unfortunately, this threat to public health is often ignored. The U.S. Department of Agriculture estimates that Americans eat more than 1 million chickens every hour. But instead of ensuring better safety measures in processing plants, the USDA requires cursory visual inspections that miss the majority of contaminants.

To keep up with customer demand, slaughterhouses operate at breakneck speeds, allowing germs to spread easily from carcass to carcass. After de-feathering, chickens are plunged into chill tanks that, by the day's end, can hold a foot or more of debris. An inspector interviewed for Atlantic Monthly noted that the rinse water is often murky, brown, and bloody. Clearly, "white meat" does not signify any degree of purity or cleanliness.

Living

While antibiotic-resistant "superbugs" can arise from the overuse of doctor-prescribed antibiotics, much of the problem stems from antibiotics used in animal agriculture. Of the more than 50 million pounds of antibiotics produced in the United States annually, about 55 percent is fed to livestock, a practice intended to prevent plagues in crowded factory farms and to accelerate animal growth rates for the sake of maximized profits.

When animal flesh is consumed, so is a not-so-healthy dose of antibiotic-resistant organisms, along with occasional traces of antibiotics themselves. And many of the drugs fed to animals are the same ones doctors prescribe every day: penicillin, erythromycin, flouroquinolones and tetracyclines.

In the early 1980s, the public debut of Escherichia coli O157:H7 meant severe foodborne disease outbreaks. While its cousins are harmless inhabitants of the digestive tract of humans and animals, E. coli O157:H7 is now blamed for 20,000 infections annually and is associated with the consumption of contaminated beef, raw milk, and water. Infections are characterized by abdominal cramping and bloody diarrhea, which can progress to hemolytic uremic syndrome, kidney failure, and even blindness. Studies from 1993 found the organism in 12 out of 50 dairy herds tested.

Other foodborne pathogens healthcare workers must contend with included Listeria monocytogenes, Bacillus cereus, Clostridium botulinum, Clostridium perfringens, Shigella, and Staphylococcus aureus.

Bigger is Not Always Better

Other uninvited dinner guests are the hormones fed to animals to speed and maximize their growth. Behind the ears of most cows raised on U.S. farms are small implants that secrete a mixture of hormones. Some occur naturally in the body (estradiol, testosterone, and progesterone), and others are synthetic (trenbolone acetate and zeranol). Since 1989, the European Economic Community has banned imports of U.S. beef containing added hormones. And studies show that consumption of animal fats alone is enough to raise hormone levels in humans. The increase is thought to cause early puberty in children consuming animal products and possibly increase their risk of developing reproductive cancers later in life.

Dairy products also harbor hormones, "natural ones" as well as recombinant bovine growth hormone, used to increase milk production. However, because cows are made to produce quantities of milk far beyond what nature intended, they often develop mastitis, an inflammation of the mammary glands, which is treated with antibiotics. And so the cycle continues.

What's Really Bugging Us?

In her book, *Living Downstream*, biologist Sandra Steingraber noted, "Indeed, the largest contributors to daily intake of chlorinated insecticides are dairy products, meat, fish, and poultry." Steingraber pointed out that the U.S. National Research Council discovered in 1991 that more than half the cattle tested in a sample of

Colorado ranches had detectable levels of pesticides in their blood serum. A common contaminant was heptachlor, a banned pesticide.

By some estimates, consumption of animal products accounts for up to 90 percent of our intake of pesticides and herbicides. Tightly confined, factory-farmed animals are given cheap feed containing pesticide-ridden grains, antibiotics (and, often, the remains of other animals—a practice that enabled the spread of mad cow disease). Each time an animal ingests pesticides, the residues of those chemicals build up in the animal's body tissues. This process is known as "bioaccumulation" and occurs especially with persistent chemicals, such as organochlorines (a group that includes DDT of Silent Spring infamy).

In 1998, the FDA detected such dangerous pesticides as malathion and chlorpyrifos-methyl in animal feed. Factory farmers also use pesticides and larvicides to control fly populations drawn by so many animals and so much manure. Toxins found in animal products such as DDT, PCBs and dioxin have been linked to cancers, nervous system disorders, fetal damage and many other health problems. Nursing infants consume fully half of their mother's total body load of dioxin.

By comparison, vegetarians have just one to two percent of the national average levels of certain pesticides and industrial chemicals. Much lower levels of DDT, chlordane, hepatochlor, and dieldrin have been measured in the breast milk of vegetarian mothers.

No Safer with Seafood

Fish is often touted as an alternative to chicken or beef. In truth, more than 100,000 Americans are sickened each year by tainted seafood. To limit bacterial contamination, the Food and Drug Administration (FDA) developed the Hazard Analysis and Critical Control Points (HACCP), which plotted inspection points throughout fish processing plants. But neither this plan nor any other actually tests the fish for disease-causing bacteria, mercury, or anything else. Such traces are generally invisible to the naked eye, and government inspectors are not equipped with the sophisticated tests that would raise red flags.

Fish carry their share of fat and cholesterol, and they also have a knack for "bioconcentrating" toxic chemicals in their muscles (the parts generally served). Swimming in the global ocean, fish pick up toxic pollution from places we would never dream of having lunch. Big fish eat little fish, and the bigger the fish, the greater the bioaccumulation of toxic chemicals in their flesh. The FDA cautions pregnant women and children against eating shark, swordfish, tilefish, or king mackerel, because of dangerously high levels of mercury. However, several environmental groups believe the list should include 20 or more additional fish, including tuna, sea bass, halibut, mahi-mahi, cod, and other commonly served varieties.

Mercury has long been associated with damage to the developing brains of fetuses and children and a recent study from the New England Journal of Medicine has linked it to an increased risk for heart attack in adults. Another recent study conducted in a fishing village in Brazil found that increased exposure to mercury was associated with decreased performance on memory, concentration and

Living

dexterity tests. Avoiding fish greatly reduces these risks and eliminates half of all mercury exposure.

Unfortunately, consumers are none the wiser. A 1997 survey of 10,000 households commissioned by the National Fisheries Institute found that the majority cited health benefits among their top reasons for eating seafood. More than three-quarters believed consuming fish to be healthier than eating cows, pigs or chickens. Most believed the quality of the seafood they had eaten was good.

But consumers looking for healthy foods need not give up. The beneficial fatty acids in fish can also be found in a more stable form in walnuts, flaxseeds, soy beans, pumpkin seeds, canola and soybean oils, dark leafy greens and other plant foods.

Moreover, taking fish and other animal food off the table makes room for a wider range of fruits, vegetables, beans and grains. Along with what they generally don't contain (cholesterol, foodborne pathogens, hormones and toxic chemicals) plant foods provide the most powerful combinations of nutrients known to prevent disease and promote good health. The result is a diet with more of what you need—and much less of what you don't.

To find out about the author, please see "About the Contributors" on pages 181-183.

"Although we think we are one and we act as if we are one, human beings are not natural carnivores...flesh was never intended for human beings who are natural herbivores."

Dr. William Clifford Roberts
Editor in Chief of the American Journal of Cardiology

Saving the Animals with Every Bite

by Jennifer Hillman, MA

"The question is not, Can they reason? nor, Can they talk? but, Can they suffer?"
– Jeremy Bentham, *An Introduction to the Principles of Morals and Legislation,* 1789

Many people love and care for animals and enjoy the good feeling that comes from finding a home for a kitten or puppy, just as others experience the joy of adopting their new found friend. We all react with repugnance at the thought of eating a cat or a dog. But are farm animals really any less worthy of our love and care? Just as with cats and dogs, farm animals are sensitive to pain and want to live happy lives.

While finding a home for a kitten saves a cat, the way to save a farm animal is to simply choose to follow a healthy vegetarian diet. Every time you choose a veggie burger, for instance, you have just taken a big step in saving the life of a gentle cow. The good news is that a vegetarian diet is so delicious that you and the cow both come out winners.

Like cats and dogs, the farm animals are sensitive creatures, but they are forced to live a much harder life than in former times. This is due to the advent of the modern method of farming known as factory farming. Factory farming cares nothing for the welfare of the animals. As with other factory methods, it often only cares about profits and efficiencies, and unfortunately that results in greatly increasing the suffering of billions of animals in the system. Most people are surprised to learn that unlike cats and dogs, most farm animals have no laws protecting them, and in the few cases where laws do exist they are woefully inadequate. Terrible overcrowding and surgery without anesthesia are just some of the ordeals that these poor creatures are forced to endure. By choosing a vegetarian diet we show, among other things, our distaste for a system that is inherently cruel and that we are willing to act to save these sensitive creatures.

In the United States alone, 35 million factory-farmed cows are raised and slaughtered every year for beef. After living very uncomfortable lives, they are rounded up and transported hundreds of miles to the slaughterhouse. They spend the last few months of their lives crowded into a feedlot, injected with growth hormones and fattened quickly in order to gain the most profit for their meat. Approximately 80% of the cattle in our country are slaughtered in large corporate slaughterhouses, where speed of production outweighs any humane considerations.

While most of us were taught to believe that milk production does not actually harm the cow, this is no longer true. Dairy cows are forced to give birth repeatedly so that they can continuously produce milk and, in many cases, are injected with Bovine Growth Hormone (rBGH) which is designed to produce an abnormally high volume of milk. This over-production continually leads to mastitis and lameness, both painful afflictions. Dairy cows are raised to spend their lives producing milk only for human consumption and when their milk production wanes after about three or four years, they are rounded up and sent to slaughter. We can help

Living

163

these dairy cows by simply purchasing alternative milks such as soy milk. These days there's even chocolate soy milk available. It's another win-win situation.

While female calves born into the dairy industry replace older dairy cows, males are often used for the veal industry. Veal calves are not allowed to nurse with their mothers, as they are taken away almost immediately after birth. The factory-farmed veal calf often spends the entirety of his 16 weeks of life chained by the neck in a crate that is built purposely so small that he cannot turn around. As he grows, it becomes increasingly hard for him to even lie down. Veal calves are fed an all-liquid diet that is designed to keep their muscles soft and to cause anemia, which in turn creates the lighter colored flesh that characterizes veal meat. The consumption of veal has become less popular partly because of the unusual cruelty involved.

Many scientists believe that pigs are actually as smart and sensitive as dogs. Yet these creatures suffer intense crowding and confinement. Some female pigs in the factory farm are raised only to produce babies for slaughter. The sow is confined for her entire breeding life (approximately three to five years) to a narrow, metal, cement-floored stall that is just barely the length of her body. In this "gestation crate," she is unable to walk or turn around and spends much of her time chained to the floor by the neck. When the female pig is just about to give birth, she is moved to a second stall where she nurses her piglets until they are weaned and sent to slaughter. She is then impregnated again and returned to her life in the gestation crate. This practice is so cruel that one state has finally enacted legislation to prohibit it. Trying the new pork, sausage and bacon substitutes will go a long way to helping these creatures and also makes for some pretty good meals.

Like all birds, chickens are capable of suffering and of feeling pain and fear. Chickens represent the largest number of animals suffering and being slaughtered on the factory farm. The "broiler" chicken, as opposed to the laying hen, is raised for meat. Kept crowded into large sheds, chickens are fed to increase their weight as quickly as possible. Because the broiler chicken is slaughtered between six and eight weeks of age, before its skeleton has fully developed, the forced growth leads to painful conditions such as bone disorders and fractures.

Scientists have determined that fish are also capable of suffering. Modern fishing methods use very long nets to catch fish. Sea mammals such as dolphins, porpoises and seals are also trapped in these nets and so become casualties of the fishing industry.

As with the dairy cow and her milk, people generally assume that laying hens are not harmed in the production of eggs. Many egg companies market to the consumer a portrayal of hens living out their lives in a natural setting. However, the factory farm shows a very different picture. "Battery cages" used to house laying hens are small wire cages, not much larger than a file drawer, in which generally six - eight hens are confined for their entire laying lives. In order to minimize the damage they do to each other as a result of the stress of overcrowding, the hens are debeaked, the beaks are sliced off with a hot blade. Hens are forced to stand on the thin wire flooring of the cages causing painful injuries to their feet. Their bodies continually rub as they are forced against the wire sides of the cage and this also creates injuries and chronic sores and infections. Intense confinement in the egg industry is yet another example of how hard factory farming is on the animals. Fortunately, the many chicken substitutes on the market provide a delicious and healthy way of saving these creatures.

Factory farming cannot afford to wait for the natural molting process to take place, during which time hens would normally lose their feathers and temporarily cease laying eggs. In order to speed up the process, and keep them laying on a tight schedule, forced molting is used. Forced molting involves periodically starving hens of food for up to two weeks and even depriving them of water for up to three days, which forces their bodies into shock and causes them to lose their feathers quickly. When their laying life is over (approximately three years), "spent hens" are also sent to slaughter, where their badly damaged bodies could never be packaged whole for consumers to view, but can only be ground to make foods such as soups or pot pies. Again the vegetarian food industry comes to the rescue with products such as egg-less egg salad and even egg replacers for baking.

Turkeys are force fed and become so large that it is painful for them to stand. Like chicken "broilers," they are forced to live in a tightly confined space and are painfully debeaked. Although ducks depend upon water to eat, swim and clean, they are completely deprived of this natural habitat in the factory farm system. Without access to water, they have difficulty keeping warm and have no way to clean themselves. Geese are used to produce foie gras or pate (meat from the liver), are tightly confined and continually force fed until their livers painfully expand to 10 times the natural size, creating this "delicacy." Try one of the turkey substitutes for a Thanksgiving dinner and save the life of a turkey.

Life on the factory farm is so hard that many of the animals become too sick and diseased to stand or walk. These downed animals or "downers" as the industry refers to them, are often not provided with any veterinary care, and with no laws to protect them, they are left to suffer and die among the other animals in the production facility. Because the meat and dairy industry can still sell these animals for food, they force them to slaughter usually by dragging and pulling them with chains or moving them with a forklift. For those that can still walk, there is evidence of production lines moving at speeds too fast to allow for humane slaughtering and well-documented cases of this have taken place right here in the Northwest. Not only is this hard on the animals, but it is very dangerous for the slaughterhouse workers as well and results in many injuries. In fact, working in the slaughterhouse is the most dangerous job in America. Some people say that if slaughterhouses had glass walls, we would all be vegetarians. Perhaps Abraham Lincoln said it best when he said, " I am in favor of animal rights as well as human rights. That is the way of a whole human being."

Saving the animals is easy. All you need to do is to make compassionate choices when shopping at the grocery store. Enjoy the many delicious alternatives to meat, dairy and eggs, and you will be saving the animals with every bite.

To find out about the author, please see "About the Contributors" on pages 181-183.

Living

"...if everyone in the U.S. adopted a vegan diet, the country's oil imports could be reduced by 60 percent."

"Likewise, the livestock industry consumes more than half of the water withdrawn in the U.S. every year."

Living

The Environmental Case for Vegetarianism

Anne I. Johnson, BA and Timothy J. Fargo, MA

Sound environmental reasons for adopting a vegetarian or vegan diet are abundant. Among them are agricultural efficiency, environmental sustainability and improved environmental health for both people and ecosystems. Animal agriculture is unsustainable on a global scale. It produces food inefficiently and it consumes resources such as energy and water irresponsibly. It also damages habitats and sensitive ecosystems. In the United States, most traditional animal agricultural practices have now been consolidated into factory farms—large, intensive operations that house thousands of animals in confined conditions. These farms have significantly altered our environment. They are creating a buildup of nutrients, toxic at high concentrations, in our soil and water. They are increasing global greenhouse gas emissions and air pollution. Moreover, they are introducing pathogens, antibiotics, pesticides and hormones into our food and water supply. Reducing or eliminating meat consumption is an action you can take now that will reap significant environmental rewards.

Agricultural Inefficiency

Why is animal agriculture inherently inefficient? It is inefficient because eating animal foods rather than plant foods wastes an enormous amount of food energy. Organisms are classified by _trophic levels_ according to the type of food that they consume. Producers, such as plants, belong to the first trophic level; they take in energy directly from the sun. Primary consumers, herbivores, belong to the second trophic level; secondary consumers, carnivores, belong to the third trophic level; and tertiary consumers, carnivores that eat other carnivores, belong to the fourth trophic level. Thus, when a human eats a plant, he or she eats on the second trophic level. By eating beef, a human eats on the third trophic level. A human who eats a salmon eats on the fourth trophic level. The higher the trophic level on which one eats, the more food energy one wastes, since about 90 percent of available food energy is lost through each successively higher trophic level. For example, if 10,000 kilocalories are available to plants in the first trophic level, at the third trophic level only 100 calories are left available for a human. Thus, a vegan, or strict vegetarian, conserves a far greater amount of food energy than an omnivore. Producing cattle for food is even more energy inefficient than the incandescent light bulb, in which 95 percent of the energy input is lost as heat to the environment.

In modern agricultural operations, animals are fed a diet of grains, such as corn, and soybeans, both of which are suitable for human consumption. In fact, cattle and other livestock consume 70 percent of the grain produced in the U.S. Animals on average consume approximately 20 pounds of protein for every pound of edible meat they produce. For example, an average steer creates less than 50 kilograms of protein for every 790 kilograms of plant protein he consumes. Thus, if over time a human chose to eat 50 kilograms of plant protein instead of cattle protein, another 740 kilograms of plant protein would be available—enough plant food for 15 additional human beings.

Living

It makes good economic and ecological sense to use grains primarily for human consumption, not to waste them by feeding them to livestock. Worldwide, the total amount of grain grown would indeed be capable of feeding the earth's human inhabitants, but 38 percent of it is fed to cattle and other livestock. In the U.S., cattle eat almost twice as much grain as the human population consumes. In 1994 David Pimentel, a professor of agricultural sciences at Cornell University, estimated that if all of the grain fed to livestock in the U.S. alone—130 million tons per year—were used to feed human beings, 400 million people could be fed. In comparison, approximately nine million humans die worldwide every year from starvation, and in the period from 1998 to 2000, 840 million people in the world were considered undernourished.

The reasons that hunger and starvation exist are often political or economic. Becoming vegetarian or vegan will not necessarily contribute to eliminating another person's hunger. Nevertheless, it can be argued that by not eating animals, vegetarians and vegans do potentially increase the supply of food available for human consumption, which would in turn make it more affordable to those in need.

Environmental Unsustainability

The production of meat is environmentally unsustainable, utilizing vast amounts of land, energy and water. Over one billion cattle currently live on the earth, foraging on 24 percent of its landmass and on 29 percent of the landmass of the U.S. Livestock grazing accounts for 85 percent of topsoil loss in the U.S. The most significant cause of desertification in dry and semidry regions is overgrazing. In addition to rangeland, the animal agriculture industry consumes fertile land as well. Two-thirds of U.S. cropland is used to grow livestock feed. In contrast, only two percent of U.S. cropland is used to produce vegetables consumed by humans. Approximately 80 percent of the world's agricultural land is used either for grazing or for growing grain to feed livestock, whereas only about 20 percent feeds human beings directly. It is easy to see how the land used to feed one meat-eater could feed twenty vegans.

Tropical rainforests support a complex diversity of life, providing habitats for nearly half of the plant and animal species on earth. Much Amazonian and Central American rainforest, however, is being cleared to turn the land into pasture for cattle to be sold on the European and North American markets. Cattle ranching in tropical rainforests not only harms native plants and animals, it also negatively impacts human populations. In the journal *Nature*, Charles Peters of the Institute of Economic Botany estimates the value of one hectare in a Peruvian tropical rainforest to be "$6,820 per year if intact forest is sustainably harvested for fruits, latex, and timber; $1,000 if clear-cut for commercial timber (not sustainably harvested); or $148 if used as cattle pasture." When trees in a tropical rainforest are burned or cut down and the landscape is cleared for cattle ranching, the thin top layer of humus is quickly eroded by the abundant rainfall. Once the soil is depleted by overgrazing, ranchers clear more rainforest, and the process of deforestation and desertification continues. In contrast, for every person who consumes a vegan diet, an acre of trees every year is spared from being cut down for rangeland.

Energy consumption per capita in the U.S. for meat production is greater than the amount of energy lesser-developed countries consume per capita for _all_ purposes. Almost half of the energy used in American agriculture is used in the livestock industry. In the journal of the American Society of Agricultural Engineers, Roller compared energy costs of producing meats with energy costs of producing plant foods. He found that "even the best of the animal enterprises examined returns only 34.5 percent of the investment of fossil [fuel] energy to us in food energy, whereas the poorest of the five crop enterprises examined returns 328 percent." It's a significant geopolitical and economic fact that if everyone in the U.S. adopted a vegan diet, the country's oil imports could be reduced by 60 percent.

Likewise, the livestock industry consumes more than half of the water withdrawn in the U.S. every year. Most of this is used to water feed crops and to rinse away livestock waste. The production of one day's food for an omnivore requires 2500 gallons of water, whereas the production of one day's food for a vegan requires only 300 gallons. A person switching from a typical meat-based diet to a pure vegetarian diet saves over three-quarters of a million gallons of water per year.

Waste and Pollution

In addition to consuming vast quantities of grains, energy, and fresh water, factory farms in the U.S. are creating massive amounts of waste and pollution. In 1997, poultry, swine, beef, and dairy facilities produced a total of 291 billion pounds of manure—130 times more waste than the human population produces. Factory farms generate such large amounts of animal manure each day that the waste cannot decompose as quickly as it is produced. Many dairy, swine, and egg-laying poultry operations pump it into holding facilities called waste lagoons, which can be up to six or seven acres in size. The waste in these lagoons is usually pumped and applied directly onto cropland or fallow land, where the nutrients and bacteria typically over-accumulate in the soil or groundwater. Worse yet, this liquid waste is often sprayed when the ground is frozen or otherwise impermeable, causing the waste to be carried away with surface runoff. The Environmental Protection Agency reports that in states where there are a high concentration of factory farms, 20 to 30 major water quality pollution problems occur each year related to waste lagoon discharges and surface runoff.

When a waste lagoon spills, overflows, or seeps its waste into the groundwater or surface waters, serious contamination can result. In North Carolina, a state with many confined hog facilities, lagoon breaches are frequent. In Duplin County, 50 miles south of Raleigh, there are about 42,000 people and 2.2 million hogs. A waste lagoon at a hog operation there ruptured in 1995 and released nearly 25 million gallons of animal manure into the New River, killing over 4,000 fish. Elsewhere in the same state, slaughterhouses operated by a division of the largest pork producer in the U.S. have contaminated the Cape Fear River almost 40 times.

Living

Ammonia from animal manure released directly into surface waters reduces the dissolved oxygen content and is thus the primary cause of fish kills. For example, the U.S. Fish and Wildlife Service reported that in 1995 in Nebraska, half of the total fish kills from agriculture investigated were from livestock waste. By 1996, three-fourths of all agriculture fish kills were from livestock waste; and in 1997 and 1998, all agricultural fish kills were due to livestock waste. In Washington State in 1998, two dairy feedlot operators suffered disastrous lagoon breaches; the Department of Ecology estimated that one lagoon emptied its entire 700,000 gallons of waste, while the other released 200,000 gallons, both into the Yakima River. The state enforced fines of only $2000 and $3000.

Nitrogen- and phosphorus-rich animal manure from factory farms can harm marine ecosystems and water quality. Scientists at the U.S. Geological Survey determined that in 88 percent of watersheds investigated in the U.S., manure contributed more to in-stream total nitrogen than traditional point sources and manure also contributed more to total phosphorus than did commercial fertilizers. When nutrients such as phosphorus and nitrogen overenrich aquatic ecosystems, beginning the process known as eutrophication, algae growth intensifies. Algae blooms block sunlight from reaching the aquatic vegetation that provides a breeding place for adult fish, a protected environment for young fish and a home for aquatic insects. The algae then decay, lowering the dissolved oxygen content to levels that cannot support fish and invertebrate life. In marine habitats, algal blooms referred to as "red tides" or "brown tides" have killed large numbers of marine mammals, while in freshwater habitats, toxins from algal blooms have poisoned humans and wildlife. The compounds emitted when blue-green algae are ingested in freshwater environments are toxic to the liver and nervous system. Algae growth can also cause drinking water to have an unpleasant odor and taste; when treatment plants use chlorine to disinfect the water, algae can react with the chlorine, creating chlorinated byproducts that are carcinogenic.

Elevated levels of nitrates are found where manure lagoons rupture or leak and also where waste is improperly sprayed onto crops or soil. The nitrogen in manure is converted to nitrates in the soil and may then migrate through the soil and concentrate in groundwater. Nitrate poisoning, also known as methemoglobinemia or "blue baby syndrome," poses a serious and potentially fatal risk to infants less than six months of age who drink water from contaminated sources. When nitrite oxidizes the iron in the hemoglobin of red blood cells, it creates a compound called methemoglobin, which reduces the amount of oxygen brought to the cells and tissues of the body. Other effects of low blood oxygen from methemoglobinemia include birth defects, miscarriages, and illness in both humans and animals. The Centers for Disease Control investigated a cluster of spontaneous miscarriages in women in LaGrange County, Indiana, in 1996. It found that nitrate was the only contaminant present at an increased level in their water supplies, at almost double the EPA's Maximum Contaminant Level (MCL). The CDC determined that the source of nitrate contamination was most likely waste from a nearby confined hog operation.

Living

170

Although the EPA has set a Maximum Contaminant Level for nitrogen-based compounds in water that is supposed to be safe for human consumption and for some fish, recent studies have demonstrated that these levels may not be protecting other wildlife. At Oregon State University, Andrew Blaustein has been investigating the role of nitrates and nitrites in declining populations of five Northwest amphibian species. He observed that some tadpoles and young frogs exposed to moderate levels of these compounds ate less, swam less energetically, grew physical mutations, experienced paralysis and died. No tadpoles or young frogs died in the tanks which had unpolluted water. The Oregon spotted frog, the most sensitive of the five species Blaustein studied, has almost vanished from its identified range, lowlands that have had concentrated agricultural use since 1960. In fact, the amount of nitrite regarded as acceptable for human drinking water killed more than half of the Oregon spotted frog tadpoles after they experienced 15 days at those levels. The EPA considers levels of nitrites that are even higher safe for warm-water fishes, although at these levels the five amphibian species Blaustein studied experienced a comparable level of mortality.

As they decompose liquid manure, waste lagoons emit ammonia, hydrogen sulfide, methane, carbon dioxide, and over 150 other odorous compounds. The primary gases produced from manure lagoons are methane and carbon dioxide, two greenhouse gases that are believed to contribute to warming global temperatures. From 1990 to 1998, methane emissions from livestock waste management increased 53 percent. In 1998, the EPA estimated that almost 13 percent of the total U.S. methane emissions originated from livestock manure.

Although generated in smaller amounts, ammonia and hydrogen sulfide are dangerous gases that can cause health problems for workers at factory farms and the people living in surrounding communities. Concentrations of hydrogen sulfide gas near factory farms in 1996 were strong enough to cause symptoms such as vomiting, headaches, insomnia, respiratory difficulties, dizziness, sore throats and blackouts. Hydrogen sulfide levels at one large hog factory farm in Minnesota surpassed the state standard 271 times in 1999 and 2000. In the six North Carolina counties where hog operations are the most densely located, ammonia emissions by swine factory farms intensified by 316 percent from 1982 to 1997. In addition to gases, particulate matter is emitted into the atmosphere, including endotoxins, the toxic protoplasm released when microorganisms die and decay.

Trace elements such as arsenic, copper, zinc and selenium are added to animal feed and are therefore found in animal manure. Although many trace elements are necessary nutrients in small quantities, elements such as arsenic and selenium are toxic at higher concentrations. Trace elements stay in aquatic ecosystems for an extended time and accumulate in the environment because they are absorbed by bed sediments or are ingested by organisms in the water. The EPA recognizes that bottom-feeding birds can suffer metal toxicity since they are drawn to shallow waste ponds and lagoons. In Nebraska wetlands, the U.S. Fish & Wildlife Service discovered that wastewater from a swine operation had elevated concentrations of copper and zinc that exceeded protection levels for aquatic life. In addition, repeated ap-

Living

171

plications of animal waste on agricultural land could cause arsenic and other trace elements to reach levels toxic to plant growth.

Salt is another nutrient in animal manure that can over-concentrate in drinking water. In California's Chino Basin, manure from local dairies contributes over 1,500 tons of salt per year to water supplies. Drinking water treatment plants must then extract this salt, at a cost of $320 to $690 for every ton. By not eating animals and animal products, we can reduce the pollution of the animal agriculture system, save the lives of sensitive species such as frogs, fish and birds, and obviate serious environmental health problems caused by the over-accumulation of nutrients and toxins.

Microorganisms such as parasites, bacteria, and viruses have the potential to infect humans and wildlife through drinking water, direct contact and the food supply. Diseases that can be transmitted to humans from animal waste include salmonellosis, cryptosporidiosis, giardiasis and colibaciliosis. Vincent R. Hill and Mark D. Sobsey, researchers at the University of North Carolina at Chapel Hill, found that the levels of bacteria in swine lagoon discharges are much greater than is permissible for municipal wastewater released onto land or into water. In May 2000, in Walkerton, Ontario, an outbreak of *E. coli* killed six people and sickened 1,300. The Ministry of Health and Long-Term Care in Ontario concluded that cattle manure runoff from a farm bordering a drinking water supply well was the probable source. In examining foodborne epidemics caused by this strain of *E. coli,* scientists have estimated that 75 percent originated from cattle products, mostly ground beef. At a dairy operation near Little Rock, Washington, state inspectors found a fecal coliform bacteria level of 130,000 colonies per 100 ml in the water in one of the drainage trenches. The state-mandated water quality standard is 100 colonies per 100 ml of water. The EPA also reports that thousands of migratory waterfowl are killed each year from avian botulism and avian cholera, which is caused by bacteria in factory farm animal wastes.

Antibiotics, Pesticides, and Hormones

Antibiotics were introduced commercially in the 1940s to control infectious diseases caused by bacteria. Today, antimicrobials are routinely added to animal feed, not only to prevent disease but also to promote faster growth in healthy animals so that they can be brought to market sooner. Whereas antimicrobials for therapeutic purposes generally are given to animals for shorter periods of time, antimicrobials for nontherapeutic uses usually are administered over an extended time. The Union of Concerned Scientists estimates the current nontherapeutic use of antimicrobials in cattle, swine and poultry to be 24.5 million pounds per year—3.7 million pounds for cattle, 10.3 million pounds for hogs, and 10.5 million pounds for poultry. In contrast, antimicrobials prescribed by physicians for humans total only about 3 million pounds a year.

As the use of antibiotics for nontherapeutic purposes spreads, more antibiotic-resistant strains of bacteria will develop, compromising our ability to use antibiotics in truly life-threatening situations. The EPA has stated that as much as 80 percent of oral antibiotics given to animals on factory farms appear in the manure unchanged; when this animal waste is applied to croplands, not only are the antibiotics and any resistant bacteria able to enter the groundwater and surface water, but they also can cause other bacteria in the soil to become resistant. For example, a form of the bacterium _Clostridium perfringens_ resistant to antibiotics was discovered in groundwater beneath land where swine manure had been sprayed. In 1995 in Minnesota, after a new class of antibiotics called fluoroquinolones was authorized for use in poultry, a study documented a dramatic rise from one to ten percent in fluoroquinolone-resistant _Campylobacter_ bacteria cultures in the people tested. Scientists were able to trace the molecular fingerprint of the strain found in people to the same strain found in animals. In Denmark, scientists demonstrated that an animal growth promoter called avoparcin had generated a significant growth in hospitals of _Enterococcus faecium_ bacteria that were resistant to the valuable human antibiotic vancomycin. Avoparcin is now illegal for use in Europe. The World Health Organization in _The Medical Impact of the Use of Antimicrobials in Food Animals_ in 1997 advised that "the use of any antimicrobial agent for growth promotion in animals should be terminated if it is used in human therapeutics or known to select for cross-resistance to antimicrobials used in human medicine." The American Medical Association House of Delegates approved a resolution in June 2001 opposing "the use of antimicrobials at nontherapeutic levels in agriculture or as pesticides or growth promoters and urges that nontherapeutic use in animals of antimicrobials [that are also used in humans] should be terminated or phased out." Choosing to eat as a vegetarian or vegan will reduce one's own involuntary consumption of antibiotics and will help to reduce the development of resistant bacteria.

Although more research is needed, it is known that both pesticide residues and hormones can be found in animal foods, in animal wastes and in the environment where feed is grown or livestock are raised. In the U.S. almost two-thirds of the total cropland is used to grow livestock feed. Agricultural pesticides are heavily used on these crops. Jeremy Rifkin in _Beyond Beef_ states that "eighty percent of all the herbicides used in the U.S. are sprayed on corn and soybeans, which are used primarily as feed for cattle and other livestock." Since pesticide residues bioaccumulate in the fatty tissues of animals, the higher the trophic level on which one eats, the more pesticide residues one ingests. Pesticides in agricultural runoff can also harm humans and wildlife.

Hormones such as estrogen and other estrogen-like compounds often found in agricultural chemicals have been found in surface waters and have been shown to disrupt the reproductive systems of wildlife. The EPA reports: "When present in high concentrations, hormones in the environment are linked to reduced fertility, mutations, and the death of fish, and there is evidence that fish in some streams are experiencing endocrine disruption." For example, in one study an estrogen hormone called estradiol was discovered in surface runoff waters originating from a field that was covered with poultry litter at concentrations up to 3.5 micrograms/liter. At levels of only 0.25 micrograms/liter of estradiol, fish frequently have gender changes, while at levels above 10 micrograms/liter fish can die.

Fish Farming

Fish farms, another type of factory farm, pollute and threaten aquatic ecosystems. A growing percentage of the fish consumed by humans today are bred in fish farms. In British Columbia, a hotspot for salmon aquaculture, 91 farms are currently operating. Not only do salmon farms pollute the water, harm marine life and introduce non-native fish and their diseases into the surrounding ecosystems, they actually deplete the number of native fish in other parts of the world. Salmon on fish farms are fed a diet of ground fish meal. To create one pound of aquaculture salmon, 2.4 pounds of wild fish must be consumed.

The Atlantic salmon was first brought to the West Coast in 1984 and is now the primary species raised in aquaculture operations in British Columbia. Juvenile salmon are raised in hatcheries and then transported to net pens called sea cages, where they continue to grow until they are taken to market. One fish farm may have 10 to 30 sea cages, each holding about 20,000 fish. The sea cages have net walls that permit clean water to enter the net cages while all waste, uneaten foods, medicines including antibiotics, and pesticides stream into the surrounding waters. Farm salmon are fed pesticides to eliminate sea lice, parasites that spread quickly among the confined salmon. Because only nets divide farmed salmon from the surrounding environment, sea lice can easily spread to wild salmon migrating past the pens. Recently Alexandra Morton, a biologist on Vancouver Island, reported that 78 percent of the 700 wild baby pink salmon she sampled were enveloped with a lethal number of sea lice.

In addition to allowing pollutants to pass directly through their walls, the nets are often ripped open by salmon predators such as orcas and sea lions, and are damaged frequently by human error and storms, all of which allow farm fish to escape to the surrounding environment. In the summer of 2000, for example, about 35,000 Atlantic salmon escaped from a farm on the northern point of Vancouver Island. Without more restrictions, the swiftly growing aquaculture industry in Europe and eastern North America could eliminate the remaining wild Atlantic salmon population in these regions. In Norway, where salmon farming has been practiced since the late 1960s, over 25 percent of spawning salmon in rivers and streams have escaped from fish farms, and in some parts of Norway farm fish now make up over 80 percent of the salmon population. Escaped farmed salmon not only compete with native species for food and habitat but spread diseases and parasites to wild salmon. Alarmingly, a company in Massachusetts is working on genetically altering the Atlantic salmon so that they can grow three to six times faster than wild Atlantic salmon.

On the Pacific Coast, the several species of native salmon coexist, but biologists warn that introduced Atlantic salmon threaten these native populations. At first the government and the salmon industry in British Columbia maintained that there would be few, if any, escapes of farm fish and that any escapees would not reach freshwater rivers and spawn. John Volpe, a biologist at the University of Alberta, however, wrote in an article entitled *Super un-Natural: Atlantic Salmon in BC Waters* in 1999 that scientists observed "the first population of *wild-reared* juvenile *Atlantic* salmon in the Tsitika River on Vancouver Island" (emphasis added). He studied interactions between farmed Atlantic salmon and wild Pacific salmon; he found that a fish that had resided in a habitat for as little as three days before another fish entered the habitat was capable of being dominant. In 1990, Atlantic salmon were first observed in Alaskan waters. Based on concerns that escaped farm fish would detrimentally affect native salmon populations, the State of Alaska has amended its constitution and now outlaws net-pen aquaculture. In contrast, in British Columbia a moratorium on new fish farms was enacted in 1985 but was revoked in September of 2002. By not eating fish, one can reduce the economic demand for factory-farmed fish, help lessen the pollution caused by fish farms, and help minimize the threat to native fish species.

Summary

Reducing or eliminating the consumption of animal foods and eating at a lower trophic level will lead to greater agricultural efficiency, increased environmental sustainability and improved environmental health. The current animal agriculture industry consumes resources in vast quantities and at an alarming rate. The large amount of land needed to raise crops for livestock feed and for grazing imperils vital ecosystems and contributes to the loss of biodiversity and native species throughout the world. Factory farms create tremendous amounts of waste and pollution; cause significant harm to water, air and land quality; and endanger the health of humans and other life by excessively concentrating nutrients and agricultural chemicals that are toxic at heightened levels. Furthermore, overuse of antibiotics in the animal agriculture industry causes increased microbial resistance and threatens the efficacy of therapeutic antibiotics. A non-animal-based agricultural system potentially would feed more people, use less water and energy, create less pollution and be a sustainable food system for the human population.

At each meal we have the opportunity to choose to eat sustainably grown plant foods that cause the least amount of pollution and damage not only to our own health but to the environmental health of our ecosystems. Health and ethics have long been two strong arguments in favor of adopting a vegetarian or vegan diet. The evidence is now clear that protecting the environment is a crucial third reason.

Please visit www.vegofwa.org/environment to read the full text of this article with complete references.

To find out about the author, please see "About the Contributors" on pages 181-183.

"Following a vegetarian diet has long been supported by many of the world's spiritual traditions. Dating back in some cases thousands of years, people of many different faiths have found a vegetarian diet an important part of their spiritual beliefs and practices. As time moves forward, more and more people are being inspired to adopt a vegetarian diet."

Living

Food and Faith

by Stewart Rose, BSc, Vice-president, Vegetarians of Washington

Whatever religious or spiritual path you follow, a vegetarian diet is a perfect fit! The world's religions have always recognized the spiritual importance of our food. Let's survey some of the world's religions and learn what they offer in support of a vegetarian diet.

In the Jewish religion there are the following three principles: saving human life and health, not causing suffering to animals and not wasting resources. All have a very solid foundation in the Bible. Indeed, nowhere can be found any commandment to eat meat. There isn't even any blessing for food that contains meat. Additional support comes from the original diet in Genesis, which was vegetarian, and the vegetarian diet spoken of in the book of Prophets. In the Book of Daniel, we see the healthfulness of a vegetarian diet over one with meat. According to the Talmud, "Kashrut teaches first of all that eating meat is itself a moral compromise...man ideally should not eat meat, for to eat meat a life must be taken, an animal must be put to death....The Torah teaches a lesson in moral conduct, that man shall not eat meat unless he has a special craving for it, and shall eat it only occasionally and sparingly."(Chulin 84a)

Many famous Jews throughout history have been vegetarians. Maimonedes, one of the most influential rabbis in history, was a vegetarian. More recently, the first chief Rabbi of the modern state of Israel, Avraham Kook Ha Kohane, and Israel's current chief Rabbi both followed a vegetarian diet. The famous Jewish philosopher, Martin Buber, was also a vegetarian. The famous Jewish scientist and philosopher Albert Einstein was also a vegetarian. Israel is said to have the second highest per capita rate of vegetarians in the world.

The Roman Catholic Church has also shown its belief in the spiritual value of vegetarianism. There have been four Catholic orders which have followed a vegetarian diet: The Trappist, Benedictine, Franciscan and Carthusian orders have all traditionally followed a vegetarian diet. Brother Ron Pickarski, a Franciscan monk, has written some of the most popular vegetarian cookbooks on the market including *Friendly Foods*. Brother Victor-Antoine d'Avila-Latourette, a Benedictine, has written two excellent vegetarian cookbooks: *This Good Food* and *From a Monastery Kitchen*. Looking beyond our personal well-being, Pope John Paul II said, "Respect for life and for the dignity of the human person also extends to the rest of creation." According to St. Francis of Assisi, "Not to hurt our humble brethren is our first duty to them, but to stop there is not enough. We have a higher mission—to be of service to them wherever they require it." These two great Roman Catholics show through their words the spiritual importance of values that are reflected by following a vegetarian diet.

From the Protestant community we have such figures as John Wesley, the founder of the Methodist church who said, "Thanks be to God, since I gave up flesh and wine I have been delivered from all physical ills." The founder of the Salvation Army, General Booth, was also a vegetarian. He credited his vegetarian diet for all his energy and vigor. When asked where he got his energy, he said, "I owe it to my careful vegetarian diet." One of the other church leaders, Colonel Moss, obtained vegetarian recipes to publish in the Salvation Army Journals.

The Seventh Day Adventist Church has been a leading advocate of a vegetarian diet for well over a hundred years. In addition to the Hebrew scriptures mentioned above, Adventists also take note of the following: "Know ye not that ye are the temple of God..." (1 Corinthians 3:16-17) "Beloved, I wish above all things that thou mayest prosper in health, even as thy soul prospereth." (III John 2) Ellen G. White, one of the founders of the Seventh Day Adventist church, advocated a vegetarian diet in several books and publications. "Vegetables, fruits, and grains should compose our diet. Not an ounce of flesh meat should enter our stomachs. The eating of flesh is unnatural. We are to return to God's original purpose in the creation of man." Approximately 55% of the members of the Seventh Day Adventist Church are vegetarians.

The Reverend Andrew Lindsey, of the Church of England, Professor of Theology at the University of Nottingham, England and research fellow at Oxford University, has written that "...vegetarianism can arguably claim to have the strongest Biblical support."

Reverend Alvin V.P. Hart, Episcopalian Priest and hospital chaplain of St. Lukes Hospital, says, "We now have scientific evidence that vegetarianism is good for the body. The greatest spiritual teachers have always known that it is good for the soul."

In the Book of Doctrines and Covenants, Section 89, written by Joseph Smith, founder of the Church of Latter Day Saints (LDS), we find the following "..flesh of the beasts and also the fowls...they are to be used sparingly ...and these God hath made for the use of man only in times of famine and excess of hunger." While not expressly forbidding the consumption of meat, the passage certainly seems to require exceptional circumstances for its use. According to Brigham Young, "When men live to the age of a tree, their food will be fruit..." Ezra Taft Benson, 13th President of the LDS church, said, "We need a generation of young people who, as Daniel, eat in a more healthy manner than to fare on the "kings meat," and whose countenances show it. But what needs additional emphasis are the positive aspects... the need for vegetables, fruits, and grain, particularly wheat... We need a generation of people who eat in a healthier manner. In general, the more food we eat in its natural state and the less it is refined without additives, the healthier it will be for us."

The four Fillmores, founders of the Unity church, actively advocated the practice of vegetarianism during their lifetimes, beginning with Charles Fillmore's original article "As To Meat Eating" published in the October 1903 issue of Unity Magazine. Lowell added the New Thought Diet section to Unity Magazine in 1906 and there were two special vegetarian issues of the magazine in February, 1911 and June, 1915. John Fillmore was editor of The Vegetarian column, which was added to Weekly Unity beginning with the October 25, 1911 issue.

Living

Many Quakers are said to have followed a vegetarian diet, consistent with their belief in universal compassion. The famous Quaker, John Woolman, said, "To say we love God as unseen and at the same time exercise cruelty towards the least creature moving by his life or by life derived from him is a contradiction in itself."

According to Science and Health With Key To The Scriptures, a major scripture of Christian Science, "God is the life or intelligence which forms and preserves the individuality and identity of animals as well as of man." (S and H p550) "The Christian Science Journal" has also contained articles advocating a vegetarian diet.

A religion in the UK, with a small but important following, called the Order of the Cross, teaches pacifism and non-violence to living beings. It requires their members to follow a vegetarian diet.

Dexter Scott King, son of Martin Luther King and a strict vegetarian, or vegan, said, "Veganism has given me a higher level of awareness and spirituality." Noted Christian theologian, medical missionary and vegetarian, Albert Schweitzer, said, "Until we extend the circle of compassion to all living things, humanity will not find peace."

Sylvester Graham was an American Presbyterian minister (ordained in 1826) who advocated a vegetarian diet. He was known for inventing the graham cracker. His "Graham Journal of Health and Longevity" preached his principles of good health, especially through a vegetarian diet.

Islam does not require the adoption of a vegetarian diet, but an argument can be made that the current treatment of farm animals would violate the Prophet Mohamed's teachings. Margoliouth, one of Mohamed's chief biographers, writes, "His humanity extended itself to the lower creation...Acts of cruelty were swept away by him." Al-Ghazzali, one of Islam's most brilliant philosophers, in his book *Ihya Ulum ul Din* states, "... Compassionate eating leads to compassionate living." The Hunza tribe, living in Northern Pakistan in the foothills of the Himalayas, follows a nearly vegetarian diet. They are famous for their longevity, often living to 100, and are often thought of as the healthiest people in the world. They have been following a largely vegetarian diet for hundreds of years and give proof to the hadith or popular saying of the Prophet Mohamed that "whoever is kind to one of God's creatures is kind to himself."

In the Buddhist religion, transmigration of the soul allows for animals to be past or future human beings. Therefore, the killing and eating of animals is discouraged. The doctrine of karma also would discourage the killing and eating of animals as doing so violates the principle of Ahimsa, which means non-violence. According to the Mahaparinirvana Sutra, "Whoever consumes meat extinguishes the seed of compassion." Buddha himself is said to have been vegetarian. It is no surprise that many of his followers also choose not to eat meat.

The Dalai Lama of Tibet advocates for a vegetarian diet, saying, "I do not see any reason why animals should be slaughtered to serve as human diet when there are so many substitutes. After all, man can live without meat...There is no justification in indulging in such acts of brutality....Still, the best way is to be vegetarian."

In China and Japan, the Buddhists were particularly careful about observing a vegetarian diet. Most notable among the many Chan Buddhists of China is Chuhung who very actively promoted vegetarianism. In Seattle, and in other parts of the country, you will find vegetarian restaurants operated by Chinese Buddhists. In his book, *The Chain of Compassion*, the famous Japanese Zen master, D.T. Suzuki, says, "Buddhists must strive to teach respect and compassion for all creation—compassion is the foundation of their religion."

Confucius was a vegetarian and many scholars believe that he introduced chopsticks in China so as to be able to eat without utensils that would remind him of the slaughterhouse.

The Hindu religion, which predates the Buddhist, shares with it the concepts of Karma and Ahimsa and is famous for promoting vegetarianism. Perhaps one of the most famous vegetarians in recent times is Ghandi who said, "I do feel that spiritual progress does demand at some stage that we should cease to kill our fellow creatures...." In the Vedic Scriptures there are many passages that support vegetarianism. In one passage it says, "having well considered the origin of flesh foods, and the cruelty of fettering and slaying corporeal beings, let man entirely abstain from eating flesh." (Manusmriti 5:49) Emphasizing the Hindu conception of the unity of all life, Srila Prabhupada states, "Everyone is God's creature, although in different bodies or dresses. God is considered the one supreme father. A father may have many children, and some may be intelligent and others not very intelligent, but if an intelligent son tells his father, 'my brother is not very intelligent; let me kill him,' will the father agree?...Similarly, if God is the supreme Father, why should He sanction the killing of animals who are also His sons?"

In the Sikh religion, originating in India, the Nahmdari sect and the Bahjan Golden temple movement are strictly vegetarian. According to Sikh scholar, Swaran Singh Sanehi, "Sikh scriptures support vegetarianism fully." The Jain religion, also originating in India, follows the Ahimsa principle quite strictly. The Jains are famous for their devotion to and advocacy of vegetarianism.

Following a vegetarian diet has long been supported by many of the world's spiritual traditions. Dating back in some cases thousands of years, people of many different faiths have found a vegetarian diet an important part of their spiritual beliefs and practices. As time moves forward, more and more people are being inspired to adopt a vegetarian diet.

To find out about the author, please see "About the Contributors" on pages 181-183.

Living

180

About the Contributors

Neal D. Barnard, MD is a nutrition researcher, an author, and the founder of the Physicians Committee for Responsible Medicine, a nationwide organization of physicians and laypersons that promotes preventive medicine, especially good nutrition, and addresses controversies in modern medicine, including ethical issues in research. Dr. Barnard is the author of seven books, including *Breaking the Food Seduction* (St. Martin's Press, 2003). He is also an adjunct associate professor of medicine at George Washington University. For more information see www.pcrm.org

Tim Fargo, MA earned a BA in Geography and Geology at Macalester College, an M.A. in Geography at University of Kentucky, and is currently working on his PhD at UCLA specializing in human-environment relationships. As City Planner for Lynnwood, WA, he drafted the Environmental Element of the Comprehensive Plan. Tim was formerly with National Oceanic and Atmospheric Administration.

Ray Foster, MD, FACS is a member of the American Academy of Orthopedic Surgeons. Dr Foster graduated from the University of Cape Town Medical School, RSA. He did his orthopedic residencies in USA and then took on a Fellowship in reconstructive surgery for peripheral nerve injuries in Vellore, South India. Dr. Foster founded NEWSTART® Healthcare Clinic in Seattle, WA where he currently practices. For more information see www.newstarthealthcare.com.

Susan Gins, MS, Certified Nutritionist, has a Master of Science from Bastyr University. Susan is in private practice as a nutritionist. She is also a media spokesperson, lecturer and teacher. Her focus is on the importance of maintaining a healthy lifestyle throughout life and the healing power of food. For more information see www.nourish.net

Jennifer Hillman, BA, MA is the Campaign and Legislative Coordinator of Progressive Animal Welfare Society in Lynnwood, WA. She was formerly a member of their Board of Directors and also spent 7 years working nationally and locally as a Public Outreach Director for Greenpeace USA. She currently serves on the Board of Directors of the Northwest Animal Rights Network. Jennifer has a Bachelors Degree in Communications and a Master of Science degree in Criminal Justice. She lives in Seattle with her 5 cats.

Anne Johnson, BA has a degree in Geography and Geology from Macalester College. She has been the Membership Coordinator and Database Administrator for Vegetarians of Washington since its founding and has worked as a Master Home Environmentalist volunteer for the American Lung Association in Seattle. Anne also has conducted environmental research at the U.S. Geological Survey. She now works for The Wellness Community in Santa Monica, California.

Marilyn Joyce MA, RD, PhD is an international radio and television personality, motivational and inspirational speaker and author of *I Can't Believe It's Tofu!* and *5 Minutes to Health*. She has 18 years experience as a nutrition and health educator and coach. Marilyn is also a Master of Yoga, a registered dietitian trained in biochemistry and human nutrition with a holistic perspective and a cancer survivor. For more information see www.marilynjoyce.com

Scott Jurek, MA, PT is a long distance trail racer and four time defending champion of the Western States 100 Mile Endurance Run. When not running, Scott works as a Physical therapist, coaches aspiring runners, offers the Stride Perfection Service at the Seattle Running Company and leads trail running camps and tours for Trail Running Tours.

Kris Kieswer is the editor of "Good Medicine" magazine, a quarterly publication of the Physicians Committee for Responsible Medicine, author of *Healthy Eating for Life for Women*, and editor of the *Healthy Eating* series of books.

Cynthia Lair is a lecturer on Whole Foods Production at Bastyr University. She graduated as a Certified Health and Nutrition Counselor from the Health and Nutrition Program (NYC). She taught the "Healthy Child Series" at the Natural Gourmet Cooking School in New York and maintains a private practice as a nutritional counselor. Cynthia has authored numerous articles for magazines. Her first book, *Feeding the Whole Family* is already in its 3rd printing . She recently co-authored *Feeding the Young Athlete* with Scott Murdoch PhD. For more information see www.feedingfamily.com

Karen Lamphere, MS, CN received her Masters degree from Bastyr University and is licensed by the Washington State Department of Health as a Certified Nutritionist. Karen is a recognized leader in the field of natural healing who loves sharing her life-long passion for nutrition by teaching a wide variety of classes throughout the Puget Sound area. She emphasizes preventive nutrition in helping people to create a blueprint for an overall healthy lifestyle. For more information see www.wholefood snutrition.com.

Reed Mangels, PhD, RD, FADA is a nutrition advisor for the non-profit, educational Vegetarian Resource Group as well as nutrition editor and columnist for "Vegetarian Journal." She recently co-authored the American Dietetic Association's position on Vegetarian Diets as well as a new food guide for vegetarians. She is a co-author of the revised edition of *The Dietitian's Guide to Vegetarian Diets*, planned for publication in the spring of 2004. Reed also wrote the nutrition section of *Simply Vegan* and the chapter on vegetarian diets for *The Pediatric Manual of Clinical Dietetics*. For more information see www.vrg.org

F. Patricia McEachrane Gross, MD attended medical school in the Caribbean where she grew up and went on to complete her Family Practice residency at the JFK Medical Center in Edison, NJ then directly entered the US Air Force. One of her duties was coordinating the Gulf War Syndrome investigations. After leaving the military, "Dr. McG" became involved in more natural ways of treating disease and maintaining wellness such as plant-based nutrition and exercise. She is currently receiving additional training in Preventive Medicine at Boston University in Massachusetts.

Cheryl Redmond is a freelance writer and editor who specializes in food and nutrition. She is the former associate food editor for "Natural Health" magazine and wrote the regular column "Natural Kitchen" as well as developing vegan recipes for the magazine. Cheryl has a degree in pastry arts and worked as a pastry chef for 10 years. She is currently working with Cook's Illustrated on a baking cookbook and building a house with her husband in southern Vermont.

Stewart Rose, BSc, Vice President of Vegetarians of Washington, is an Orthodox Jew originally from New York. He earned his Bachelor of Science degree at the State University of New York. Stewart and his wife Susan were spiritually inspired to become vegans many years ago. They moved to Washington 10 years ago and for the past two years he has devoted much of his life to being Vice President of Vegetarians of Washington, helping the organization grow so successfully. Stewart and Susan currently reside in Bellevue, WA with their cat, Belle.

Greg Scribner, MD is board-certified in Internal Medicine with an interest in using lifestyle methods to treat disease. Dr. Scribner graduated from Loma Linda University School of Medicine in 1986, moved to the Northwest in 1991 working with the Adventist Health System until 1999. Since the end of 2000 he has been in private practice with a special interest in a natural approach to the treatment and prevention of disease. He has a major focus on diseases which affect adults and the elderly. Dr Scribner currently practices in the Washougal, WA area.

Amanda Strombom, MA was inspired to become a vegetarian after reading the book *Fit for Life* by Harvey and Marilyn Diamond. She is originally from England, holds a Masters degree from Cambridge University and worked as an information technology consultant for a major accounting firm before starting a family. She came to Washington seven years ago where her interest in vegetarianism continued to grow. In 2001, she joined Stewart Rose and two other friends who had just founded Vegetarians of Washington. As President of Vegetarians of Washington, she devotes a major portion of her life helping people to improve their diet.

Heather Woods, ND graduated from the John Bastyr College of Naturopathic Medicine after earning her Bachelor's Degree in holistic medicine from San Francisco State University. Heather became a vegetarian when she was in the fifth grade long before most people had heard of such a thing and attributes much of her own good health to this. She favors vegan and/or vegetarian cuisine and has encouraged patients to eat lower on the food chain for over 15 years. She recently moved to Port Townsend, where she is writing a book on regaining and maintaining optimum health.

Many wonderful people have joined Vegetarians of Washington. We meet their needs by creating a positive atmosphere where they can socialize, have fun, eat great food together, and reinforce their excellent choice to follow a vegetarian diet.

About Vegetarians Of Washington

Vegetarians of Washington is an independent, nonprofit, all volunteer organization made up of people from all walks of life. We are the largest vegetarian organization in the Northwest. We are affiliated to the International Vegetarian Union, North American Vegetarian Society and the Provender Alliance.

You don't need to be a vegetarian to join. Many join Vegetarians of Washington just to learn a little more about it all. We believe in providing a "can do" atmosphere where everybody proceeds at their own pace and just does the best they can.

At our gourmet monthly dinners, held at the Mount Baker Club in Seattle, you can enjoy a delicious multi-course meal from a different local restaurant, chef or cookbook author each month and meet lots of interesting people at one convenient location.

We also hold free informative nutrition and cooking classes at locations throughout the Puget Sound, and fun social events such as hikes, picnics and Veggie Bowling. Our members receive a free subscription to the quarterly Vegetarian Journal magazine, published by the non profit Vegetarian Resource Group. This unique magazine is packed full of recipes and the latest nutritional information. Our discount program entitles members to discounts from over 58 local restaurants and businesses.

Our biggest event of the year is Vegfest, held in the Seattle Center in March each year. At this two day event, you can taste free food samples from over 80 companies, see cooking demonstrations by chefs from all over the country, hear the latest information on nutrition from our speakers and choose from a huge selection of vegetarian books. Last year, we handed out over 130,000 samples of food.

The Vegetarians of Washington community education program includes presentations to schools, colleges, churches, programs for disadvantaged mothers and children, hospitals, patient support groups, health clubs and community health fairs.

Many wonderful people have joined Vegetarians of Washington. We meet their needs by creating a positive atmosphere where they can socialize, have fun, eat great food together, and reinforce their excellent choice to follow a vegetarian diet. Please join us! For more information, please visit us on the Web at www.VegOfWA.org or give us a call at 206 706 2635.

To join, visit www.VegOfWA.org/joinus.html or copy the form on the back of this page, complete it and mail it in.

Membership Application

I /We would like to join Vegetarians of Washington.

Annual Fee *(Please check appropriate level)*

☐ $20-Individual ☐ $35-Family ☐ $50-Supporter ☐ $100-Patron

Full Name(s) *For family memberships, please provide names of all family members who require a membership card.*

_____ _____

_____ _____

_____ _____

Address _____

City _____ State _____ Zip _____

Day Phone _____ Evening phone _____

Email *For family memberships, more than one email address can be provided if you wish. Please provide your email address so that we can send you newsflashes and reminders. We respect your privacy. Your contact details will not be shared with anyone, without your prior permission.*

_____

_____

As part of your membership, you will automatically receive a free subscription to the quarterly publication, *Vegetarian Journal,* by mail unless you indicate to the contrary here:

☐ I prefer not to receive the quarterly *Vegetarian Journal* magazine.

Method of payment ☐ VISA ☐ MasterCard ☐ Check enclosed

__ __ __ __ - __ __ __ __ - __ __ __ __ - __ __ __ __   Exp. date __ __ / __ __

Cardholder signature _____

Date _____

Please make checks payable to:
Vegetarians of Washington
PO Box 85847
Seattle, WA 98145

We are an independent 501(c)3 non-profit organization. If your company offers matching gifts, please enclose form with your payment.

Please Give Us Your Feedback

We invite you to help us prepare for the next exciting edition of *Veg-Feasting in the Pacific Northwest*. Tell us about a vegetarian or very veg-friendly restaurant or a natural food store that you would like to see included in our next edition, or to help us update our reviews, please send us your comments about an establishment you visited that is in this current guide. Thank you!

Please include the store's business card or restaurant take-out menu if available.

☐ Restaurant ☐ Natural Food Store *(please check one)*

☐ New establishment ☐ Updated review *(please check one)*

Full name of establishment _____

Address _____

City _____ State _____ Zip _____

Phone ___(___)_____ Email or Web site _____

Information _____

_____

_____

_____

_____

_____

_____

_____

_____

_____

Your name _____

Address _____

City _____ State _____ Zip _____

Phone _____ Email _____

Please visit our Web site, www.VegofWA.org/vegfeasting, or copy this form and mail it to

Vegetarians of Washington
PO Box 85847
Seattle, WA 98145

Restaurants and Natural Food Stores Reviewed in Washington

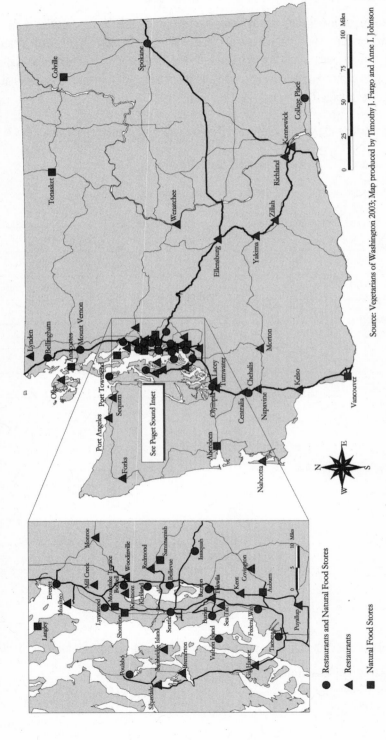

Source: Vegetarians of Washington 2003; Map produced by Timothy J. Fargo and Anne I. Johnson

● Restaurants and Natural Food Stores
▲ Restaurants
■ Natural Food Stores

Restaurants and Natural Food Stores Reviewed in Oregon

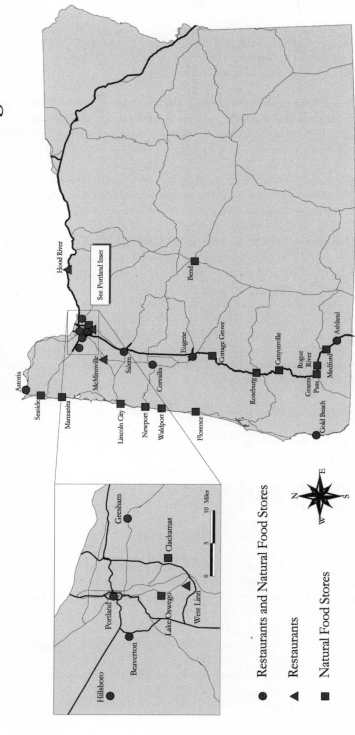

Source: Vegetarians of Washington 2003; Map produced by Timothy J. Fargo and Anne I. Johnson

● Restaurants and Natural Food Stores

▲ Restaurants

■ Natural Food Stores

Famous People, Famous Quotes

"Although we think we are one and we act as if we are one, human beings are not natural carnivores...flesh was never intended for human beings who are natural herbivores."
Dr. William Clifford Roberts
Editor in Chief of the American Journal of Cardiology

Adam Smith: *"It may indeed be doubted whether butchers' meat is anywhere a necessary for life. Grain and other vegetables...afford the most plentiful, the most wholesome, the most nourishing and the most invigorating diet. Decency nowhere requires that any man should eat butchers' meat."*

Immanuel Kant: *"If [man] is not to stifle his human feelings, he must practice kindness towards animals, for he who is cruel to animals becomes hard also in his dealings with men. We can judge the heart of a man by his treatment of animals."*

Did you know that Paul McCartney and Ringo Starr of the Beatles are vegetarians?

Did you know that Hank Aaron who broke Babe Ruth's home runs record for one season was a vegetarian?

Did you know that Charles Darwin was a vegetarian?
"The love of all creatures is the most noble attribute of all man"

Did you know that George Bernard Shaw was a vegetarian?
Animals are my friends...and I don't eat my friends

Did you know that Benjamin Franklin was a vegetarian?

Did you know that Susan B. Anthony, leader of Woman's Suffrage movement, was a vegetarian?

Did you know that Steve Jobs, Founder/CEO of Apple Computer and CEO of Pixar, is a vegetarian?

Did you know that Leo Tolstoy was a vegetarian?

Did you know that Leonardo Da Vinci was a vegetarian?
"I have from an early age abjured the use of meat, and the time will come when men such as I will look upon the murder of animals as they now look upon the murder of men."

Did you know that the famous anthropologist Jane Goodall is a vegetarian?

Henry David Thoreau: *"I have no doubt that it is part of the destiny of the human race, in its gradual improvement, to leave off eating animals."*

Abraham Lincoln: *"I am in favor of animal rights as well as human rights. That is the way of a whole human being."*

Did you know that Einstein was a vegetarian?
"It is my view that the vegetarian manner of living by its purely physical effect on the human temperament, would most beneficially influence the lot of mankind."

Did you know that Isaac Newton was a vegetarian?

Did you know that Thomas Edison was a vegetarian?

Did you know that Confucius was a vegetarian?

Did you know that Johnny Weismuller, a world swimming champion and later the star of the Tarzan movies, was a vegetarian?

Did you know that Albert Schweitzer was a vegetarian?
"Until he extends the circle of his compassion to all living things, man will not himself find peace."

Did you know that Dr. Benjamin Spock, author of the all-time best seller and classic book, *Baby and Child Care,* (a standard for parents for the past 50 years) was a vegetarian?

Did you know that Dr Dean Ornish MD, a Noble Prize Winner in medicine, is a vegetarian? Dr Ornish discovered that a lowfat vegetarian diet will open clogged arteries.

Did you know that Desmond Howard, Super Bowl MVP, was a vegetarian?

Did you know that Carl Lewis, Olympic gold medalist in track and field, was a vegetarian?

Did you know that Bill Pearl Bodybuilder, Mr. America, Mr. Universe was also Mr. Vegetarian?

Did you know that Martina Navratilova and Billie Jean King, tennis champions, are both vegetarians.

Did you know that Gustav Holst, the famous Classical Composer, was a vegetarian?

Did you know that Eddie Vedder of Pearl Jam is a vegetarian?

Did you know that Mr. Spock (Leonard Nimoy) is a vegetarian?